A VIOLENT HOMICIDE

As the garage door slowly opened, Reno Police Department detective David Jenkins observed what he believed to be a dead adult woman lying facedown in a pool of blood, toward the front of the garage. Jenkins subsequently determined that the woman was indeed dead, likely the victim of a very violent homicide. She was lying in front of two vehicles, one of them a dark gray Lexus SUV and the other a gold Jeep Cherokee, both with Nevada license plates. It appeared that the vehicles had been moved into the garage following the violence.

As Jenkins walked slowly around the garage, he gave everything a once-over, a cursory examination to try and get an idea of exactly what he was dealing with. Among the things that he noticed, aside from a female dead body lying in a pool of blood, were what appeared to be bloodstains on the Lexus and the Cherokee, and on their tires. There were drag marks made in blood where the dead woman's body had apparently been moved, and there was blood spatter on the garage walls. It was not a pretty sight.

Jenkins would remember it as being among the more gruesome crime scenes of his career.

RAGE

GARY C. KING

PINNACLE BOOKS
Kensington Publishing Corp.
http://www.kensingtonbooks.com

PINNACLE BOOKS are published by

Kensington Publishing Corp.
119 West 40th Street
New York, NY 10018

All Kensington Titles, Imprints, and Distributed Lines are available at special quantity discounts for bulk purchases for sales promotions, premiums, fund-raising, and educational or institutional use. Special book excerpts or customized printings can also be created to fit specific needs. For details, write or phone the office of the Kensington special sales manager: Kensington Publishing Corp., 119 West 40th Street, New York, NY 10018, attn: Special Sales Department, Phone: 1-800-221-2647.

Pinnacle and the P logo Reg. U.S. Pat. & TM Off.

ISBN-13: 978-0-7860-2139-0
ISBN-10: 0-7860-2139-X

First Printing: July 2010

10 9 8 7 6 5 4 3 2 1

Printed in the United States of America

For Teresita

Years of love have been forgot,
In the hatred of a minute.
—Edgar Allan Poe

Justice and power must be brought together,
so that whatever is just may be powerful,
and whatever is powerful may be just.
—Blaise Pascal

PART I

RENO

1

Reno, Nevada, has always been a rough-and-tumble kind of town, even during its meager frontier beginnings when it was little more than a gateway to the gold-mining town of Virginia City, nestled in the rugged hills some twenty miles southeast of Reno. Mark Twain began his writing career in Virginia City, where he worked as a reporter for the *Virginia City Territorial Enterprise*. Many things have changed, of course, from the time when Reno, part of the Silver State, made itself known as the birthplace of gambling and brothels. This incarnation happened shortly after a man named Charles August Fey, a Bavarian, who had immigrated to the U.S. when he was about fifteen, invented the country's first mechanical slot machine and named it the Liberty Bell. He had placed it in a San Francisco saloon, where it proved to be very popular, and the rest, of course, is history. Gambling did not become legal in Nevada, however, until Governor Fred Balzar, on March 19, 1931, signed a bill into law legalizing it. Although Nevada has more mountain ranges than any other state—a little-known fact—the state is perhaps recognized more for the fact that it is a place where people come and lose money.

Although once fueled by tourism and quickie divorces, Reno nowadays is feeling the effects of the nearly mortally wounded national economy. A number of well-known gambling hotels and casinos, such as Fitzgerald's, now sit dark and idle, and the once-bustling downtown gambling center, located on Virginia Street, where the famous arched neon sign proudly proclaims that Reno is THE BIGGEST LITTLE CITY IN THE WORLD, struggles today to draw in customers willing to part with their money. The area is rife with homeless people and panhandlers, and some resorts provide shuttles to their guests to travel a mere three or four blocks, due to safety concerns. Even though the city averages less than seventeen murders per year, gang violence has clearly increased, as have crimes related to drug usage.

Many of the city's nongaming enterprises are still thriving and prosperous, particularly south of the city where there are a number of newer housing developments that serve as bedroom communities for commuters who work at the state capital, Carson City, or in nearby Sparks, just east of the city. A visitor to this once-thriving metropolis of approximately 210,000 people cannot help but wonder, however, which cards the future holds for Reno.

In recent years, Reno had been the site of a number of high-profile diabolically plotted cold-blooded murders. One of the more recent ones involved a dashing millionaire swinger named Darren Roy Mack, forty-five, his ex-wife, Charla, thirty-nine, and their divorce judge, Charles "Chuck" Weller, fifty-three, who had a reputation for angering many people whose cases were heard by him. This was the tragic story of an attractive couple who had it all—whose sex lives were unabashedly over-the-top, but who made no secret of the fact that they were swingers, and how, after ten years of marriage and a bitter divorce, it all came crashing down. The downward spiral culminated in murder, a sniper-style attempted murder, and an international manhunt that generated headlines across the country. It was a story that the residents of the Biggest Little City in the World would not easily forget.

It was approximately 11:00 A.M., on June 12, 2006, a Monday, that Reno's 911 emergency-response telephone systems lit up like a Christmas tree. The police began receiving reports that shots had been fired in the downtown area, presumably from the fourth or fifth floor of a parking garage on First Street, near the newly opened Mills B. Lane Justice Center. One of the first calls that came in was from someone inside that building, which houses family court, as well as the Washoe County District Attorney's Office, located on South Sierra Street. The person who placed the call hurriedly put a police officer on the phone, who identified himself as Officer Jones, of the Reno Police Department (RPD).

"I think there's . . . a sniper inside a parking garage, just north of the family court building," Jones told the 911 operator. "I think there was a gunshot from the parking garage. I don't know if there's anybody down or not in the family court building. I'm gonna check and see if we have injuries or not. I don't know yet."

There were several moments of silence as the 911 operator attempted to enter the information from Officer Jones into her computer. It seemed like a tense moment for the operator as she attempted to get her computer to function properly. Jones suggested to the operator that she have police officers set up a staging area in and around the Mills B. Lane Justice Center and the parking garage, approximately two blocks away. The operator informed Jones to stand by, because her computer had gone down and she needed to walk to the radio operator's room to relay the emergency message. When she came back on the line, she asked Officer Jones if there was any additional information that he could provide. His response was that he had no further information at this point. However, the operator informed Jones that they had received another report, almost simultaneous with his, that the shooting had come from the fourth floor of the parking garage in question. Because their system was down, the 911 operators and the radio operators were yelling and screaming across the room to one another in an effort to coordinate all the information that was coming in almost faster than any of them could handle.

Seconds later, another call was received at the 911 emergency center from a caller requesting medical assistance. The caller provided the emergency dispatcher with the family court building's address, and instructed the dispatcher to have paramedics use the Sierra Street entrance when they arrived. The caller calmly explained that there had been a gunshot, and that one of the judges had been injured. She explained that he was located on the third floor of the building.

"Is there anyone with the judge right now?" the dispatcher asked.

"Yes, there are deputies with him," the caller explained.

"Is it clear to enter the building?"

"Yeah, it's clear."

Someone could be heard talking on a police radio that the shot or shots had not originated inside the building, but had come from a different location on the outside of the building.

"Are you with the patient now?" the dispatcher asked.

"No."

"How old is this person?"

"In his fifties."

"He's a male, correct?"

"Yes," responded the caller.

"Is he conscious?"

"I don't know."

"Is he breathing?" the dispatcher asked.

The caller explained that the victim was breathing and talking, but had suffered a gunshot wound. The 911 operator had not yet been able to ascertain which part of the victim's body had sustained the gunshot. It could be heard in the background conversations that it had been Judge Chuck Weller who had been shot. Apparently, the shot came through the third-floor window of his chambers on the north side of the building. Police officers and deputies, the caller said, were currently blocking all traffic at Sierra and First Streets, as well as all along Island Avenue, a street that ran east and west the length of much of the city's man-made river walk, which the window in the judge's chambers overlooked. The Truckee River runs through the center of town, and the river walk had been created to help beautify the downtown area, at a tremendous cost to taxpayers during recent revitalization efforts.

As additional calls were made to the 911 dispatch center, there were no reports of eyewitness accounts, nor were there any reports of descriptions of a potential suspect or suspects. At one point, Officer Jones called back to the 911 center to determine whether or not a SWAT team had been dispatched to the area. Amid all the confusion, not to mention the frustration with a computer system that had crashed, the dispatcher finally told Jones that a SWAT team had not been dispatched yet. Jones asked to be notified when a SWAT team was en route, and asked that he be contacted by the team, because he believed he could be of assistance to them, at least logistically. In the meantime, precious minutes continued to pass, allowing ample time for the gunman to escape as the police attempted to get organized sufficiently to deal with the problem at hand, while others simultaneously dealt with the 911 computer system crash. While everyone worked feverishly to sort out exactly what had happened, all police units not involved in the downtown sniper shooting were advised to switch over to a secondary frequency.

Within minutes the entire downtown Reno area was literally crawling with cops, and it began to look like a war zone. Police cars were blocking off traffic so that the affected area could be isolated, allowing no one, except for police and paramedic units, in or out of the area. As the area was being locked down and sealed off on the ground, helicopters circled the area and offered whatever assistance they could from the air. As the police continued to take control of the situation and get organized, courthouse employees began to report that bailiffs had charged into Judge Chuck Weller's chambers, guns drawn, and literally threw another judge, who was curious about what had happened, onto the floor for his own safety, in case the sniper began shooting again.

Before long, reports began coming out of the family court building, which sits adjacent to the main

Washoe County Courthouse, where some of those seeking to provide assistance had come running from, indicating that Weller had been shot while standing in front of a window inside his third-floor office. According to those who were providing information updates, Weller's office faced the parking garage located to the north and was clearly visible from the family court building. Investigators would determine later that the shooter had a straight shot into many of the building's windows, including those of Weller's chambers.

Initial reports indicated that Weller had been hit in the torso area of his body, and it appeared that one of his staff members, Annie Allison, who served as his administrative assistant, had also been injured. However, police officers soon clarified that Allison had most likely not been shot at directly, but rather had been hit by glass or bullet fragments, or both. At one point during all the activity, Weller was said to have stood up and calmly instructed that someone notify his wife of what had happened and to instruct her to get out of the house, because the judge feared that the shooter might come after her next.

The injured judge and Allison were promptly taken by paramedics to a nearby hospital. During the short drive, Weller reportedly told one of the paramedics that he thought he may have been shot by "Darrell" Mack, who he claimed was a likely suspect. Although he hadn't realized it at the time, he had incorrectly identified the alleged shooter's first name, and would later state that he had meant to identify the suspected shooter as Darren Mack, a man whose divorce case he had recently presided over. Throughout the entire shooting ordeal, as tense as it had been, Weller had remained calm—so calm, in fact, that a fellow judge had characterized him as "the calmest person there."

By the time that Weller and Allison had entered the emergency room of the nearby hospital, the Reno PD had set up a command post near the area of the shooting, and the methodical search for the sniper suspect was well under way. Additional law enforcement personnel were brought in, including deputies from the Washoe County Sheriff's Office (WCSO), and the city's SWAT team was ready and standing by in the event that the sniper had not left the area and began shooting again.

The scene in and around the Mills B. Lane Justice Center was chaotic, with people running out of the building to reach a place of safety, making calls on their cell phones, as they tried to make sense out of what was happening. Washoe County undersheriff Mike Haley was among those who were in the midst of all the confusion and pandemonium.

"We're certain the shot came from outside," Haley later told news reporters. "We can't speculate now where it came from. We have to establish the height of the window. It could have come from a variety of locations to the north."

A tourist told the reporter for the *Reno Gazette-Journal* that he had heard a loud explosion while parking his car inside the First Street parking garage, shortly after 11:00 A.M. The tourist described the explosion as sounding like that of an electric transformer blowing up. It was noted that if the tourist had been inside the same parking garage as the shooter, the sounds of the gunshot or gunshots would have appeared amplified dramatically because of the echo effect inside the structure and may very well have sounded more like an explosion than a gunshot.

One witness told KRNV-TV's News 4 reporters that he had heard two gunshots prior to all the commotion inside the justice center and that which occurred a short time later outside on the streets. He described getting into an elevator in the building and how "people started scattering up there on the third floor." He explained that "a deputy got in front of us and somebody said, 'Someone got shot. We heard a pop.'"

Another witness described how he had hidden behind a concrete pillar as "everything was starting to go crazy all over the place." Cops, he said, were suddenly everywhere.

"We were walking downtown near the building, and we heard a gun," said yet another witness. "We all just ducked."

Another witness described how he had seen an armed man inside a parking garage located near the justice center at the time of the shooting.

Meanwhile, the police continued to evacuate people from the justice center, but many other people, at least two hundred, were simply ordered to stay put and remained locked down for the next several hours. Employees at the justice center and at the adjacent courthouse had begun closing the curtains and blinds inside their offices, terrified that the shooter might not have finished what he had set out to do. Most of those ordered to remain in the various judicial buildings were inmates in the holding areas, as well as those who worked in various capacities at the courthouse and the justice center. They would not be allowed to leave until the entire area had been cleared by the police. The justice center, as well as the Washoe County Courthouse, would end up being closed for the remainder of the day as a WCSO helicopter continued to search from the sky the downtown area for the suspect, and two

SWAT teams continued looking from the ground for the shooter. According to Reno's police commander Steve Pitts, one of those SWAT teams was inside the courthouse searching for the person responsible for firing the shots. The streets surrounding the justice center, including a wide area that extended from Virginia Street to Rainbow Street, and from Court Street to the Truckee River, remained sealed off to vehicles and pedestrians until late into the evening as the police asked visitors to the downtown area to stay away.

A police command post was set up near Sierra and Second Streets, and yet another SWAT team assembled at the Silver Peak Restaurant & Brewery. The downtown library was also closed, as was the nearby building for Washoe County Social Services. The people inside those buildings were also instructed to remain inside until the area had been cleared.

In the meantime, it was revealed by the *Reno Gazette-Journal* that family court judge Chuck Weller had indeed suffered a gunshot wound to the chest. He was reportedly stable, but doctors at Washoe Medical Center reported his condition as serious to critical. He remained in the hospital following surgery to treat his wounds. Annie Allison reportedly only suffered superficial wounds to her hip, left arm, and neck, and was released from another hospital following treatment. Because the judge was being treated at Washoe Medical Center, the emergency room there remained under heavy security, and everyone attempting to gain entry was carefully scrutinized.

Emergency room physicians who provided medical treatment for the injured judge discovered injuries caused by "bullet fragments" in the area of his chest. The injuries ranged in size from one centimeter to five centimeters and were discovered beneath the skin and in muscle tissue. Doctors also found "a sizeable foreign body in the lower left flank wound," which they believed might be useful for "forensic purposes." The "bullet fragment was removed from the lower left wound" and was sent to the investigators, according to police and medical reports.

Reno investigators soon learned that Allison, employed by Washoe County as Weller's administrative assistant, had hurriedly gone into Weller's office at the onset of all the commotion. From the information that had so far been obtained, it appeared—but was not yet confirmed—that two shots had been fired and that Allison had perhaps walked into Weller's office at the time of the second shot. She had been injured by broken glass or bullet fragments then.

According to Undersheriff Haley, there appeared to be some confusion as to how many times the judge had been shot.

"Anytime you are struck in the chest, you have the potential for serious consequences," Haley said.

Haley also said that he did not yet have any information on whether Weller had been shot by a random sniper, or if he had been targeted for a reason.

"Judges in the family court try a lot of cases, and some of them are volatile," Haley added. "But it could also be someone wishing to target anybody."

As the search for Darren Roy Mack continued, Reno deputy police chief Jim Johns confirmed that Mack was indeed the chief suspect in connection with the downtown shooting. Based on information gleaned from witnesses and other sources, such as video surveillance cameras, Mack was believed to be driving a silver Ford Explorer. It was pointed out that the vehicle may have been a rental. Mack's personal vehicle, police believed, was a 2003 orange Hummer, which was located in the driveway of a relative's home. Johns also indicated that the Reno Police Department's bomb squad was investigating whether or not explosives had been placed in or on Weller's personal vehicle parked at the courthouse, because a bomb-sniffing police dog had indicated the presence of such material in the judge's car. As the police investigation into the midmorning shooting at the Mills B. Lane Justice Center continued, the detectives looking into the background of their chief suspect, Darren Mack, learned that Mack was known to own several firearms. Since he had not been located to be brought in for questioning, police urged anyone who might have seen him to call 911.

Concurrently, investigators learned that Darren Mack was the owner of a successful business in downtown Reno, known as Palace Jewelry & Loan, located on South Virginia Street, only a few blocks from the justice center. The business was basically an oversized pawnshop that dealt mostly in jewelry and diamonds. When investigators showed up at the pawnshop, with the hope of questioning Mack about the morning's events, Mack, of course, was not there, and no one at the shop knew where he could be found.

That same afternoon, the police received a tip that Mack might be inside a home located on Chipmunk Avenue in Washoe Valley. WCSO deputies set up a secure perimeter around the vicinity of the home, but a subsequent search of the house and adjacent areas failed to turn up any sign of Darren Mack.

Many things in an investigation of this magnitude and intensity occur simultaneously pursuant to individuals doing their assigned jobs. One of the things that occurred early that afternoon was that police had issued an all points bulletin (APB) for Darren Mack, which described him as a white male with brown hair and brown eyes, five-eleven, and weighing between 190 and 220 pounds. They reiterated the fact that it was possible he was driving a silver Ford sport utility vehicle (SUV), possibly an Explorer, and accelerated their warnings that he may be armed and dangerous.

Although the police didn't know it yet, the case was about to take a dramatic turn that same afternoon and lead them into an upscale condominium community, south of the city. It was nearing midafternoon when veteran Reno Police Department detective David Jenkins received a telephone call from a person expressing concern about the safety of Darren Mack's estranged wife, Charla. The caller, Daniel "Dan" Jacob Osborne, asked Jenkins to meet him at a house on Humboldt Street in Reno.

When Jenkins arrived at the Humboldt Street address, at approximately 1:30 P.M., Osborne nervously explained that he had been an invited guest of Darren Mack at Mack's condominium located on Wilbur May Parkway. He had been staying in an on-and-off capacity since late May 2006 or the first part of June 2006. Osborne explained that he had known Darren Mack for roughly thirty years, and that they had been friends ever since high school. The previous evening, said Osborne, Mack had asked him if Osborne would be available to give Mack's eight-year-old daughter, Erika, a ride to the home of Darren Mack's mother. Osborne apparently agreed, and Mack told him that Erika's mother, Charla, would bring the child to his Wilbur May Parkway residence at approximately 9:00 A.M., on June 12, 2006, a requirement of their joint custody.

On the morning of June 12, Osborne explained, he drove to Darren Mack's residence, taking his dog along with him. He said that he had left the dog inside the car, and had left the windows open. Shortly after his arrival at Mack's condominium, a woman he had never met before but had presumed was Darren Mack's ex-wife, Charla, dropped off Erika. According to Osborne's account, Erika's mother arrived in a Lexus sport utility vehicle. Mack, who was at home at the time, had asked Osborne to stay with Erika in the upstairs area of the condominium while Mack met with his ex-wife outside or downstairs in the garage. Such meetings were not a part of the court-ordered divorce settlement—the parent dropping off or picking up the child was required to remain inside the vehicle.

Several minutes later, Osborne's dog, Rusty, began barking frantically, obviously excited about something. As Osborne prepared to go to the lower level of the condominium to find out why his dog was making such a fuss, Darren Mack entered the dwelling through the door that led to the garage. Osborne had arrived at that same door, which led to a stairway that provided access to the garage, in time to see Darren Mack walking up the stairs with a towel wrapped around his hand. Without saying anything to him, Mack walked past Osborne and went into the master bedroom.

In his statement to Detective Jenkins, Osborne explained that his dog had followed Mack into the condominium. Osborne said that he had immediately noticed that his dog was covered in a substantial amount of wet blood after Erika pointed it out to him, from its muzzle to past the dog's chest area. When he had examined the dog for injuries, Osborne said, he had not found any. He said at that point he had assumed that the blood on the dog must have come from Erika's mother.

It was after observing such a large amount of blood

on his dog, Osborne told Jenkins, he began to fear for his and Erika's safety. He then decided to leave the residence through the front door. As he was leaving the condominium unit, Osborne said, he had noted that Erika's mother's SUV was still parked outside the condo unit. He further stated that when he dropped Erika off at Mack's mother's home, he had expressed concern to the woman about the child's mother's well-being. Osborne said that he had told her that he suspected that Darren Mack had somehow harmed Erika's mother.

He explained to the seasoned detective that he also called the Reno Police Department earlier that day to file a report about his concerns, and to request that officers check on the situation at Mack's townhome. Reno police officers had been sent to Darren Mack's condominium unit inside the Fleur de Lis complex on a report of a domestic disturbance. When they rang the doorbell and knocked on the door of Mack's condo unit, there was no answer, and they left a few moments later without taking any further action. Jenkins later confirmed that this had indeed been the case, and that officers had gone there to investigate the possibility of a domestic disturbance at or near the time of the downtown shooting.

During the course of their conversation that afternoon, Osborne related to Jenkins that Mack had shared with him for the past several weeks details about the difficult divorce that Mack and his estranged wife, Charla, had been going through. Osborne said that Mack had verbally expressed his ill feelings toward Charla, and he had expressed dislike, as well as contempt, for certain members of the legal profession involved in his divorce. He had specifically expressed ill feelings toward the judge who was handling their divorce.

Osborne also told Jenkins that he believed that Erika's mother had been injured or killed and was still inside the condo. At that point, Jenkins and Osborne drove to the Fleur de Lis complex on Wilbur May Parkway, south of the city, just off South Meadows Parkway. By that time, it was nearly midafternoon. They would be shocked, but not surprised, by what they found there. It somehow suddenly seemed very disturbing that Darren Mack would use his eight-year-old daughter, his own flesh and blood, to lure his estranged wife to his townhome so that he could do her harm. But, as many would learn, Mack was that kind of guy.

2

During the approximate twenty-minute drive from the Humboldt Street address, where Jenkins had met up with Osborne, to the Fleur de Lis luxury town-home development, Osborne and Jenkins, a thirty-two-year veteran of the Reno Police Department, continued discussing what Osborne knew about Darren Mack, and what he had observed at Mack's condominium earlier that day, as well as what he had seen and heard on other occasions there. Among the things they discussed during the short drive was the fact that Darren Mack had recently been operating a new silver Ford Explorer SUV, which Osborne knew that Mack had rented at Budget Rent A Car. Although it did not seem that Osborne knew why Mack had rented the Ford Explorer, he told the detective that Mack had been driving the vehicle almost exclusively since he rented it.

When they turned off onto South Meadows Parkway, they passed near the residence of Nevada state controller Kathy Augustine and that of her husband, Chaz Higgs, en route to Mack's townhome. Jenkins didn't know it yet, but he would be investigating Augustine's murder in less than a month after she allegedly had been poisoned by her husband with the powerful paralytic drug succinylcholine.

Although, remarkably, Reno has so few murders given its population size, most are either domestic or gang-related killings that typically are none too challenging. But here, amazingly, were two unusually high-profile investigations that were nearly back-to-back, both particularly challenging, which Jenkins would be investigating simultaneously.

The Fleur de Lis luxury townhome development had been a $75 million, forty-acre project that had opened its doors in mid-July 2003. The development boasted a twenty-thousand-square-foot clubhouse, and Phase 1 of the project had quickly sold out, despite the hefty price tags of between $190,000 and over $300,000, which was considered a lot of money for a condominium unit in Reno. Most of the units ranged in size from 1,600 square feet to 1,900 square feet. The gated development was constructed in a somewhat European style, with an abundance of natural stone, wood, and glass, and a mountain setting served as its backdrop. There were waterfalls and streams running through the property, exquisite landscaping, and elaborate gardens. Each of the units had two full bathrooms, a laundry room, a courtyard at the entry, a covered patio, and an attached two-car garage.

After passing through the gated entry guardhouse, which faced Wilbur May Parkway, Jenkins and Osborne soon arrived at Darren Mack's unit and parked in front of it. After getting out of Jenkins's car, Jenkins instinctively looked at the driveway as he approached the closed garage door and observed several small red stains on the concrete, located near the outside of the door's entrance. Jenkins's experience told

him that the small red stains were most likely blood
that had dried. At Jenkins's urging, Osborne provided Jenkins with the code number for the electric
garage-door opener. Osborne explained that he knew
the code because he had been sharing the unit with
Mack on an on-and-off basis for the past few weeks.
Believing that he would find an injured or dead
person on the other side of the garage door, Jenkins
quickly entered the code to open it. As the garage
door slowly opened, Jenkins observed what he believed to be a dead adult woman lying facedown in a
pool of blood, toward the front of the garage. Jenkins
subsequently determined that the woman was indeed
dead, likely the victim of a very violent homicide. She
was lying in front of two vehicles, one of them a dark
gray Lexus SUV and the other a gold Jeep Cherokee,
both with Nevada license plates. It appeared that the
vehicles had been moved into the garage following
the violence.

As Jenkins walked slowly around the garage, he
gave everything a once-over, a cursory examination to
try and get an idea of exactly what he was dealing
with. Among the things that he noticed, aside from a
female dead body lying in a pool of blood, were what
appeared to be bloodstains on the Lexus and the
Cherokee, and on their tires. There were drag marks
made in blood where the dead woman's body had apparently been moved, and there was blood spatter on
the garage walls. It was not a pretty sight. Jenkins
would remember it as being among the more gruesome crime scenes of his career.

Knowing that he needed a search warrant before
going any further, Jenkins called the Reno Police Department to request additional resources. When additional units arrived, he made what he termed a "quick

protective sweep inside the residence to check for additional victims or injured persons," with the assistance of Sergeant Mike Lessman, of RPD's SWAT team, and others. He determined that there was no one else inside the residence.

During the protective sweep of the condo unit, Sergeant Lessman pointed out to Jenkins that he had observed several items inside the master bedroom that he recognized as material that could be used to build a bomb or some other incendiary device. Needless to say, Jenkins had no trouble securing a search warrant for Mack's condominium.

Among the things that Jenkins and the other investigators had also noticed during the protective sweep of the condo was a Budget Rent A Car rental agreement lying on a landing at the top of the stairs, observable from just inside the front door. Jenkins would add it to the search warrant request of potential items of important evidentiary value. He later confirmed that the rental agreement had been for the silver Ford Explorer SUV, which Osborne had told him about earlier.

During the process of examining the crime scene, Jenkins and others tentatively identified the victim as Charla Mack. Without disturbing the body, Jenkins could easily observe that the victim had suffered severe cutting-type injuries to her upper torso and neck area. A more precise extent of the victim's injuries would be determined later during the autopsy. As he continued noting his observations, Jenkins wrote that he could see drag marks from the area beneath one of the parked vehicles in the garage that were several feet long and ended near the front of the garage, where the victim lay. When he looked inside the front passenger seat of Charla's Lexus, he saw the keys to the vehicle lying there, and they appeared to be saturated with dried blood. Jenkins also noted the presence of "blood transfers" on areas of the vehicle's interior that were consistent with the SUV being moved after the violent incident that had taken place there.

Upstairs, inside the residence, Jenkins discovered an empty sheath lying on the floor of the master bedroom's walk-in closet. The sheath, he noted, had been manufactured to hold a Gerber dagger. The master bedroom, he reflected, was where Daniel Osborne said that he had last seen Darren Mack.

Along with Detective John Ferguson, Jenkins found several boxes of firearm ammunition strewn about the floor in one of the bedrooms. The detectives also found an empty rifle case that contained a receipt for the purchase of a Bushmaster .223-caliber rifle. The receipt for the rifle bore Darren Mack's name as the person to whom the rifle had been sold. A witness would later describe Mack's Bushmaster rifle as having been equipped with a laser sighting device.

As they moved through the condo unit in an organized manner, Jenkins noted the presence of a Dell desktop computer in the kitchen. A number of e-mails that had been printed lay near the computer. There were also several other documents that had been computer generated that referred to Judge Weller. There were also a number of handwritten documents, mostly notes, lying nearby. The investigators opined that the notes appeared to be in Darren Mack's handwriting. Some of the documents particularly caught the investigators' attention; these contained allegations that Judge Weller was corrupt and displayed favoritism with regard to some of his rulings. Based on what was said in the documents, it appeared that Mack had a low opinion of Weller.

As the afternoon turned into evening and darkness approached, it was decided that the search of Darren Mack's townhome would be suspended until first thing the next morning. After the victim's body had been removed from the residence and taken to the morgue, located near downtown, the condo unit was sealed, and sentries were posted outside to stand guard all night.

After the body found in the garage had been positively identified as that of Charla Mack, along with the evidence that had so far been seized and the disparaging remarks about Judge Weller had been considered—not to mention the fact that Judge Weller had been shot earlier in the day by a sniper believed to be Darren Mack—it became easier to see how everything began to fit neatly together. It became clear that Charla's slaying had occurred first, after having been lured to Mack's condo to drop off their daughter, Erika, and had thus started off the day's events. Apparently on a mission from hell, Darren Mack then went after Judge Weller by securing a place on the fourth or fifth floor of the First Street parking garage, where he had a clear view of the window of the judge's chambers. While it wasn't yet known how long Mack had been lying in wait to shoot the judge from his vantage point, Jenkins and his colleagues reasoned that Mack's window of opportunity had occurred soon after he arrived. This reasoning, of course, was based upon the fact that investigators believed that Charla had been killed sometime around midmorning—a conclusion arrived at, in part, because of Osborne's statements to Jenkins. After factoring in the time that it takes to drive from the South Meadows area to downtown Reno, and the time it must have taken for Mack to locate an advantageous parking space where he could get the judge clearly in his sights, it did not leave much time or room for the unexpected to occur. That alone was a strong indication that Mack's actions that day were not spontaneous but were part of a well-planned scheme that he had put into play that morning. There were still many unknown factors, of course, that would have to be figured into the timeline, and Jenkins knew that the precise details of the case would not be known until everything began to come together as the investigation moved forward.

At one point that day, Jenkins became aware that several bullet fragments suitable for comparison analysis had been collected as evidence from Judge Weller's chambers, as well as from his person. However, the rifle that Mack had allegedly used to shoot the judge first had to be found, and the likelihood of that happening diminished with each hour that Mack remained on the run.

As much as the cops might have liked it to be, the drama of day one was not over yet. At around eight-thirty that evening, someone reported a possible sighting of Darren Mack at the Reno-Tahoe International Airport. As a result, heavily armed police officers closed and secured the airport's parking garage and subjected everyone wanting in or out of the structure to a car-by-car search. They also questioned the drivers, as well as the passengers of each vehicle, during the search process. Airport police, along with federal agents, also searched flights that were still on the ground awaiting clearance to depart.

"Flights were held for some time this evening, just to make sure this suspect somehow didn't make it past security checkpoints," airport spokesman Brian Kulpin said to reporters from News 4, KNRV-TV. "There are a lot of procedures put in place so that doesn't happen. But in a case with this profile, we wanted to make sure we're covering all the airport."

All of the police activity at the airport naturally caused numerous flight delays, with flights being held at the gates. He said that there were also some flights in which aircraft were brought back to the gates and searched.

"People immediately got on their cell phones," said a passenger who, along with all of the other passengers on his flight, was escorted off the plane by police. "I was one of them. We all wanted to know [the latest information]. . . . I called a friend of mine who works for a radio station to see if he knew anything, and pretty much everybody said it was all word of mouth. . . . 'They got the sniper.'"

Nothing, of course, could have been further from the truth. Darren Mack had not been found at the airport, and all of the airport security personnel had been provided with flyers resembling wanted posters that described Mack—complete with color photo. Airport security personnel were asked to keep an eye out for the wanted man, but to use extreme caution if anyone spotted him.

This was all big news for a small city like Reno, and the local news media were, of course, all over the story. Before the day had ended, News 4 was reporting that they had a number of court documents pertaining to Darren and Charla Mack's divorce. Among the things being reported was the fact that Charla had asked for custody of their daughter, as well as more than $10,000 a month in child and spousal support. Charla's attorney had filed a motion asking that Darren Mack be held in contempt of court because he had purportedly not complied with the orders requiring him to pay child support. The television station also revealed that Mack, a millionaire on paper, had recently filed for bankruptcy protection.

News 4 also reported that it had found an eBay website with a profile of Darren Mack and his family, complete with photos. For reasons that were not entirely clear, Mack's eBay website was quickly removed after Mack had become a major news item. However, it had contained the following statement while it existed: **My name is Darren Mack, and I am the ... owner of a small business in Reno, Nevada.** Mack also explained how his family had owned and operated small businesses in Nevada for nearly a half century, and went on to describe his pride of carrying on the family business left to him by his parents, which had been left to them by their parents. He described how jewelry and diamonds had been a major part of his life from the time, at age seven, he was introduced to the business by his father. He explained his personal commitment to excellence, and how he was a fair dealer with integrity. He concluded by pointing out the fact: **[I am] married to a lovely young lady and have three beautiful children.**

Two of Mack's children, Jenkins would learn, were from a previous marriage.

3

The next day, Tuesday, June 13, 2006, while the more political personas of the Reno Police Department were busy holding press conferences about the shooting of Judge Chuck Weller and the murder of Darren Mack's ex-wife, Charla, investigators such as Detective David Jenkins and his partner on the case, Detective Ron Chalmers, were much closer to the front lines of the investigation. They busied themselves by resuming control or direction over the crime scene processing at Darren Mack's Wilbur May Parkway townhome. Armed with a search warrant authorizing an additional search of the premises, the investigators were now specifically looking to seize: rifle ammunition; rifles; rifle aiming devices, to include scopes and/or lasers; spent shell casings; indicia of the purchase, ownership, and/or possession of rifle ammunition, rifles, and rifle aiming devices; a Dell brand desktop personal computer; computer data storage media, to include disks, hard drives, CD and DVD drives and disks; printed or electronic copies of any e-mail correspondence regarding Judge Weller; and documents and/or writings alleging corruption and favoritism by Judge Weller. Experience reminded the cops that they would likely have to revise their affidavit for a search warrant at least a couple of more times as the case continued to evolve, and they recognized that one of those times would be to search for and to confiscate alleged bomb-making materials observed in Mack's bedroom a day earlier by Sergeant Mike Lessman.

Aside from items such as the ammunition that had been observed a day earlier, Jenkins and Chalmers, among others, noted the presence of ten 1-pound jars of Tannerite, each recognizing its potential for misuse. Tannerite is typically used in long-range target practice in which the shooter would place the material in a bottle or can and set it up a great distance away from where they would be firing at it. When the shooter hits the target, such as a soda or beer bottle filled with Tannerite, the target explodes, in a relatively small way, and allows the shooter to see from afar that he has hit the target. If the Tannerite were somehow attached to a blasting cap, it would explode if the blasting cap went off.

"There were materials that could have made a bomb," said Sergeant Lou Gazes, chief of the Washoe County Consolidated Bomb Squad.

It was pointed out by Gazes and others that the substance can be purchased via the Internet. However, ten jars of the material, police said, would be barely enough to make a small explosive device, and there were no detonation devices anywhere in the condo. Nonetheless, they had to view the Tannerite as suspicious, particularly after bomb-sniffing dogs had alerted their handlers to the possible presence of explosive material on, in, or near Judge Weller's vehicle at the justice center—even though an explosive device had not been found. The police later downplayed the significance, if any, of the Tannerite found in Mack's townhome, and publicly stressed that Mack had probably not possessed the Tannerite for the purpose of making a bomb but had, instead, used it for its intended purpose.

By the time the investigators had finished searching Mack's condo, they had bagged up all of the items mentioned, and had amended their search warrant so that they could also remove other items: miscellaneous papers found in a hallway closet, Mack's address book, the May 2006 issue of *Soldier of Fortune* magazine, swabs from various locations inside the unit, such as the front panel of a living-room chair, walls, the shower door of the master bedroom bathroom, various locations inside the garage, and so forth. They also removed many boxes of different brands of ammunition, most of it .223-caliber, and a folding knife from the top of the dresser in the west bedroom. Also confiscated was a variety of literature on exposing corruption and fathers' rights, a VHS tape titled *Your Honor,* another VHS tape titled *The Case Against Lawyers,* and another called *Court Corruption.* They also took water samples from the sink traps in the master bedroom, apparently looking for blood that Mack might have washed off after coming out of the garage.

Interestingly, one of Jenkins's and Chalmers's colleagues, Detective Shanna Wallin-Reed, found a yellow legal pad on Mack's kitchen table. The writing appeared to be in his handwriting, but the cops knew that it would take the expertise of a handwriting analyst to say so for sure after comparing it to actual known samples of Mack's penmanship. Nonetheless, the writing appeared to be a "to do" list. Among the things written on the notepad was *Dan take Erika to*

Joan, and another mentioned the condo's garage door being open prior to *end problem.* It also said to put *Lex in garage,* and *lock home.* Another reference at the end was *Parking garage—if yes,* which Jenkins, Chalmers, and Wallin-Reed reasoned had been related to Mack's plan to shoot into Judge Weller's chambers from the parking garage located near the justice center. At that point, the investigators did not know whether Mack had written the "to do" list before or after Charla had been killed.

The detectives recalled Osborne's statement about the garage door having been open when Charla arrived and began talking with Mack, but that it had been closed only moments later, the approximate time that Osborne began thinking that something terrible was happening downstairs.

It was becoming clearer by the hour that Darren Mack had been a man with a plan, a mission of murder. Nonetheless, many of those involved with the case could not help wondering how Mack could viciously and cold-bloodedly murder his daughter's mother in the garage while the child watched television upstairs. Some people believed that Mack had set up his wife's murder, using the only opportunity to see her afforded him by the court-mandated arrangement involving Erika.

At one point, Jenkins and Chalmers reviewed some of the photographs that had been taken a day earlier of the garage crime scene, and those taken inside the judge's chambers. One photo depicted one of Charla Mack's arms, covered in her own blood, outstretched across the garage floor in the direction where one of her yellow-and-aqua sandals lay. Another depicted what appeared to be a knife hole in Charla's blood-soaked T-shirt, near the neck area, and various others that depicted a number of suspected knife wounds—including the fatal wound that appeared to have perforated an artery in the area of her upper chest.

One of the photographs showed Charla's body lying facedown on the garage floor. She was wearing a pair of blue pants and a T-shirt, but was barefoot. A white towel covered her right arm, and there was a swath or track of blood, nearly the width of her body, that extended across the floor from the area of the front of the garage, indicating that she had been dragged to the location where she was found. A thick rivulet of quickly coagulating blood that had long since stopped flowing extended from the area of her neck to the area beneath her Lexus, which was parked near her body, making it a gruesome crime scene, even for weathered detectives.

At a later time, the detectives obtained video surveillance photos of the Ford Explorer believed to have been driven by Darren Mack at the gated condo development and at the downtown Reno parking garage, from where they suspected he had shot the judge. The problem with those photos was that they were out of focus and unclear, and the driver of the vehicle could not be seen. The photos also failed to show the Explorer's license plates.

However, the video surveillance tape helped Jenkins and Chalmers piece together a timeline of sorts regarding the downtown sniping event. They noted that the Explorer, silver in color, had entered the parking garage a few minutes before 11:00 A.M. and depicted the vehicle as it was driven to the fifth floor, where its driver parked it in a space that allowed a clear, unobstructed view of the justice center and of the windows of Judge Weller's chambers.

Fifteen to twenty minutes passed when the SUV

backed out of its space, pulled forward a few feet, and then backed up into the same space so that the rear of the Explorer now faced the judge's chambers. A few minutes later, the video captured the vehicle's rear hatch being opened at the approximate time that Weller had been shot. The video also captured the Explorer after its rear hatch had been closed, as well as when it left the parking garage. Investigators would later determine that the parking garage was, according to a police affidavit, *where the shot that struck Judge Weller is suspected to have been fired from based on the trajectory.*

Later, at the Washoe County Morgue, a definitive autopsy performed on Charla Mack's body by Katherine Raven, a forensic pathologist, included, of course, clear details of the wounds she had sustained that resulted in or contributed to her death. Deep knife cuts, some greater than two inches in length, were noted on Charla's legs. She had sustained a long cut along the inside of her right arm, and there were what appeared to be slashing wounds on other parts of her body, including one of her wrists, that may have been defensive wounds as she had attempted to fight off her knife-wielding attacker. She had also sustained a large, deep cut on the left side of her neck, near the collarbone, that Raven determined had cut Charla's carotid artery, esophagus, and trachea "in half." Raven determined that Charla died as a result of at least seven stab wounds, including those to her forearm, wrist, elbow, and lower legs. Raven said that the wounds to her forearm, wrist, elbow, and lower legs were also consistent with defensive wounds.

Although the cops did not know it yet, Darren Mack was long gone by the time investigators were busy searching his townhome. Of course, they were beginning to put the various aspects of the investigation together by then. It would not be long before the various pieces to the puzzle began to fit into place, becoming more interconnected with each passing hour. By then, the detectives would be able to see at least some of his movements as Mack attempted to elude the long arm of the law.

Although gut feelings told investigators that they didn't have to look any further than Darren Mack as a suspect in the cases, Reno deputy police chief Jim Johns was still referring to Mack as a "person of interest" whom police wanted to question about his wife's murder and Judge Weller's shooting.

"He is known to have access to firearms," Johns told local media reporters. "We don't have enough to say that he is a suspect in the shooting, at this time, but it is an obvious connection."

As Detectives Jenkins and Chalmers, as well as others, continued running down leads and collected background information on Darren Mack and his deceased ex-wife, Charla, they learned that the couple had been married on May 13, 1995, at Lake Tahoe, California, just across the border from Lake Tahoe, ada. They had remained together, for the most til Charla decided to file for divorce in Febru-

ll, Charla was asking for custody of their born in 1997, within two r divorce papers, filed for divorce, and although she had reportedly been in a number of movies previously, including *Poison Ivy* and *Heaven,* she had not been employed outside the home for many years. She complained that she had no income or ability to support herself or the child at that time. On the other hand, she said, Darren was fit and able-bodied and had sufficient income to provide *substantial permanent alimony* to allow her to *maintain the standard of living enjoyed during the marriage.* Her primary reason for seeking the divorce was incompatibility. She also sought to be awarded reasonable costs associated with filing the divorce, including her attorney's fees. She also sought joint legal custody of Erika, which would allow Darren frequent and reasonable visitation with the child. She also wanted to be awarded her sole and separate property that was not included in the assets and liabilities that would be divided equitably by the court.

Darren, of course, objected to the terms of the divorce settlement that Charla had been seeking and filed a complaint and counterclaim, contending that Charla was an emotionally unstable woman, and that it was in Erika's best interest that the court award custody of the child, *but* he, not Charla, sh awarded primary physical custody of the gi *specified visitation rights* for Charla. While principle to short-term divorce, he partic episodes had escalated while her emotional stability had rapidly declined to such an extent that *she has become incapable of taking care of* their house and property on Franktown Road in Carson City; as such, she was not providing a clean, sanitary, and safe living environment for their child. He emphasized in his complaint that Charla's actions and behavior were not in the best interests of their child. His petition further asked that the court order a *comprehensive psychological evaluation* of Charla prior to *establishing a visitation and/or parenting plan* for Erika.

Darren also complained that despite the fact that Charla had not worked outside the home for many years, she was capable of being employed and equally capable of paying child support with regard to Erika. He specifically asked that both parties pay for one half of any and all out-of-pocket noncovered medical, health, dental, and orthodontic care for the child.

On May 24, 2005, despite Darren Mack's counterclaim against his wife in the divorce proceedings, Washoe District Family Court judge Chuck Weller ordered that Darren Mack pay $849 per month in child support and to provide $10,000 per month in alimony to Charla. The alimony amount reportedly was determined by the fact that Mack's income was approximately $44,000 per month. Weller further ordered that Darren and Charla share joint custody of the child, alternating weeks.

The divorce was certainly a bitter one, and if allowed to stand as ordered, it was certainly a costly one in a monetary sense to Darren Mack. It was easy to see why someone who was making $44,000 per month would protest vehemently about having to pay an ex-wife $10,000 per month on a permanent basis. But why, the detectives wondered, would someone—like

Mack—risk losing it all through the act of cold-blooded murder that could ultimately lead nowhere but the big house?

As the intensive multifaceted investigation continued, Jenkins obtained Darren Mack's cell phone records in the hope that they might allow him to track his suspect's movements on the day of Charla's murder and the shooting attempt on the judge's life. Mack was known to carry a Sprint Treo smartphone, blue and silver in color, a device that also can be used to send and receive e-mail and access the Internet. Such devices, also known as a personal digital assistant (PDA), act as a miniature computer as well. Jenkins similarly obtained the records for Charla's cellular telephone as well. It wasn't long before Jenkins and his colleagues could see that Darren Mack got onto Interstate 80, the primary—if not the only—East-West route between Reno and Sacramento, and had begun driving west toward Sacramento, California, shortly after 11:00 A.M., presumably right after he made the attempt on the judge's life.

Jenkins was further able to determine from the cell phone records, as Darren's phone connected to a number of cell phone transmission towers that day, that Mack, or at least his phone, had been in the vicinity of the justice center at 10:55 A.M. Nineteen minutes later, the cell phone had made a connection to a tower near Boomtown, a major hotel and casino located seven miles from downtown Reno, just off Interstate 80, at the base of the Sierra Mountains. After that, the cell phone had connected to towers near Verdi, which is near the California border but still on the Nevada side, and a short time later, it connected to a tower near Truckee, California.

There was little doubt that Darren Mack was heading

west toward Sacramento. The cell phone's final connection to a tower occurred near the Boreal ski area at Donner Summit, and that is where the cell phone connections to the various towers ended. One of the primary questions on everyone's mind was whether Darren Mack was truly going to Sacramento, or had he only been attempting to make it look that way? Had he, in actuality, planned to double back and head off in a different direction after ditching his cell phone? At this juncture, no one knew for sure what he was up to or where he was heading.

That same day, while detectives attempted to map Mack's movements, it was reported that Charla Mack's cell phone had been found lying on the side of Interstate 80, a short distance west of the Robb Drive exit. Jenkins and his colleagues presumed that Mack had tossed the phone out of the Explorer's window as he drove west toward Sacramento. Although there had been no sign of the Ford Explorer that Mack was believed to have been driving, the cops had to consider whether he had abandoned it somewhere or was still driving it to some as yet unknown destination.

Among the next steps that the detectives had taken in their efforts to track Mack's movements was to obtain information on his finances—primarily information on his credit card usage. They also had to consider that since he was heading toward Sacramento, he might be inclined to go to the airport there and attempt to take a flight to another city. As a result of that effort, Jenkins soon learned that Mack, or someone, had used one of his corporate credit cards when exiting a parking garage at the Sacramento International Airport, at approximately 2:30 P.M.

Why had Mack stopped at the airport in Sacramento?

Had he gone into the terminal to attempt to take a flight to another location, only to determine that things were too hot for him to try to get on an airplane? Had he stopped there long enough to gather his thoughts in an attempt to decide what he would do next? Or had he simply gone to the airport to create a ruse of sorts in an attempt to throw the cops off his trail? The truth of the matter was that Jenkins and his colleagues really had no idea why Mack had gone to the Sacramento airport—but Jenkins would make it a priority to try to find out.

Judging by the information obtained from Mack's cell phone records, coupled with the knowledge that it typically only takes a little more than two hours to make the 132-mile trip from Reno to Sacramento, Jenkins and his colleagues figured that he must have gone directly there, based on all of the aforementioned information they had collected thus far. An issue that seemed to trouble Detective Chalmers was the fact that the credit card used when exiting the Sacramento airport parking garage could have been used by someone other than Mack, particularly since it had been a corporate card to which other people, including employees of Palace Jewelry & Loan, may have had a copy of. While it seemed like a small detail, it was nevertheless one that needed to be ironed out and resolved.

Before the second day of the investigation had come to a close, Darren Mack was officially charged with the murder of his estranged wife, Charla, and the attempted murder of Judge Chuck Weller. A warrant for his arrest had been issued by Washoe County, according to Reno deputy police chief Jim Johns. Specifically, the warrant was for one count of open murder with the use of a deadly weapon, which could potentially make the case a death penalty case. However, District Attorney (DA) Richard Gammick said that his office had not yet decided whether to seek the death penalty. It was also announced that a $2,500 reward had been offered for the arrest and conviction of Darren Mack by Reno's Secret Witness program. Darren Mack clearly was now a wanted man, and the Reno police detectives had officially issued a nation-wide APB for him. They also alerted police agencies across the borders in Canada, as well as Mexico, to be on the lookout for him, and later upgraded the alert to include overseas destinations. It was cautioned in the APB that Darren Mack should be considered armed and dangerous.

"We would like to resolve this situation in a peaceful manner and let the justice system run its course," Johns said.

4

Darren and Charla Mack were a glamorous couple, by nearly anyone's standards. Darren, a handsome former bodybuilder, had reportedly made millions running the family business, Palace Jewelry & Loans. He had made at least enough money that he and Charla, an attractive eye-catching brunette, could both afford to drive luxury vehicles and to purchase a large Tudor-style house situated on several acres in a semirural area approximately halfway between Reno and Carson City. The house, surrounded by many tall trees, sat back a considerable distance from the street on Franktown Road, a Carson City address, and had a man-made lake in the backyard. It could easily be described as a dream home, one that anyone would be proud to own.

As the murder and attempted murder investigations continued (both cases would eventually be rolled into one), investigators learned that Darren and Charla Mack's marriage had turned south several months before Charla ever filed for divorce. The couple actually separated in July 2004, more than six months before the papers were filed. In addition to the items covered in

Darren and Charla's legal filings, such as custody and alimony issues, the cops learned more about the terms of Judge Chuck Weller's orders, including the fact that Weller had ordered the temporary joint custody of the child because he felt that it better served Erika if her relationship with both parents was kept intact. They also learned that Darren had proposed taking $100,000 from his and Charla's bank account to pay for the cost of both of their attorneys. Since the money that he proposed to use would come from an account that they would eventually split anyway, as part of the divorce settlement, his offer amounted to little more than a fifty-fifty split with regard to covering the attorneys' costs—perhaps a fair proposal, but far from gallant considering his wife's employability after the divorce. Charla had reportedly worked as some type of consultant prior to the birth of their daughter, and had not worked anywhere for at least seven years, preferring instead to stay at home with their daughter. In addition to not having much work experience, Charla also did not have a college degree.

Weller also ordered that the noncustodial parent would pay child support in the amount of 18 percent of that party's gross monthly income. However, according to Nevada state law, the child support amount is capped at $849 per month. Since it had been shown that Mack's monthly income was around $44,000, and that Charla's income was zero, Weller had ordered that Darren be the parent who would pay the child support. Weller also ordered Darren to pay Charla $10,000 per month to help her with the costs of running a household, and granted Charla temporary exclusive possession of their Franktown Road house, until it could be sold as part of the divorce. The proceeds of the sale, of course, would be split fifty-fifty when the sale occurred. In the meantime, Weller ordered Mack to pay the bills associated with that house, including the mortgage, and any expenses related to taxes, lawn, gas, electric, pool/Jacuzzi, TV/satellite, insurance, water, alarm, garbage, pest control, and telephone. Furthermore, according to Weller's order, Mack was not allowed inside the house without first gaining Charla's permission—mostly standard stuff in a divorce case. However, Darren had found much fault with the judge's decisions and it had made him angry—very angry. But had it made him angry enough to murder his wife with such unleashed savagery, and then go and try to pick off the judge with a rifle from a distance?

One of the ways in which Mack had shown off some of his anger was when he had appeared on Reno television station KRNV-TV a few weeks prior to Charla's murder and assault on the judge. He had then told anchor Shelby Sheehan that he believed that Judge Chuck Weller was corrupt. Sheehan said on air that Mack and another person, purportedly a friend of Mack's, had provided documentation to the news program that he hoped would support his claims that Weller was not always impartial in the decisions that he handed down. Sheehan said that Mack had "alleged improprieties in the way Weller handed down verdicts, and claimed Weller based some or all of his decisions on donations to his campaign." According to Sheehan, Mack and his friend had also provided documents in the form of legal motions that Mack believed showed that a number of Reno area lawyers did not want "to do business in Weller's courtroom."

Although the media seemed intent on indicting Judge Weller, at least in part, for what had occurred, most news agencies neglected to mention that a divorce judge didn't have to be a bad guy, a monster like Weller was being made out to be, to cause one of the parties in a divorce settlement to suffer. There were insinuations that he may have somehow deserved what had happened to him. However, it goes almost without saying that one party in a divorce is going to suffer more than the other, whether it is emotionally or financially, or both.

Another matter uncovered during the early stages of the investigation was how Mack had taken issue with Charla's request to the judge that their daughter receive psychological therapy, and that Mack should pay for it. Mack questioned whether their daughter even needed therapy. He had asked that an alternate psychologist evaluate the girl to make that determination. As it turned out, Weller denied Charla's request, thus making Mack's issues about the therapy moot.

Following her separation from Darren, Charla and Erika lived in the large Tudor-style home on Franktown Road and struggled to make ends meet, with the house in danger of going into foreclosure. Darren, meanwhile, enjoyed attending swinger conventions and gatherings in Las Vegas, San Francisco, and at other locations, some of them out of the country. Darren quickly got behind on his ex-wife's alimony payments, as well as the mortgage payments that he had been ordered to make on the Franktown Road house, which at the time had been worth more than $1 million. It was not immediately known whether Mack had gotten behind on most of his court-ordered payments due to his lavish and swinging lifestyle, or whether he had deliberately withheld the funds in an attempt to make life more difficult for Charla. Between May and August 2005, Mack had only paid Charla $9,000, according to court records, and had filed a Chapter 7 bankruptcy in August 2005. Mack also filed a lawsuit through the family's business, Palace Jewelry & Loan, which was little more than a demand that Charla return a number of expensive jewelry items that Mack's business had supposedly only loaned to her, including a diamond ring purportedly worth nearly $200,000, as well as a $13,000 Rolex watch.

Within the first year of our marriage, Charla had written in a court filing, *Darren sold my wedding ring off my hand. I was very upset and hurt.* She said that he had replaced it, presumably with the ring that he was demanding back, and had *promised he would never sell it or other gifts out from under me.* The point of her court filing, of course, was to respond to the lawsuit and to counter Darren's claims that the jewelry had been loans, when they had, in fact, been gifts to her.

During the course of the divorce, the utilities at the Franktown Road house, where Charla and Erika lived, were turned off due to nonpayment. At a subsequent court hearing, Mack had been ordered by a judge to pay Charla $2,000 so that she could pay the utility companies and have energy and water turned back on. Despite the judge's order, it had taken three days for Charla to obtain the money from Mack.

"Despite his claim of bankruptcy, Darren Mack has continued to maintain a lavish lifestyle after the couple's separation, and has traveled outside of Reno with various women, almost every weekend, to alternative lifestyle or swing parties," said Shawn Meador, Charla's attorney, in Charla's response to the family business lawsuit filed by Mack. "In fact, he was in Mexico with a young woman at such a party on the date his bankruptcy petition was filed." It seemed Darren was spending his money wildly, while his wife struggled to keep up with the household bills.

Court records also showed that Mack had gone on vacation to Costa Rica in the time frame in question, and had attended out-of-town swinger conventions at the pace of once nearly every two weeks, apparently with little or no regard for the well-being of his daughter and ex-wife. By this time, Charla and Erika *were entirely dependent upon Mack for their financial support,* according to court documents.

According to Meador, Mack had on prior occasions surreptitiously entered the house on Franktown Road with the purpose of stealing personal items from Charla—despite Weller's order that he not enter the house without Charla's permission. Meador said that prior to the divorce being finalized, Mack had made a settlement offer that he advised her not to refuse. If she failed to accept this offer, Mack allegedly claimed that he would file bankruptcy and leave her with nothing.

She didn't accept or reject the offer, Meador asserted in a court filing. *Instead, she requested Mack provide her with the basic financial information to evaluate the proposal. Mister Mack is now following through with that threat.* Meador further claimed that the lawsuit in which he demanded that Charla's jewelry be returned was little more than his way of using *hardball litigation to destroy his estranged wife. . . . Mrs. Mack desperately needs this court's assistance to protect her from his abusive litigation tactics.*

Jenkins and his colleagues had learned about a My-Space profile on the Internet that had Mack's picture on it and was named "toomuchfun." Whether it was really Mack's MySpace site or not remained to be seen. Considering, however, that it had his picture on it certainly made it seem likely that it was his profile.

The details for the toomuchfun MySpace profile indicated that the person was male, forty-five years old, an Aquarian, divorced, and had graduated from Reno High School in 1979. The profile also indicated that he was a proud parent and business owner. It said that he was on MySpace for networking, dating, serious relationships, and friendship. He listed Reno as his hometown. The profile indicated that his sexual orientation was straight, said that he was five-eleven and that he was athletic. It indicated that he did not smoke or drink. In his "Interests" box were links to what appeared to be several nightclubs and/or swinging sites, mostly in California, Nevada, and Arizona locations. Toomuchfun's objective indicated that he was hoping to meet a beautiful, sensual, sexual, smart, fun woman with a respectful attitude and enjoy all life has to offer. Get ready for too much fun. Chillingly, the person who had created the MySpace account in question had logged on to it the day before Charla had ended up murdered in Mack's garage, and the last log-in was shown as having occurred on June 23, 2006. Based on the personal details, the photograph, and the swinging aspect included in the profile description, it certainly seemed plausible that the profile was Mack's, and provided another twist to the already bizarre case.

It was not long before another bizarre twist occurred. It turned out that a woman, Alecia Biddison, whom Mack had met online three months earlier, possibly in February or March, had gone on a date with Mack and they had spent part of Sunday, June 11, 2006, target-practicing together. Mack and Alecia had both been readers and posters on an Internet blog devoted to voicing complaints about Judge Chuck Weller—she'd had her own differences with Weller, and that had certainly not hurt her chances of hitting it off on a good note with Mack. She had apparently heard the news about the courthouse shooting of Judge Weller, and had tried to reach Mack by telephone to inform him about it. However, she failed in her attempts to reach Mack without thinking, even for a moment, that he somehow had been involved in the violence at the downtown justice center—despite the fact that she recalled that he was a good marksman. When the phone calls failed, Biddison decided to try sending Mack a text message about the shooting incident, but he never responded.

"I immediately text-messaged him, saying, 'Judge Weller's been shot. Call me,'" Biddison said later. "And I didn't hear back from him. . . . What came into my mind was 'I've got to call Darren and tell him this. This is unbelievable.' I mean, we knew lots of people didn't like Judge Weller, and rightly so."

After learning that Darren Mack was the prime suspect in the downtown shooting—and suddenly concerned that she might also be suspected by the police of somehow being involved in the act of violence because of her association with Mack—Biddison decided to call an acquaintance in law enforcement to find out. She also wanted to know what she should do, and whether or not she should go back to her home. Relieved that she was not under suspicion of being involved, Biddison became disconcerted when she learned that Charla Mack had been stabbed to death, and that Darren Mack was the prime suspect in that case, too.

Jenkins and Chalmers soon learned of Biddison's

concerns as the information flowed through the law enforcement pipelines. The detectives, naturally, wanted to learn more about how Biddison and Mack had met online, and more pointedly about Mack's activities on an Internet blog critical of the judge. While it was not their top priority at this time, the information was duly noted and it would be a matter that they would eventually look into. Meanwhile, Darren Mack remained on the lam.

They also learned that Mack held two exclusive and expensive memberships valued at approximately $70,000 at the Canvasback Gun Club. He was, after all, known as a hunter and a sportsman. In addition to the Bushmaster .223 semiautomatic rifle that they knew Mack owned, Jenkins and Chalmers also learned that he owned a .40-caliber Smith & Wesson handgun. Because of his connection to the pawnshop, he also had easy access to a number of other firearms that had been brought into the shop. He also held a federal firearms license and a permit to carry a concealed weapon.

5

A number of people around town who knew the Mack family considered them to be snooty and smug. They were, after all, a wealthy family who had been in Reno for a long time, and their business ventures—particularly Palace Jewelry & Loan—had been successful. Perhaps they were sometimes resented because of their success. Or perhaps because they were well known throughout the area and, in turn, knew a lot of the prominent townsfolk, and regularly rubbed elbows with those in positions of power and money. In many people's eyes, particularly other Nevadans, that meant that they were a cut or two above the masses, and were not hesitant to utilize the benefits of their connections for their own interests. They were perceived by some to have "juice," a term that refers to a long Nevada tradition of using one's connections to powerful and influential people for mutual benefits, a tradition that likely even predates the decades of when the Mafia outwardly ran things in Las Vegas and Reno. Nevada is, after all, a different kind of place. History has shown that the state attracts—

if it doesn't create—some unusual and often unsavory characters.

On the other hand, there were just as many people—perhaps even more—who claimed that the Mack family was friendly, down-to-earth, and that there was nothing to suggest that they were not completely on the up-and-up. They ran their business by the book, just like they had done since it opened in 1958, long before it had passed to Darren Mack. Darren Mack had no criminal record, and had been personal friends with Washoe County district attorney Richard Gammick. When Charla Mack ended up brutally murdered and a violent attempt had been made on Judge Chuck Weller's life, many people—whether they liked the Mack family or not—were bewildered about what could have gone wrong in this golden boy's life. Why would he risk losing *everything* just because he could not handle the divorce settlement?

The trigger mechanism that had set Darren Mack's morning of violence into action certainly seemed to be the terms of the divorce settlement, which the detectives viewed as a primary motive almost from the outset of the investigation, along with his hatred toward Judge Weller. During the course of their investigation, however, Jenkins and Chalmers would learn that Mack was not the only person to have been upset over dealings with Judge Weller. In fact, violence, or at least the potential for violence, goes with the territory of working in any family court system, not just Washoe County's. Family court judges, such as Weller, make emotionally charged decisions, such as which parent is awarded custody of the children and which parent pays child support and how much, and issues a visitation order to which the parents of the child must adhere. It is little wonder, then, that a major area of concern for family court judges and others who work within that system is the nagging perception of the threat of violence lurking nearby. Sometimes, as in Weller's case, the violence did become a reality.

In the aftermath of the attempt on Weller's life, the feelings of many of the people who had gone up before him suddenly became newsworthy. The judge was denigrated on a number of websites: He was referred to as Hitler, accused of being abusive, and described as being a bully, among other things. Some of the people who posted to the sites charged that he decided his cases before actually hearing them, that he was similar to a tyrant, and that he was often unsympathetic to people's problems. One poster referred to him as a monster with a God complex.

One father, John Parsons, went before Weller in 2005 to ask for additional visitation time with his children, but Weller purportedly refused his request and instead ordered him to pay additional child support.

"Weller is very abusive," Parsons said. "He's a monster. He's destroyed everything I've worked for."

Parsons indicated that he had met Darren Mack at a support group for parents who had lost custody of their children as part of their divorce settlement. He claimed that he and Mack discussed their feelings with each other about Weller, and that Mack had expressed being upset about having to pay so much child support. Parsons said that Mack had gotten "the extreme royal shaft," and had filed a Chapter 7 bankruptcy "because he was getting nailed." Parsons said that he was not sympathetic toward the judge.

"I think karma finally came back to bite him,"

Parsons said. "Hopefully, Weller will have a change of heart in the way he deals with human beings."

While Weller was not without critics, he obviously had his share of supporters as well. Ken McKenna, an attorney who had known Weller for at least twenty years, described the judge to the Associated Press as serious and efficient, traits that were sometimes mistaken as being abrupt and unsympathetic by those whose lives were basically being restructured by a third party who, in most instances, had the final say over the outcome. According to McKenna, such traits in a judge—while not necessarily improper—can breed resentment, bitterness, and anger among those whose lives are being sorted out during the divorce process.

"People's lives are being affected to the core of their beings," McKenna said. "Mothers are being taken away from their children. Children are being taken away from their fathers. People tend to lose their reasonableness and they act irrational. It is a very scary situation."

Weller, a married man with two daughters, was born in New Jersey. He graduated from St. Joseph's University in Philadelphia in 1974 and from Georgetown University Law Center in 1977. Weller and his wife, Rosa, moved to Reno in 1982, where he opened up a private practice and specialized in divorce and custody cases. He was host of *Chuck Weller and the Law,* a legal-advice radio program that ran for several years, and wrote a legal column for the local newspaper, the *Reno Gazette-Journal.* The radio program and the newspaper column, of course, significantly raised the level of his visibility within the community.

Weller, who had initially been opposed to the construction of the $86 million Mills B. Lane Justice Center, where he would ultimately carry out his duties as a judge, and, of course, be shot in the process, landed on a committee after moving into the new building in which he recommended that the prisoner-holding facility be shared between the city and the county. His recommendations were accepted and implemented, resulting in the savings of millions of taxpayer dollars, not to mention the gaining of taxpayer respect.

Obviously, Darren Mack had not been one of those taxpayers who had viewed him with such esteem.

In fact, it had only been about three weeks before the downtown shooting and Charla's murder that Darren and Charla Mack had appeared before Weller after their agreed-upon divorce settlement had fallen apart. It was during that time frame that Mack had requested that negotiations be renewed, and he had asked to be heard by a different judge. Weller, however, disagreed, and he ordered the settlement that Mack had been so upset about into effect.

As Jenkins and Chalmers continued looking into the details of the divorce proceedings between Darren and Charla Mack, they found transcripts of two hearings that shed some light on the degree of anger that each had displayed toward one another. In any divorce case, animosity and accusations typically fly back and forth between each party. But in Darren and Charla's divorce, things frequently became very heated, and the allegations toward one another were often viewed as outlandish. For example, Darren once accused Charla of sending viruses to infect his computer, and on another occasion, Charla charged that Darren had hired a private investigator to try to form a dating relationship with her through a popular online dating service. Darren accused Charla and her lawyer of lying regarding some of the support payments he had made to her, and he argued that he had receipts to prove his accusations.

After Weller ordered their divorce settlement to take effect, things only seemed to go more downhill. At one point, Charla and their daughter moved from the house on Franktown Road that they had all once shared as a seemingly happy family. She purportedly refused to reveal her new address. Darren's lawyer, Leslie Shaw, told Judge Weller that Darren had the right to know where his daughter was residing, and after discussing the issue, Weller agreed and ordered that Charla disclose her new address. Weller also ordered Darren and Charla to stay away from each other's residences—except when one or the other dropped off or picked up Erika for visitations. Weller also ordered each to respect the other's privacy, and that any such violations would not be tolerated.

Although many of the discussions between Darren and Charla that took place in Weller's courtroom and inside his chambers could be described as heated, the most severe talks centered on Darren's support payments to Charla, who was claiming, through her attorney, Shawn Meador, that she was broke and had run up more than $13,000 in legal fees to Meador. In one such discussion, Meador claimed that she "owes me a fortune." Charla had incurred more than $36,000 of debt, much of it in the form of loans, simply to survive. Darren and his attorney, however, countered the claims by telling Weller that he had been paying 40 percent of his income to his ex-wife.

"Your Honor, I paid her sixteen hundred dollars a month," Mack retorted during the discussions. "Even though Mr. Meador has lied many times on the record in stating that I haven't. I will give you bank records. He lies over and over and over again on this thing."

"Sir, if I had ruled in your favor, right now, whether or not she would be saying it out loud, she would be thinking very similar thoughts about either me or your counsel or you," Weller said.

Weller told Mack that the system was not a perfect one, and that it is often perceived as "not nice" when a judge rules against someone. He suggested that if Mack was not happy with the ruling, he could go forty miles south of Reno to Carson City and appeal his decision to the state supreme court.

6

While still in the early stages of the investigation, Jenkins and Chalmers learned that Darren Mack had called a cousin, Jeff Donner, in Northern California within three minutes of having shot Judge Chuck Weller. When Donner's cell phone rang at 11:19 A.M., with an excited Mack on the other end, Donner had no idea, yet, of what had transpired that morning in Reno.

According to the account that the investigators would eventually hear, Mack had purportedly made a plea to his cousin not to let him down and to promise to carry his message to the public about everything that had occurred inside Weller's courtroom regarding his and Charla's divorce proceedings—particularly if anything happened to him. Little else was said during that conversation. Understandably, this had left Donner feeling confused about why the telephone call had even been made. Things became clearer to him, of course, as the day wore on, and news of Charla's death and the attempt on Weller's life were released to the public.

Donner explained to the investigators that Mack had not discussed anything else with him, and that he had not called him again. He said that he did not know Mack's whereabouts, but indicated that Mack had spoken with him in prior telephone conversations regarding the judge.

"He talked about how this judge ruined his life, and would ruin his mother's life, and that his child would be taken away," Donner explained, adding that a person who is "broken and snapped to that extent" needs to have someone who is willing to "look into what may have occurred in that courtroom that would precipitate" such acts of violence. Nonetheless, Donner said Mack was not a violent person, and he did not know him to use or carry knives. He explained that Mack, however, had said that he feared for his safety, and Mack believed that Charla would try to do him harm. As a result, Donner said, Mack began carrying a gun.

"By all of his reports," Donner said, "she is responsible for the violence in the marriage. He shared many times over the past year that he feared for his life, and feared she would either shoot him or have him shot."

In a cooperative effort, the Reno police had their colleagues in the town where Donner resided search his house for signs of Mack or his possible whereabouts, to no avail. They turned up nothing.

Evidence in the form of another divorce court record did surface, however, that corroborated Donner's statements about Mack fearing for his life. It was a temporary protection order against Charla, which Mack had filed in February 2005 soon after Charla had filed for divorce. In the court document, Mack had stated that Charla had been verbally and physically abusive toward him throughout their marriage—basically from the time they were married in 1995 until they separated in July

2004. Mack stated that Charla had threatened him many times, and purportedly had said, "If you leave me, I will kill you." He claimed that while they were on a Carnival cruise in the Caribbean in October 2003, Charla had punched him so hard that it had knocked him back onto a table in the vessel's disco lounge. He complained of having been hit in the neck with a toilet-cleaning brush that caused an injury that drew blood, and that he had to have his fingers set on two occasions as a result of Charla's attacks against him. He cited her mental state, and claimed that she used alcohol excessively.

I believe her totally that she will make good on her threats and am in terror of Charla, Mack wrote in support of his protective order application.

Mack also accused Charla of infringing upon his allowed time with their daughter following their separation, and said that she took Erika from his mother, Joan Mack, after showing up at a basketball game that one of his sons from a previous marriage was playing in. Mack had excused himself to go to the bathroom, he wrote, and when he returned, Charla had taken Erika from his mother and left with her *on my time.* He wrote, *It was as if she was taunting me to start a confrontation,* and claimed that he would not obtain *peaceful time* with Erika, unless he received the protection order. However, for reasons that were not immediately clear, Mack had withdrawn the request for the protection order a short time later.

Mack's cousin made a public plea on Wednesday evening, June 14, 2006, for Mack to surrender. Donner said that he would help him if he was in California, and that his family in Reno would assist him in surrendering, if he was still in his hometown. He urged Mack to give himself up without resisting. It was not known whether Mack had heard the plea or not, but neither the police nor anyone else heard anything from the fugitive that evening or, for that matter, anytime soon.

As additional details of the Mack divorce—and the events that led to it—continued to surface, an astute uninterested observer in all likelihood should have been able to see what was heading down the pike. Three months after Mack had filed for Chapter 7 bankruptcy protection for himself, leaving Palace Jewelry & Loan out of it, Palace Jewelry & Loan had filed the lawsuit against Charla, according to instructions from Joan Mack, Darren's mother and business partner, in which the business sought the return of a 4.33-carat platinum ring, valued at $195,000, as well as the return of the 18-karat Rolex watch, valued at $13,000. Although Charla had repeatedly claimed that the jewelry had been given to her by Darren, Joan Mack said that Darren had personally signed the expensive items out of the business and had loaned them to Charla. By November 2005, Joan wanted them returned to the business. According to settlement hearings heard by Judge Weller, the lawsuit demanding that the jewelry be returned seemed to only make matters worse in deciding on who got what. Two months later, however, despite all of the friction, it began to *seem* like Charla and Darren might be able to reach an agreement, after all.

By January 2006, according to court records, it was agreed in principle that Darren would pay Charla $480,000 so that she could purchase a house and a car. Furthermore, Darren agreed to pay Charla an additional $500,000 in yet-to-be-determined installments over a five-year period, and the money would be placed in a special account from which Charla could draw on as needed. Under that plan, Charla would be able to continue receiving approximately $10,000 per month in temporary spousal support payments, as originally ordered by Weller. The money was to have been obtained from Darren's retirement fund. Darren was behind in the spousal support payments, to the tune of $31,000, but it was agreed that the debt could be settled for a $15,500 payment from Darren—to be paid at the same time that he was supposed to make the $480,000 payment. The agreement also called for Darren to pay for Erika's orthodontic treatment. Both Darren and Charla would each pay 50 percent of the child's school tuition, day care expenses, and health insurance premiums. It seemed that the $1 million payout by Darren was sufficient to settle their financial disagreements, but they still needed to iron out their differences regarding personal property.

Among the items at issue was a feather given to Darren years earlier by an Indian chief. The feather, the precise significance of which was not known, had meant a lot to Darren, and he was adamant that he wanted it returned to him. He claimed that it was the only thing "that's really of any significance to me," and Charla agreed to return it to him, despite the fact that he allegedly had removed items from the house, which they once had shared, while she was out of town.

"All I want is my feather," Darren had said.

"In honor of the integrity of how this has played out," she said, "he came in with four movers and a U-Haul while I was out of town and took a ton of stuff. And I think that in the spirit of this . . . I'll give you the feather."

"All right," Weller said. "He gets his feather."

Darren, however, then brought up the fact that they owned a $10,000 television, which was inside their Franktown Road house. Darren argued that they should sell the television and split the proceeds, saying that it would "probably only fit in that house."

Weller disagreed, and ordered that Charla could keep the expensive television.

There was also the issue of the so-called "family photographs," which Darren wanted destroyed. The photos in question were at that time in the possession of Charla's attorney, Shawn Meador.

"Oh, the sex photographs?" Charla said. "Okay."

"Yeah, let's get over that issue," Meador commented.

"Sex photographs," Mack's attorney, Leslie Shaw, said. "We'll say it as many times as we need to."

"All right," Weller interjected. "Let me stop you."

According to reports in the *Reno Gazette-Journal,* Darren had wanted to examine the photos *again,* to ascertain that none were missing. It was agreed that Mack could review them again, after which Meador promised they would be destroyed. When they had finished and all of the details had been agreed to, the plan was to have the order finalized by January 20, 2006. Naturally, that did not happen.

Little by little, the agreement began to fall apart, and it was evident by May that there were still problems, chief among them the lawsuit against Charla demanding the return of the ring and the Rolex. During the January negotiations, Weller had said that the lawsuit would be dropped if Charla returned the ring and the watch to Palace Jewelry & Loan. It had seemed like the simplest and most sensible solution to the problem.

"Moreover, we'll have to get the necessary signature of Mr. Mack's mother," Weller had said. "It's my understanding that part of this agreement is she will drop her litigation against Mrs. Mack . . . and also, I think what we're talking about is, ma'am, you're not going to sue him or his mother or the business, and that they're not going to sue you anymore. That this resolves all claims among the business, the mother, Mr. Mack, and you."

However, by this time, Joan Mack had made it clear that she did not want to sign any releases stating that she would not sue Charla Mack. Without obtaining her signature on the releases, a legal issue would be created if the January agreement had been so ordered into effect. It would bring into question whether the agreement could be enforced, since the agreement had included the jewelry in question, and Meador was quick to point out that Charla "would have an action for breach of contract," if Joan Mack failed to adhere to the agreement.

Since Mack's attorney, Leslie Shaw, had agreed on his client's behalf that they were willing to go ahead with the January 2006 settlement agreement—*if* Joan Mack signed the necessary releases—it was decided that Joan Mack would be asked to come in to one of the meetings in May to determine whether she would sign, or would not.

In response to questioning by Weller and, occasionally, the attorneys representing both sides, Darren's mother confirmed that she had been the person who had originally approved the lawsuit against Charla after previous attempts to get her to return the jewelry had failed. When asked by Weller if she would drop the suit against Charla if the items in question were returned to her store, she readily agreed that she would. However, Weller took the questioning a bit further.

"Are you willing to go beyond dropping the case and release any and all claims that Palace may have against her?" Weller asked. "I mean, as you're probably aware, there's suspicion among all these people that something else is going to happen, and I think what everybody's trying to accomplish is that when we resolve this, it's resolved, and that there will be no further trouble."

Joan Mack's response was that she still had concerns over things that she was "not comfortable with," and told Weller and everyone present that she would not be willing to sign the releases that everyone was wanting her to sign. She said that she would drop the lawsuit in question, if the jewelry items—namely, the ring and the watch—were returned to the store. However, she would not rule out the possibility of future lawsuits by signing the releases. Her stance on the situation raised some eyebrows, but it soon became clearer why she had taken the position not to sign the releases.

According to what was said at one of the meetings, an independent accounting firm was conducting an audit of Palace Jewelry & Loan, and an investigation was being conducted as well. According to Shaw, the audit had turned up "inaccurate recordkeeping of items taken out of inventory, like the watch and the ring, and that reflects that Charla Mack has taken far more personal property than is involved in that lawsuit," Shaw said. "That's what I was told."

Shaw said that a list of items had been compiled as a result of the audit and it included stereo systems, televisions, and other electronics equipment that had been taken out of the store's inventory, and the matter needed to be resolved. Meador, Charla's attorney, contended that it was Darren Mack who removed items from the store on a regular basis. Meador said that Darren would take electronics, such as games, and other items out of the store to give them to his children. Adding to the confusion, he would later return some of the items he had purportedly taken and would, in turn, take new items for a while.

Meador brought up the fact that there could be reasons for Charla to sue Joan Mack and Palace Jewelry & Loan, but he said that she would be willing to sign releases agreeing not to sue, if Joan Mack did likewise. Now irritated, Joan Mack reiterated her position of agreeing to drop the original lawsuit—if the ring and the watch were returned. However, she became increasingly incensed about how the issue of releases from future lawsuits had gotten into the mixture of the divorce settlement.

"I guess I'm a little miffed here," Joan Mack said. "There was nothing ever said about releases or having anything to do with settlements or anything to do with the divorce case. It was simply to get some merchandise back in the store that had never been paid for. It was very simple to me, and it had gotten very convoluted, because I was brought into something here that I had no knowledge of. I was not at the settlement conference for any divorce proceedings. So as Palace's representative, I know nothing about . . . how I was brought in or how Palace was brought into the divorce."

She said that she had spent $70,000 in legal fees surrounding the issues of signing or not signing the releases, but she had not been swayed into changing her decision to not sign them. Shaw took the position that the judge should delay making his ruling until everyone could work out their differences. Shaw, on behalf of Darren, proposed that a new judge be assigned to the case so that a new settlement conference could be conducted, but Weller flatly refused.

"I'm going to rule today," Weller said. He also told both sides that they needed to make their final decisions on everything that had occurred so far, which meant, for all intents and purposes, that Darren and Charla, and their lawyers, had a very short time in which to make their decisions about who got what, and whether or not to sign releases guaranteeing no future lawsuits.

"Is there any possibility now, in the few minutes before I make a ruling, to resolve this?" Weller asked. "So I mean," Weller continued, "is that if we're going to have settlement discussions, the time to have them is before a ruling, because I fear that by ruling, all I'm going to do is ignite a confrontation. One side is going to win, and the other side is going to lose. You're better off right now for negotiating than you're going to be after. Whoever wins is going to think, 'Wow, this is great,' and savor it, and the other side is going to be terribly offended, blame the judge, blame the other lawyer, blame the other party, blame somebody other than themselves."

Shaw argued that rushing to decide the outcome of the divorce case would not do anything to resolve the issues brought up at the settlement conferences, and he made a last-ditch plea to have the case brought before another judge. He also suggested that "any agreeable third party . . . attorney . . . [or] retired judge . . ." would suffice, and enable them to "talk settlement."

Meador, however, was quick to voice his disagreement with such an idea.

"Mr. Mack made a deal and now wants out of it," Meador argued. "He wants this court to find that the deal this court brokered, put on the record, confirmed, and approved was completely illusory."

When it came time to make his ruling, Weller indicated that he thought that Darren Mack had been involved in negotiations with his mother regarding the divorce settlement. As a result, Weller said that he was duty-bound "to do everything that he could to keep the business and (Darren Mack's) mother from initiating a lawsuit against Charla Mack," and that he had made his decision and would rule on it.

"I wish that based upon some of the things I've said, and your own self-interest, that you guys could have come up with something that I could rule on that would make you both happy," Weller said in announcing that he had ruled in favor of Charla and was ordering into place the agreement reached in January.

Weller ordered that each party could take $50,000 from their community property account, held with Smith Barney, to pay their attorneys.

Because Charla Mack had contested the custody arrangement agreed upon in January, Weller set a new date for an additional custody hearing. However, due to the events that would occur on June 12, 2006, the custody hearing would not be held—at least not the one for which Weller had set a new date. In the meantime, Weller had granted both parents temporary joint physical custody of Erika, saying that there was "nothing in the record that suggests that the child won't thrive in the care of both parents, jointly." Weller also pointed out that the child would be better able to develop a relationship with her half brother and half sister under such an arrangement.

Weller ordered that Darren and Charla would each have physical custody of Erika on a week-on/week-off schedule, and that each would take custody of Erika on Mondays at her school for the remainder of the school year. Darren had assured the court that he would arrange his personal schedule so that he would never be out of town on the weeks in which he had custody of Erika.

The parent relinquishing custody will drop the child off at school at the beginning of the school day, Weller wrote. *The parent acquiring custody will pick the child up at the end of the school day. During summer vacation custody shall exchange Mondays at 9 a.m. at the home of the parent acquiring custody. The parent relinquishing custody shall drive and shall remain in the car during drop off. The parent acquiring custody shall remain in the house during drop off.*

In retrospect, the words that Weller wrote were chilling in many ways, right down to the day and time of custody exchange. He had deliberately set boundaries for the couple to follow because of past inappropriate behavior, but on that fateful Monday, June 12, 2006, at 9:00 A.M., both had failed to adhere to those boundaries. Once Weller set pen to paper and signed the order, Darren would have forty-eight hours to pay Charla the agreed-upon $480,000, plus the additional agreed-upon $15,500.

In the meantime, Darren set out to determine who had sent out his bankruptcy notices to "hundreds of vendors and pawnshops, all pawnshops in Northern Nevada that we know of and to diamond vendors in Los Angeles and New York." Darren was concerned, not to mention angry, that vendors had begun voicing their concern that it was Palace Jewelry & Loan that was in bankruptcy, and not only Darren. Aside from being angry over the erroneous perception that the notices had created with his vendors, he and his vendors were alarmed that news of his personal bankruptcy might impact Palace Jewelry & Loan's ability to acquire the merchandise it needs to operate on.

When Judge Weller had voiced his concern about setting into motion a confrontation over his decision, he had no idea of the magnitude it would entail.

7

According to his mother and others, Darren Mack spent much of his childhood growing up in Northern Nevada, and remained there during most of his adult life. The exceptions, of course, were his numerous vacations and weekend trips out of town that pertained to his swinging activities. He graduated from Reno High School, and earned a college degree playing baseball on a scholarship at the University of Nevada—Reno (UNR). In 1998, Darren told a reporter for the *Reno Gazette-Journal* that he began helping out with the family business, Palace Jewelry & Loan, when he was about seven years old, particularly during the summer months.

"I worked here every summer," he told the newspaper reporter. "I would walk from St. Thomas School to work here every day after school. It was in my blood."

His mother and father, Joan and Dennis Mack, began their successful business venture in 1958, when they opened up a small pawnshop on Second Street in Reno. With nothing to sell, the couple started their business by putting many of their wedding presents up for sale. According to Joan Mack, it had not taken long for the business to take off, and within a little more than a decade, the business expanded to the point where they needed to move into larger quarters. In 1969, Joan's parents helped their daughter and her husband acquire the much larger site on Virginia Street, a block or so north of the city's famous downtown arch landmark, where the shop remains today.

"Everybody loved my husband and my father," Joan Mack said to the reporter. "We all had the same philosophy. We didn't have to step on anybody to get ahead. Dennis always had such a good heart, and so did my dad."

After Darren had turned twenty-one years old in 1982, he was given the position of store manager. He held the manager position for the next four years, until his father died in an airplane crash in 1986, at which time he was made president of his parents' company. A short time later, Darren and his mother split ownership of the business, with each owning 50 percent. Ownership of the thriving business made Darren and his mother worth $5 million each.

With mother and son each doing their share at running the business, they were able to make time to take care of personal political interests, particularly issues that adversely affected the small-business community with which they were so closely aligned. They also became involved in trying to get eminent domain laws changed so that an affected owner could, hopefully, negotiate a fair price for his or her property rather than simply being forced to take what was being offered anytime someone wanted a property. According to Darren's brother, Landon Mack, Darren established the Nevada Pawnbroker Association. He eventually became politically active on the state level by lobbying for issues beneficial to Nevada's pawn industry, and he often showed up at state hearings regarding the pawn-shop business. According to those who knew him, Darren was always working to improve the industry and its image.

Many people who knew Darren Mack and his family, including Nevada governor Jim Gibbons, who was U.S. representative Jim Gibbons running for the office of governor at the time of the crimes, reeled with shock at the charges being alleged against Darren. It was nearly impossible for anyone to believe that he would have destroyed what he had worked so hard to build. Gibbons declared the events of Monday, June 12, an "absolute surprise." He was also obviously sad-dened by the news he had been hearing over the past couple of days.

"My heartfelt sympathy goes out to all the victims of this week's violent and tragic events," Gibbons said to reporters. "The family and friends of Charla Mack are in my prayers."

Darren Mack was also a conundrum of sorts. On the one hand, he worked hard to portray an image of a dedicated family man who let it be known that money was no object if it meant spending it to have his three children in his sole custody or—at the very least—easily accessible to him so that he could main-tain a spirit of closeness with them. On the other hand, here was a man who also embraced the persona of a swinging playboy who belonged to swingers' clubs, many of them out of town, and frequented In-ternet dating sites—a man who also ignored the di-vorce judge's order for support and alimony payments that were, in part, intended to benefit his child with Charla. This was a man who had gone so far as to file for bankruptcy in an attempt to avoid making some of those payments. It just did not make a lot of sense that a smart guy like Darren Mack would make such bad choices, decisions that would not only cost him the fortune that he had worked so hard to make, but that likely would also cost him the best years of his life.

The Mack family's history also showed how they reached out to the community, particularly in their support of sports programs, especially baseball. Darren and his family started the Hooligan League, which provided an opportunity for thirteen-year-olds to play on a baseball team. Joan Mack, with the assistance of other members of the community, helped obtain a playing field for the games, as well as uniforms and gear, such as bats, balls, and gloves. Joan Mack also gave back to the community by serving on the Washoe Foundation medical board for many years. With these kinds of backgrounds, the charges against Darren seemed unreal.

The investigation conducted by Jenkins and Chalmers revealed that Darren's first marriage, to nineteen-year-old Giselle Butler, had occurred on June 1, 1986, in Glenbrook, Nevada, located along Highway 50 in neighboring Douglas County, near the eastern shore of Lake Tahoe—an idyllic setting if ever there was one. The marriage produced a son, Jory, within a year, and a daughter the following year. However, the marriage could be described as tumultuous at best, and would be short-lived. Darren suspected his wife of having an affair with a psychology professor whose class she had taken at Truckee Meadows Community College. Despite confronting her about the purported affair, Darren believed that she continued the liaison. He filed for divorce in 1991. Three months after the divorce became final,

Giselle moved in with the professor, and then married him in July 1994. Darren and Charla were married the following year.

The divorce settlement between Darren and Giselle had been a speedy one. Both parties had agreed to joint custody of their two children, with Giselle maintaining physical custody, except for when it was Darren's turn to have the children with him. According to court records, Darren had agreed to pay $500 per month in child support for each child, and had further agreed to pay his ex-wife $2,300 per month in alimony. The alimony agreement called for those payments to end in 1996, or when Giselle married again—meaning that Darren ceased paying her the $2,300 a month in July 1994.

Even though it had seemed like everything had been settled to each party's satisfaction, Darren and Giselle continued to squabble over actual physical custody of the children, particularly when it came to their plans for vacations. Their continued disputes also involved disagreements over which schools the children would attend. In 1997, Darren retained a lawyer to file a motion on his behalf asking for physical custody of the children, in which he had accused his ex-wife of wanting "total control" regarding their children. Although his motion was denied, their disagreements continued.

By 1998, Giselle and her new husband decided that they wanted to relocate to Nevada City, California, located about eighty-five miles southeast of Reno, near Grass Valley, to bolster their careers. Darren, however, had not liked the idea. He had always made it known that he wanted his children to live near him, and he felt that Nevada City was too far away. Darren voiced his opposition to the move in court, and Giselle's request to move and take the children with her was denied by the judge who had handled their case all along, family court judge Scott Jordan. Giselle, however, defied Jordan's ruling and moved to Nevada City, anyway, taking the children with her and her new husband.

While the dispute over Giselle taking the children out of state with her against the judge's ruling continued, Darren's son, Jory, who was ten at the time, had been injured while he and his sister were staying with Darren and Charla. According to the initial report, their dog had run into the boy and had caused him to fall down at Darren and Charla's home on Sunday, March 22, 1998. Although details of the incident were sketchy, Giselle called the Washoe County Sheriff's Office and asked for a child abuse investigation after the children were returned to her home.

When an investigator came out to take the report, the boy said that after the dog had caused him to fall, he had struck the animal to make him run away. Afterward, according to what the boy told the investigator, Charla allegedly walked over to him and struck him on his arm and his chest. The investigator was also told that the boy's chest had become swollen as a result of being struck. The boy told the investigator that Charla had cried over the incident and had apologized to him, but that he was now fearful of her and did not want to see her anymore.

Darren's first wife informed the detective that she had heard about violent altercations between Darren and Charla, including some in which people had witnessed them fighting with each other in public, including inside stores, yelling and screaming at each other. During this child abuse inquiry, Darren's daughter with Giselle was questioned by the investigator. The girl acknowledged that she recognized the fact that Charla was her stepmother, who lived with her father, and abruptly recounted an incident in which she claimed that Charla had slapped her dad "across the face at the airport." She said that Charla had slapped her dad because "they were really mad at each other."

Although the charges of child abuse did not hold up, and the investigator who looked into the case determined that such charges could not be substantiated by what she had learned, Judge Scott Jordan nonetheless required Charla to attend parenting classes for stepparents, which she completed in 1998. Despite the judge's orders against Giselle moving with the children to Nevada City, the arrangement and the disputes continued between Giselle and Darren, until 2004. The divorced spouses finally agreed that the boy could live with Darren and Charla, leaving the girl to live with Giselle and her husband. After Darren and Charla separated, Jory divided his time between the various households.

After Charla had been killed, and Darren had gone on the lam, reporters with the *Reno Gazette-Journal* attempted to speak with Darren's first wife to get her thoughts about what had happened. Obviously shaken by the events that had occurred, she declined to be interviewed. It turned out that she and her family had left town to stay with friends at an undisclosed location—they would remain there until Darren Mack was apprehended.

8

As they continued investigating Darren Mack's background, it was amply clear to Jenkins and Chalmers that Mack was wealthy—just precisely *how* wealthy remained to be seen. There were a number of issues regarding his wealth that needed to be reconciled, and most of the issues turned out to be discrepancies purportedly created by Mack himself after the divorce proceedings between him and Charla had gotten well under way. It appeared that he had made efforts to try and hide his assets, or at least a significant portion of them, when it became clear to him that he was losing control of the situation. It was also clear that he and Charla liked to live large, so to speak. With a $500,000 line of credit at Wells Fargo Bank, there was no struggling, at least not financially, both before and after Charla had given birth to their daughter—their only child together—in 1997. They sent Erika, as well as Darren's children from his first marriage, when it was their turn to be with Darren and Charla, to an expensive private school, Montessori. A stay-at-home mom by then, Charla sometimes helped out at the school in a number of ways, both personally and financially.

One of the teachers at the school had positive, fond memories of Charla, and said that she believed the kids "were really close with her." The teacher described Charla as a good mother and a good person, in general, "who took care of her kids."

A former director at the school chimed similar praises for Charla.

"Everybody loved her," the former director said. "She was vivacious, smart, the kids ran up to her and loved her. She was a lot of fun. She was a joy in my life, and my life was enriched by knowing her."

The 5,700-square-foot home on Franktown Road, with its five bedrooms, five bathrooms, a workout room, an in-ground swimming pool, and the acreage it was situated on, also required considerable financial input for its upkeep, but with Darren's hefty monthly salary, it was not a problem. Neither was the town house he moved into and paid $3,300 per month for, after he and Charla separated. He also easily afforded Charla's Lexus and his orange Hummer, along with the many swinger trips he went on and the family vacations, including ocean cruises, that were a normal part of their lives.

However, a number of people, including Jenkins and Chalmers, would wonder whether he could have afforded his and Charla's lavish lifestyles on the kind of money he reported when he filed for bankruptcy. After all, he had reported to Wells Fargo nearly a year before Charla's death that he and Charla were worth approximately $13 million together, and had listed his own worth on his financial statement to the bank at nearly $11 million. After Judge Weller had ordered him to pay Charla $10,000 per month in alimony, his financial situation suddenly changed, the detectives noted. In August 2005, when he filed the Chapter 7 bankruptcy, he was suddenly worth about half of what he had reported to Wells Fargo earlier in the year. During the bankruptcy, he claimed that his assets were worth approximately $4.3 million, and that he had liabilities of approximately $2 million. As they studied his financial history, the detectives discovered that Wells Fargo had contested the claims that Mack had been making, and filed a formal complaint with the U.S. Bankruptcy Court in Reno. The bank also provided inconsistencies in Mack's financial claims to the court.

Among the inconsistencies reported by the bank was the fact that he had told Wells Fargo that his share in Palace Jewelry & Loan was valued at $5 million, but he had told the bankruptcy court that it was worth only $550,000. Mack told the bank that he owned $3 million worth of commercial real estate, but he told the court that the real estate was worth only $450,000. His financial statement to the bank had stated that he was half owner of a U-Store-It venture, and his share was valued at $325,000, but he told the bankruptcy court that he owned 100 percent of the U-Store-It, and said it was worth $350,000. He told the bank that he held a promissory note from Palace Jewelry & Loan for $1.1 million, and that he was being paid nearly $12,000 per month toward the note, yet he reported the value of the note to the bankruptcy court at $470,000. When it came to his personal property, he had told Wells Fargo that it was worth more than $150,000, but he told the court that his personal property was worth a mere $16,000. On and on, it went, leaving many people—including Charla's lawyers, Wells Fargo, the bankruptcy court, and the cops— wondering just how much he really was worth. The bank's purpose, of course, in providing the court with all of the discrepancies was to try and prevent Darren's debt to the bank from being discharged in the bankruptcy proceeding.

The financial discrepancies were enough to give those examining his actions under a magnifying glass cause to be suspicious of his character. The fact that Charla was still attempting to collect on the divorce court orders for the child and spousal support payments that he was supposed to have been making on a regular basis sealed the deal. The fact that he was vacationing in Mexico when one of his attorneys filed his bankruptcy petition for him did not help further his cause, either. After all, here was a guy who obviously was having trouble deciding how much he was actually worth. Or, depending upon one's point of view, he was having difficulty concealing his true net worth. He was not paying court-ordered child and spousal support, but he was vacationing south of the border. It didn't end there, however.

It was also shown that Mack had taken another vacation to Costa Rica, also after filing for bankruptcy protection. He had purchased an airline ticket for his new girlfriend to travel from Texas to be with him in Reno, according to a motion filed by Charla's attorney, in September 2005, in an attempt to force him to pay the amounts owed to her for support. Charla's motion also pointed out that Darren had attended swinger conventions over the past several months in Las Vegas and San Francisco, sometimes traveling to those cities every other week. Charla also alleged that he had taken young women with him to these swinging events. She also accused him of trying to destroy her through his financial and legal maneuvering. She said that at one point he had even transferred 1 percent of his ownership interest in Palace Jewelry & Loan to his mother, which effectively made Joan Mack the majority owner. The latter decision allegedly was made *after* he had agreed that all assets would be frozen until after the divorce had been declared final.

Darren had been portraying Charla to Judge Weller for some time as someone who was emotionally disturbed and had accused her of being violent and abusive toward him throughout their marriage. During their final meeting with Weller on May 30, 2006, he had asked the judge to order Charla to undergo a psychological evaluation with a psychologist that he had chosen. He also had claimed that Charla was emotionally unfit to have custody of eight-year-old Erika, which had been one of the reasons for his request for her to undergo a psychological evaluation. Charla, however, told Weller that she was not comfortable seeing a psychologist who she did not know, particularly one who Darren had selected. Weller sided with Charla about seeing that particular psychologist, but he ordered that both Darren and Charla undergo an evaluation by a mental-health professional who they both could agree on. If they could not agree on a psychologist, the court would select one for them, Weller had told them.

As it turned out, given the short time frame left before the violence of June 12 began, neither of them would undergo the evaluation. Instead, Charla would be killed, the judge seriously wounded, and Darren Mack would be on the run from the law. His status as a champion for fathers' rights would also be seriously discredited.

9

Charla Mack was characterized by family members and friends as a vivacious and energetic young woman whom Darren had met in May 1994 during a trip to Los Angeles where he had been scheduled to speak at a seminar. One of his relatives said that he was a "great motivational speaker" who belonged to a self-help organization, which the relative did not name. Charla, who had been twenty-seven at that time, had been running a florist shop in Los Angeles when Darren came into her life and swept her off her feet. The petite, beautiful brunette had shared Darren's passion for self-help education, and she was fond of singing country music. Charla had seen Darren as accomplished, secure, and stable. She had been attracted to him physically. To her, he had seemed like the ideal guy, and she almost immediately wanted to be a part of his life, even though he was the father of two children from his earlier marriage. After she had gotten to know him a bit, he had seemed like such a wonderful father, someone whom she had not even wanted to try and resist—at least not at first. In practically no time at all, Charla's and Darren's families perceived that the couple was deeply in love with each other, right from the start, and nearly everyone felt that their prospects of having a happy life together were very good. Eight years before her death, in a twist of irony, Charla purchased space on a Reno billboard honoring her husband. Mack's photo appeared on it, along with copy that read: "The Mack Family Presents: Darren Mack. 1998 Father/Husband of the Year. A unanimous decision by his wife, Charla, and his three wonderful children."

But according to Charla's mother, Soorya Townley, about sixty, the perceived happiness was short-lived, and Darren and Charla began fighting in a "big" way, "loud, dramatic, and emotional." At first, they were always quick to make up, also in a "big" way, and Townley characterized the fighting and make-up episodes as "their passion."

After only a few years of being married, Charla actually began making plans to leave Darren. She likely would have done so—but she discovered that she had become pregnant with Erika. As a result, according to her mother, she decided that she would do her best to make the marriage work.

Shortly after Erika was born, the family moved into the $1.6 million home on Franktown Road. They prospered, in part, by making a living off of those who were compelled by their own financial needs to bring their valuables into Palace Jewelry & Loan, where they either pawned or sold outright items of value that only brought them a fraction of their true monetary value. Those who did not return to get their valuables out of hock, of course, lost them forever, because they would be sold at a substantial markup—thus, a handsome profit for the Mack family. Of course, pawned items were not the only items sold at their store, and the relatively small sum paid out to those pawning their goods helped make up for the risk taken by the establishment. After all, there was no guarantee that every item brought into the store would quickly sell later on, if at all.

Later on, as the case began making national headlines, Soorya Townley told MSNBC's *Dateline* correspondent Victoria Corderi that behind all of the pretense and façade being put forth by Darren and Charla, their marriage was still crumbling, despite Charla's best efforts to please her husband. In fact, their lives, at Darren's urging, began to transform into the sordid world of swinging.

"Darren came in and gave her an ultimatum," Townley said during one of the *Dateline* interviews. "Right after the birth, when she was still nursing, he said, 'You either do this or I'm leaving you.'"

Swinging, of course, often brings complete strangers into a couple's lives for sex. According to Townley, Darren's travel plans included visiting exotic adult-themed resorts, some as far away as Jamaica, and to strip bars—both local and at a distance. Darren also experimented with the drug Ecstasy, and introduced the sordid lifestyle to Charla. In an attempt to save their marriage, Charla went along with what Darren wanted, at least at first. But she was not happy about it, and repeatedly asked Darren to leave the kinky lifestyle behind. She finally demanded it.

"She just finally put her foot down and said, 'I don't want to do this anymore.' And that's when they started having serious problems," Townley said.

There are two sides to every story, however, and Darren's brother, Landon Mack, disagreed with Townley's version of events on the *Dateline* program.

He claimed that his brother had never compelled
Charla to do anything that she had not wanted to do,
and that the swinging lifestyle that they had engaged
in had been agreed upon mutually. He said that Charla
had her own demons, including a brutal temper.

"I watched Charla hit my brother so hard, it knocked
him over a bar table in a disco," Landon Mack said.

According to Darren's brother, the marriage continued to worsen to the point that Darren decided to
move out of the family home in the autumn of 2004.
The following February, Charla had filed for divorce,
an action that brought Judge Chuck Weller into their
lives. That was when the accusations began flying, alleging that Darren was hiding his money and assets,
and with a purported $44,000 per month in income,
Darren had not even come close to being bankrupt.
Darren had claimed that Weller had imposed "an impossible situation" upon him, and that he had consulted
with his attorneys for possible solutions, including bankruptcy. Weller had given Darren a few days to pay what
he owed to Charla, or he would lock him up in the
Washoe County Jail.

"From the very first meeting, Judge Weller . . . had
already made a ruling that Darren was wrong, Charla
was right," Landon Mack said.

As a result, according to Landon Mack, Darren's
hatred for Weller had only grown stronger with each
new ruling or determination that the judge had
made. Mack, it seemed, was on a mission to get his
side of the divorce story, particularly about how he
had felt that he was being mistreated by Weller, out in
front of the public's eyes. It had been during one of
those heated moments long before the day of violence had occurred that Mack had met Alecia Biddison and had won over her support.

"He went to people saying, 'Look at my case. Look at what's going on. Look at how these decisions are being made. Somebody intervene and help,'" Biddison told *Dateline*.

According to Landon Mack, Darren had sought assistance from state senators and other judges, with a common complaint that his case was not being handled fairly by Reno's family court system and Judge Weller.

In a statement shown on *Dateline*, Weller said that "some of Mack's apologists appear to have divorced themselves from reality in order to maintain their support for him. They have made similar outrageous attacks on me, other judges, and lawyers involved with the case. These attacks on the judicial process and those of us who administer it have been shown to be false."

Even Mack's longtime friend, Prosecutor Richard Gammick, who had counseled Mack during his first divorce years earlier, said that the divorce between Darren and Charla was "really getting under his skin." Gammick said that Mack had become "really obsessed with it, to the point that's about all he could talk about."

Following the meeting with Weller in which Weller had ordered Mack to pay Charla more than $1 million over a five-year-period, Darren's demeanor had suddenly changed—for the worse. Weller's administrative assistant, Annie Allison, recalled that when Weller had returned from that meeting, he had looked at her and said, "That guy gave me the look of death."

Many wondered whether Mack had snapped at the point when he had given Weller "the look of death," three weeks before the crimes occurred, or whether he had actually reached his breaking point closer to the time of the actual crimes. Had being involved with the family court system in both his first divorce and that involving Charla caused him to snap and go into a violent rage? He had, after all, been involved with the family court system in one manner or another, particularly matters involving child support and custody, for nearly a decade. In any case, the evidence that was piling up against Mack now clearly showed premeditation.

After Weller had been released from the hospital and was whisked off to a secure and secret location to be with his wife and family while the cops continued to search for Darren Mack, the local television news anchor Shelby Sheehan, on whose show Mack and a friend had appeared to offer their views of Judge Weller, told a *Reno Gazette-Journal* reporter that Mack's friend had shown up at the television station again, amid all of the news about the case that continued to flash across television screens and topped front pages of several area newspapers. The same person, who was not named in the reports, also talked with police detectives.

Among the things the friend related to the cops and reporters was the fact that he had spoken with Mack on the telephone approximately two hours before Weller had been shot, Sheehan told the reporter. According to Sheehan, Mack's friend had said that Mack had not sounded "great," but also did not "give any indication he was about to do anything." The friend purportedly told Sheehan that he did not believe that Mack was capable of the level of violence that had been committed.

"But then when he started to talk it through with the authorities," Sheehan said, "he was talking about how Darren felt he had lost everything. He had lost his family, he had lost a lot financially, his home, and he felt he didn't have any other options."

Sheehan said that Mack's friend had confirmed to her and the investigators that Mack knew "how to use weapons." Sheehan also told the reporter that during her first meeting with Mack, he was "very pleasant, very nice, very calm, and seemed like a very intelligent man.

"But I do remember him saying," Sheehan also said, "'Shelby, my case is over. I lost. I'm moving on.' But he also said, 'I don't want any more families going through what my family has gone through.' He really felt he was unjustly dealt with in the family court."

In the meantime, it was revealed that if the bullet that had struck Judge Weller had been only a half-inch lower, it likely would have killed him. As it was, the bullet had lodged itself in an area just below the judge's left collarbone, slightly above his heart, and had, fortunately, missed other vital organs and major arteries. One of Weller's friends and colleagues, senior judge Charles McGee, issued a public statement: [Weller was] *in good spirits and basically out of the woods.* Weller, safe and on the mend from his gunshot wounds after being relocated to a medical setting, where his condition could continuously be monitored, issued the following statement:

I would like to thank everyone for the outpouring of support . . . for me and my family. I would especially like to thank the court deputies, Washoe County Sheriff's Department, the Reno and Sparks police departments and the Federal Bureau of Investigation for their help and assistance. I am especially grateful to the emergency medical personnel and the fine people at Washoe Medical Center for their work in saving my life.

Additionally, I want to offer a personal note of thanks to the many people of Reno, Sparks, and the rest of Washoe County and around the country who have expressed their support and offered their prayers. With your support, and the help of God, my family and I will get through this difficult time.

I also want to give my deepest sympathies to the children and family of Charla Mack. It is my hope that the community will join me in reaching out to that family in what has truly been a tragic and senseless crime.

Annie Allison, I thank God, suffered injuries that were treated quickly and that will cause her no lasting disability. I am thankful that she was not injured more severely or killed in this incident.

Similarly, Annie Allison issued a public statement:

I would like to extend my deepest gratitude to the law enforcement, medical personnel and others who came to Judge Weller's and my assistance. Their response to Monday's events was remarkable.

I am deeply saddened by the murder of Charla Mack and extend my sympathy and prayers to her family. The impact of this event will take time to heal, both physically and emotionally, but I am confident that both Judge Weller and myself will make full recoveries and return to serve the families of Washoe County. Please continue to pray for Judge Weller and for the family of Charla Mack.

In any investigation of such intensity, the facts continue to be revealed, either directly to the police as a result of interrogation or simply because one or more witnesses step up to tell what they know, either to reporters or to the police. Such had been the case regarding the shooting of Judge Weller inside his chambers.

McGee, who had talked to detectives and reporters, it was revealed, said that he had stopped in the justice center on the morning of June 12, 2006, and had made lunch plans with Weller. He had excused himself briefly and had gone into the office next door to Weller's so that he could make a telephone call when the shooting occurred. It had been a few minutes past 11:00 A.M. when McGee had left Weller's office. Weller, he said, had been standing beside his desk with his administrative assistant, Annie Allison, standing nearby when the gunfire erupted.

"I heard the shatter of glass and a thump," McGee said. "I thought somebody had tripped on a glass coffee table."

When McGee returned to see what all of the commotion was about, Weller was lying on the floor, bleeding from the wound in his chest. Everything had happened so quickly, McGee said. Within a few seconds, a bailiff ran into the room and pushed McGee to the floor, then applied pressure to Weller's wound while waiting for medical personnel to arrive. One of Allison's legs had been injured by the fragments of flying glass. McGee, as well as others, had characterized Weller as being very calm that morning, despite the violence that had occurred.

At some point, Weller had told McGee that someone had placed an advertisement in the *Big Nickel* advertiser, claiming that Weller had a Harley-Davidson motorcycle for sale. The ad had listed Weller's home address and telephone number, and people had begun showing up, asking to see the motorcycle. McGee said that Weller had told him that he believed the ad "was intentional harassment" against him and his family, and feared that the ad was somehow related to the shooting.

"It is so frightening," McGee said. "It's an assault on

the entire system that was designed to solve problems without violence."

McGee characterized Weller as "a warm and loving human being."

By Thursday, June 15, 2006, after four days of intensive investigation and the week quickly drawing to a close, Darren Mack was still missing, and police had few, if any, solid leads to his whereabouts—despite hundreds of tips that had been coming in daily. Some people believed he was still somewhere on the West Coast, hiding out, while others believed that he had fled the country. Nonetheless, the FBI officially joined the manhunt and issued a federal warrant for unlawful flight to avoid prosecution.

According to Reno police lieutenant Ron Donnelly, the FBI had also been asked to help with technical assistance, specifically to use their more sophisticated equipment to try and clear up grainy surveillance video at Sacramento International Airport, where Mack was believed to have used his corporate credit card. Donnelly also said that investigators were working in twenty-four-hour shifts, and were being assisted by other law enforcement agencies to try and solve the mystery as to Mack's whereabouts.

"Mack is resourceful and has connections and really could be anywhere," Donnelly said. He had even previously held a student pilot certification, making fleeing by plane a possibility, albeit a remote one. "This is a highest-profile and labor-intensive investigation. There are so many moving parts to the investigation. We have tremendous manpower working around the clock."

According to Donnelly, Weller had expressed

concerns about Darren Mack to the detectives after being shot, because he had allegedly been abusive to the judge, not to mention angry, during the divorce and child custody hearings.

"The judge said he made a lot of angry comments accusing the judge of wrongdoing," Donnelly said.

Somewhat ironically, Weller had been the victim of a shooting several years earlier. In 1978, shortly after he had graduated from Georgetown University Law Center in Washington, D.C., he was shot by a robber.

That time, I just stood there, Weller recalled in a statement released by a Las Vegas political consultant. *This time, from experience, I knew enough to get down as soon as I was hit.*

Police investigators were naturally sensitive to criticism that began circulating in the local media about why they had taken so long to interview Daniel Osborne on the day that Charla Mack had been killed. To many people, particularly the cops, the criticism seemed unfair considering everything that had occurred that morning. In reality, when one considered all that they were dealing with, they really had gotten to Osborne fairly quickly. In defense of their actions, however, Donnelly said the delay that had been perceived was due to all of their "resources being concentrated on finding the sniper."

People who had known Darren Mack seemed surprised by the acts of unleashed savagery that the police believed Mack was responsible for committing. One person, Toni Lackey, who had worked briefly as a jeweler for Mack in 1999, and also had known Dan Osborne, was one of those who had expressed surprise over Mack's violence.

"He always had a nice polite demeanor to him,"

Lackey said. "Dan and I have lost a lot of sleep over this. . . . I knew how much Darren hated the judge and that he was furious with him, so I called Dan and said, 'Did you know the judge was shot?'"

Another person, Kathleen Winn, of Phoenix, Arizona, who was a friend to both Darren and Charla, and had acted as their mortgage broker, also expressed surprise at the revelations surrounding the morning of June 12. Winn, who had spent considerable time with the couple, had formed Parents Advocating for Court Reform in her state. She had been aware of some of their issues, but she had not realized the degree of Darren's distress with the family court system in Reno and, in particular, with Judge Weller. Had she known, she would have offered to help him in some way, she said.

"I think there were some signs that no one put together," Winn said. "He may have presented a sane picture, but he was not thinking right. A lot of times, the emotion of divorce takes over, but that doesn't justify [his actions]."

Winn said that one of the reasons that prompted her to form Parents Advocating for Court Reform was to provide a means for people who were disgruntled with the system to voice their concerns. She suggested that the people advocating tighter security measures in family courts should focus their energy on giving people dissatisfied with the system an outlet in which they can vent their concerns and emotions.

"Darren Mack wasn't heard or wasn't able to express what he felt about the judge," Winn said, "so he took it into his own hands. Security measures won't fix a problem like that. . . . Divorce court is so humiliating. It's just a business venture where assets are broken up . . . and emotions run high. In this situation, they got out of control and cost someone their life. It's a real tragedy. . . . Who really loses is the three children who ultimately lost both their parents."

Winn recalled an episode in 2002 in which Darren had been stricken with the dreadful disease meningitis. He had nearly died from the disease, but it had brought Darren and Charla closer during his recovery.

"This is so shocking because Charla and Darren went through some really tough times together, and when he was getting a divorce from his first wife, Charla was so understanding and supportive," Winn said. "Then to have things flip around, and both of them be involved in the same kind of divorce is just heartbreaking."

Meanwhile, Father's Day was just a couple of days away and everything indicated that the "Father of the Year" would be spending his day alone, running from the long arm of the law. Instead of being showered with love and gifts from his children, Darren Mack would be spending Father's Day not knowing what the future held for him.

10

As the cops worked literally around the clock in their efforts to find Darren Mack, they recalled that the last reported actual sighting of their prime suspect in the murder of Charla Mack, and the attempted murder of Judge Chuck Weller, had been by Mack's friend, Dan Osborne. Osborne had told police that he had agreed to meet with Mack at a Starbucks, located near Mack's Wilbur May Parkway townhome. According to Lieutenant Ron Donnelly, Osborne had left the townhome almost immediately after realizing that something was amiss, which had been shortly after seeing his dog soaked in blood and witnessing Mack walking toward his bedroom with a towel wrapped around his hand. Donnelly said that Osborne was driving with Erika to her grandmother's home when he received a call from Mack requesting the meeting for coffee at Starbucks.

"Mack had said something like, 'Hey, why did you leave so soon? How about going with me for some coffee?'" Donnelly said. "He said he wanted to meet Osborne and his daughter. So they met for coffee."

But what had they talked about while at Starbucks? What could they have talked about in the presence of the little girl? Had the meeting been a ploy by Mack to try to buy additional time? Had he asked Osborne not to call the police immediately? According to what Osborne had told the police, he had informed Mack's mother, Joan, that something may have happened to Charla. It was after the conversation with Joan Mack that Osborne had placed the 911 call to the police, which had occurred at 11:11 A.M., in which he had expressed his concern that Charla Mack may have been killed. He also told the 911 operator that the police would likely find Charla's SUV parked outside in front of the unit—that was where it had been when he left earlier with Erika. Seven minutes later, Reno police officers were dispatched to the townhome on a call of potential domestic disturbance. They were soon diverted to the activity that was occurring downtown, though. Nonetheless, a team of officers eventually arrived at 11:33 A.M., but they had found no one home at the Wilbur May Parkway address, nor had they seen any vehicles parked outside. The team of officers had reported their findings and had left the condo at 11:40 A.M.

Something just did not feel quite right, in particular why it had taken so long for Osborne to notify the police of his suspicions. After all, nearly two hours had elapsed from the time of the perceived violence at the Mack townhome until Osborne had called 911. It was possible, of course, that fear for his and Erika's safety may have been the reason for the delay. Whatever the reason had been, it had given Darren Mack a substantial head start on the police.

Among the many things that were occurring simultaneously insofar as the investigation was concerned was the discovery of additional information. For example, police learned that Mack and his family owned other pawnshops outside of the Reno area, in Southern Nevada, as well as Arizona, making it necessary to check with employees of these shops to determine whether or not Mack had shown up at any of them. Although it turned out that he had not, surveillance was nonetheless set up over the next few days—just in case.

"By virtue of what he does for a living, he has unlimited access to guns," Donnelly said. "He would have the potential to have any type of weapon, too."

Because of Mack's status as a fugitive from justice, federal authorities suspended his firearms license and permit to carry a concealed weapon. During the course of many inquiries, investigators also discovered that Mack had recently purchased tactical gear typically used by police SWAT teams. He had purportedly made the purchases online.

The cops soon realized that the Bushmaster rifle owned by Mack and believed to have been used in the attempt on Weller's life was the same type of semiautomatic weapon used by sniper killers John Lee Malvo and John Allen Muhammad in a string of murders on the East Coast, particularly around Washington, D.C., in 2002.

Because they were aware that Mack had made considerable use of online dating services, including Match.com, detectives began tracking down the numerous women whom he'd had contact with, warning them that Mack was a dangerous man. They also asked the women to tell them immediately if Mack attempted any kind of contact.

The cops still had no idea as to his whereabouts, of

course, and were still on the lookout for him in central and Northern California as they continued to run down Secret Witness tips and possible reported sightings. Because of Mack's known ability to fly a small aircraft, authorities notified a number of small airports to also be on the lookout for him, despite the fact that his student pilot certificate was no longer valid. The police had also not ruled out the possibility that Mack had fled to another country and they had alerted the U.S. Department of Homeland Security just in case he attempted to use his passport at a border crossing or at a major airport.

According to Dønnelly, literally "hundreds and hundreds of Secret Witness reports had been received from Des Moines to Miami—into the wee hours of the morning. One of these tips is going to be a good one," he said.

John Walsh, of *America's Most Wanted* (*AMW*) television show, sent staff members to Reno to gather information about Mack and his alleged crimes so that they could put it up on their website and begin preparing for a televised episode. Much of the information that was known about Mack and his alleged crimes made it onto the *AMW* site before the end of the first week of the investigation.

Soon after the FBI had become involved in the case, so had former FBI profiler Clint Van Zandt, if for no other reason than to offer his professional two cents' worth in an effort to assist the Reno detectives. Having been involved in a number of high-profile cases over the years, including that of the Unabomber, Van Zandt pointed out that his involvement was unofficial, and anything he said was the result of studying media news reports. He had not seen the case files, but offered his analysis of the case through contact with *Reno Gazette-Journal* reporters, in the hope that it might provide some help. He made it abundantly clear that he was not offering up an official profile.

One of the difficulties in this case was in attempting to determine whether the killer was organized or disorganized, which he pointed to simply by asking questions.

"What's interesting in the Mack case is you see this potentially disorganized confrontation with his wife at his house," Van Zandt said. "He's at the house, and there appears to be no preplanning necessarily, because his friend is there to pick up the daughter. The sheath (for the knife) is found upstairs in the bedroom. Did [the] wife get the knife to protect herself? Or to attack him? Did he go up and get it? Did he drop the sheath while retrieving the knife? Did he go to the bedroom to get it as a weapon of attack?"

Van Zandt indicated that he was not convinced that Mack had brought the knife with him, if it turned out that Mack had, in fact, killed Charla. If he had not brought the knife with him, that would, of course, serve to downplay any preplanning or premeditation on Mack's part. Van Zandt indicated that it was possible that Mack had obtained the knife from inside the house after Charla had arrived, or that he may have wrested it away from Charla. In the case of a lack of preplanning on Mack's part, it was possible, Van Zandt said, that emotions may have played a part in setting off Darren or Charla "so much that one or the other came up with a weapon, and he wound up using that to kill her."

If Van Zandt's analysis was correct, then Mack was an anomaly. Here was a guy who had allegedly committed a violent murder while in an emotional state of mind—certainly not characteristic of an organized killer. Then he regained his calm demeanor and went on to carry out the attempted murder of Judge Weller *after* having coffee in the company of his daughter with an old friend from his high school. He suddenly fit the characteristics of an organized killer, going on to carry out an intense and seemingly preplanned sniping incident, after which he vanished, seemingly without a trace.

"Where I have to consider the preplanning is in a short time he has coffee with his friend, goes across town, takes the rifle to a perfect vantage point, and shoots the judge," Van Zandt said. "That's a hell of a shot. I mean, that is an absolute hell of a shot, especially for someone knowing they had already committed a homicide."

It did not seem likely to Van Zandt, or to the police, that Mack could have decided to kill his divorce judge on the spur of the moment. It would have taken a fair amount of planning and forethought, particularly finding the location from which he could easily carry out the sniping incident at the appropriate time. Besides, the cops had found considerable evidence inside Mack's townhome that pointed to him planning the violent events—both of them—right down to using the court-ordered visitation routine of dropping off the child to get at the spouse.

According to Van Zandt, the person who shot Weller knew ahead of time where he could get off a good, clear shot of the judge, a location from where he could likely escape afterward. The shot, after all, had been accurate, and an emotional person lacking the ability of clear thinking—who had already killed another person that morning—likely would not have been able to accomplish such a feat from that distance.

"It's hard for me to believe he was able to put that together within two hours, without some type of forethought or planning," Van Zandt added.

The fact that Mack was also an accomplished big-game hunter seemed to bolster Van Zandt's theory of Mack being able to pull off such a shot, at nearly two hundred yards.

"So he was practiced in the long shot and probably made long shots in the past," Van Zandt continued. "So we have one killing that looks like an unplanned, emotional outburst, and another cold, calculated [attempted] killing that suggests planning and forethought. My challenge would be to put these two aspects together. . . . For this guy to be able to do this, get out so quickly and stay gone, suggests planning, money, maybe even setting up another identity. It used to be easier to fake identification, but even though it is more difficult nowadays, you can still do it with enough information, create enough of a new identity to get out of the country."

Van Zandt believed that if Mack was capable of planning all of the steps required to shoot the judge, such as purchasing equipment, staking out the location, and so forth, it seemed unlikely that he would go that far without having in place a good plan of escape. In addition to speaking with local reporters, Van Zandt went on television and, like others, urged Mack to give himself up—at least for the sake of his children. However, due to Mack's self-centered characteristics, Van Zandt did not believe that he would do so.

"When I look at this guy's background, I think he is

the sun, and everyone else [is] the planets that circle around him," Van Zandt said. "I think he's the most important person in his own mind right now, and his children are probably secondary."

It seemed clear, no matter how things turned out—whether Mack gave himself up or not—that the ones who would likely suffer the most because of Mack's purported actions would be his three children. In a few short hours, Darren Mack had destroyed everything that he had spent much of his life building. This seemed especially true of the lives of the people closest to him.

In the meantime, on Tuesday, June 20, 2006, a private memorial service commemorating Charla's life was held at Mountain View Mortuary in Reno. Approximately five hundred people, mostly friends and family, were in attendance. Family members asked the media, particularly writers and photographers, to respect the family's privacy as they mourned their loss.

In a news release, the mortuary's director wrote: *This tragic event has deeply traumatized two wonderful families who are experiencing their own grief and are working feverishly to provide the love, nurture, caring and assistance in the grief process of three beautiful children . . . and this* celebration of life *needs to protect them from any further trauma of having their private emotions aired on the evening news.*

Darren Mack's mother and his brother attended the funeral service, along with Darren and Charla's daughter, Erika, and showed their support for Charla's family through their attorney, Scott Freeman.

"Everyone's thoughts and prayers are with the family," Freeman said. "And everyone wishes Charla's family the best."

Charla's body was buried afterward at Mountain View Cemetery, located nearby.

Because the police believed that Mack was armed and dangerous, they were naturally apprehensive concerning the possibilities for what could happen next. They really did not know Mack's frame of mind, and if he had snapped completely, it was always possible that he could still harm others, or even himself. They were also concerned about the amount of ammunition that had been found inside Mack's townhome, along with the other explosive material. If he had an ample amount of either with him, it could spell trouble yet to come.

"What concerns us is the weapons for that ammunition have not been recovered," Lieutenant Ron Donnelly said. "The question is, where are those weapons? Everything's a concern because he acted out in a violent, irrational manner. We can't assume anything. I don't know what's driving this man. . . . We haven't found anything yet to show that he planned to manufacture an explosive. But we can't rule that out."

According to Donnelly, police were more than a little dismayed by the fact that no one had seen or heard from Darren Mack since June 12. He indicated that the police were also frustrated because the rented 2006 silver Ford Explorer had not been found, either. No one knew whether he had ditched the vehicle, or whether he was still driving it.

"You'd think it would have been found by now,"

Donnelly said, referring to the Explorer. "But it could be in a garage, or the plates could have been swapped. . . . There's a chance he's still around. We keep checking everything to make sure we didn't miss anything."

Part II

Mexico

11

As the Reno police investigators, as well as agents of the FBI, continued their search for Darren Mack, tips of possible reported sightings began pouring in from around the country and from other countries. Many of the tips were quickly discounted as having little or no merit, while the more potential ones were given additional scrutiny. One such reported sighting that investigators from both agencies considered as having value had come from the region of San Jose del Cabo, Mexico, which is located near the more well-known, and quite possibly more popular, tourist destination of Cabo San Lucas. Although the area is very much desert in nature, the humidity is often high because of the nearby sea, making it seem hotter than it is in reality. The outlying terrain is not much to look at, but the resorts try to make up for the dry desert look by having beautiful flowers growing on the grounds—the bougainvillea and the red hibiscus seem to be favorites—and *palapas,* which are open-air thatched roof structures found on the beach, are somewhat popular with the tourists.

As it turned out, Mack was reportedly seen in the health club at the upscale Melia Cabo Real hotel and resort, big with the younger crowd and adorned by women in bikinis and buff men. Seldom is a person seen without a margarita in his or her hand. Virginia Delgadillo, an attractive and shapely young blond woman who checked guests in and out of the club, and was there to make certain that their needs, if any, were attended to, would later recall for police that a man who looked a lot like Mack had worked out inside the health club on two or three occasions around June 14 through June 15. She remembered him because he had been so obvious when he checked her out during his visits. He typically wore a tank top and shorts when visiting the health club. She said that she thought he was handsome, and he had large muscular arms, which were exposed to his shoulders. However, it bothered her the way he continuously looked at her, often staring through one of the mirrors at her body, which was often clad in tank tops and short skirts. She said that his aggressiveness caused her to flush and feel embarrassed. It got to the point where she would stay concealed, partly hidden from view, behind the counter when he was there. Displaying a serious demeanor, he rarely spoke to anyone else but her while inside the club. His routine during each of his approximately hour-long visits included twenty minutes on the treadmill and lifting weights for the remainder of the hour. He only came in during the morning hours, she said.

On his first visit to the health club, he had asked Delgadillo whether he needed to sign in. She had told him that yes, it was necessary, and directed him to the sign-in sheet attached to a clipboard. Although it appeared to Delgadillo that he did not want to sign the sheet at first, he nonetheless relented and scrawled something on it, but the name that he had written was not legible. She later learned, as did the cops, that the room number he had entered on the form had been unoccupied during his stay. The shady attitude that he had displayed remained with the health club assistant, and she had no difficulty recalling the incidents to the cops.

Likewise, Chad Ruff, a United Airlines pilot, contacted police officials and reported that he, too, had seen Mack working out at the Melia Cabo Real's health club. He had run on a treadmill next to Mack one morning. After Ruff had returned to the United States he had seen news reports on television about Mack, along with his photo, and had remembered him. As a result, Mexican officials, in a cooperative effort and spirit, showed up at the resort with Mack's photo. Upon seeing his picture, Delgadillo identified Mack as the man who had visited the club during the week in question. It was a major break in the case, as it was the first positive identification of Mack that had placed him in a specific locale since he had fled Nevada. The positive sighting, of course, launched a massive search for the fugitive in Mexico.

As the manhunt and investigation ensued, David Jenkins, along with a number of other investigators from the Reno Police Department, special agents with the FBI, as well as *federales,* a slang term for the Mexican federal police, learned that Darren Mack's June 2006 visit to the Melia Cabo Real had not been his first. As it turned out, according to hotel records, Mack had stayed at the resort for nine days in November 2005, where he had shared a $170-per-night room with a woman who had not been his wife. Barely three months after Mack's bankruptcy had been filed, he and the woman had gone there as part of a swinger's group called Eutopia. The group stayed at the hotel from November 16 to November 24, and according to what desk clerks told investigators, the group had literally booked the entire hotel for that period. During the so-called convention, many people walked around un-clothed—some even had sex in public areas, such as the lobby and the swimming pool. A desk clerk told investigators that it did not matter to hotel manage-ment if people chose that type of behavior—after all, it was a convention. Delgadillo also confirmed that many of the convention guests worked out in the health club while in the buff. According to a bellman, Darren Mack, whether clothed or naked, was always in the company of several women.

As investigators conducted interviews with hotel personnel, sometimes in the open-air lobby as a light breeze blew in off the ocean and wild birds flew through the first-floor public areas, both of which made the 100-degree temperatures somehow seem more bearable, they learned that Darren Mack had checked in to the hotel on this latest trip under an as-sumed name. When they had checked the hotel's records, the cops also learned that he had apparently not used any known aliases, such as "Darren Stone" or "John Smith," names that police sources said they be-lieved he had used elsewhere. Apparently, Mack had paid for his room with cash this time around, leaving few traces of him having been there.

Because Mack had paid cash for everything, the telephone in his room had not been turned on, forcing him to make calls from pay phones at other locations—often inside the hotel. Investigators learned that he had asked a clerk on a few occasions to make local calls for him from the hotel's front desk, which the clerk had done. But after three or four such requests, the clerk had become irritated and told him that it was against the hotel's policy to make calls for guests from the front desk. Detectives were unable to determine who it was that Mack had called in the Cabo area, and the clerk did not recall the numbers he had dialed for him.

Of course, Mack was no longer a guest at the hotel by the time the cops arrived. In fact, despite the headway made in the case, he was still nowhere to be found.

As the cops continued running down leads, they had no way of knowing whether the tidbits of information would lead them to the elusive Darren Mack or not. One thing seemed certain, however—by the time they had wrapped up interviews at Melia Cabo Real, they were almost certain that Mack had left the area. They had no idea how he had left town, whether by bus, taxi, or private vehicle—his missing SUV was still unaccounted for—but taxi drivers did not recall transporting anyone matching Mack's description to the airport, bus station, or out of town.

As the case became more tightly wound, the cops had reason to believe that Mack may have journeyed from Cabo to the town of La Paz, situated below the midway point of the Mexican state of Baja California Sur. While they were not saying *why* they believed he may have made the trip, they learned that it would have taken approximately two and a half hours if he traveled by bus or other vehicle, such as a taxi, using the often one-lane, winding, and hill-laden Highway 19 through the desert. It was a rough drive for even the most experienced of drivers. The trip would have taken even longer traveling along Highway 1. Taxi fare for the trip would typically cost $150 to $180. Although La Paz has an international airport, investigators could not find anything to indicate that he had flown there, either through a private charter or public airline.

Investigators believed that Mack was familiar with this part of Mexico, which encompasses Cabo and La Paz, as well as Mazatlan and Puerto Vallarta, just across the Sea of Cortez from Baja California Sur. He had reportedly visited Puerto Vallarta within the past year, and had checked in to the posh Grand Velas All Suites & Spa Resort with a young woman. The cops considered that it was possible that he had traveled to La Paz so that he could catch a ferry across the Sea of Cortez to the Mexican Riviera coast.

During that time of the year, the ferries made the crossing from La Paz to Mazatlan on Tuesday, Thursday, and Saturday, leaving La Paz at 3:30 P.M. The journey typically takes eighteen hours, putting passengers into Mazatlan at approximately 9:00 A.M. the following day. Naturally, the police could find no clue that Mack had made the journey—no one recalled seeing him, and ferry passengers are not required to show any identification to make the trip. He would have been in big trouble, however, if he had been carrying any of the weapons that he was believed to have left Reno with, because ferry passengers are required to have their baggage X-rayed prior to boarding. If he had brought the weapons illegally into Mexico, he would have to have disposed of them prior to making such a trip.

Although the routes that he had taken through Mexico to get to his destinations were not known, that was all about to change.

12

In the aftermath of the carnage of June 12, 2006, the police, as well as the district attorney's office, had confirmed that Darren Mack had indeed crossed an international border and they had placed him at a specific location in Mexico before losing his trail. Although publicity that had been broadcast via major media outlets, such as CNN, MSNBC, and others, had brought in tips of Mack sightings from a number of locations around the world, the events that began transpiring on Monday, June 19, 2006—exactly one week to the day after Charla Mack had been killed, and Judge Chuck Weller injured—showed that Mack was in Mexico. The question, of course, was whether he was still there. They found out that he was, soon after the telephone rang in the Washoe County District Attorney's Office, at approximately 2:30 P.M.

The caller was Darren Mack, and he wanted to speak to his friend Richard Gammick, the district attorney. Gammick, who naturally wanted to speak to the fugitive pawnbroker, was frustrated when he picked up the telephone and found that there was no one on the other end of the line. He figured he must have picked up the wrong line, so he quickly tried another.

"Darren," Gammick said. "I picked up the wrong line. You there?"

"I'm here," Mack responded.

"Good."

"Did you get my e-mail?" Mack asked.

There was some discussion about which e-mail Darren had been referring to, because, according to what Darren said to Gammick, there had been more than one. Apparently, Mack had sent Gammick a list of conditions pertaining to his surrendering, and both Mack and Gammick wanted to make certain that they were both referring to the same e-mail as they discussed the conditions of surrender. Gammick later said that Mack had told him that he was somewhere close to Puerto Vallarta, but Mack had suggested that they meet in Mazatlan if his list of conditions could be met. He obviously wanted Gammick to travel to Mexico.

Mack's first condition was that he would surrender only to Richard Gammick "and who he wants to bring" with him. He expressed his trust in Gammick, and said that he was unarmed and would go peacefully. Gammick assured him that the condition would be met. His second condition was that he wanted two other people to accompany Gammick, whom Mack named as Mike Laub and Mel Laub, friends of his. Gammick said that he did not think he had a problem with the request, depending upon what Mack had "in mind." Mack agreed with the prosecutor's analysis.

Another condition that Mack apparently wanted was the death penalty.

"I will ask for the death penalty and want it agreed on prior to surrender," Gammick told him. "I got to look at all the aggravating, um, we've got aggravating circumstances here, we've got laws that have to be met. I cannot promise you we're going to get you the death penalty."

"That's fine," Mack responded. "I just want it to be on record that I'm not going to fight that."

Gammick told him they would get everything in writing.

Mack explained that he had been defending himself from "yet another attack from Charla." He also said: "On another note, if I would have wanted Weller dead, he would have been."

Gammick told him that he was charged with open murder in connection with Charla's death, and that he had not yet been formally charged with shooting Judge Weller, because the shooting was still under investigation. He said that they would deal with the issues one at a time. Mack responded that he wanted Weller alive so that he could expose the corruption he perceived Weller was committing.

Another condition of Mack's surrender was that he wanted his family and children to be able to see him when he was returned to Nevada.

"That's going to be up to the mom and the kids and everybody," Gammick told him.

"I understand," Mack replied. "I just want access to them if they want to see me. . . . I just want to know from you if that works out, are you going to support that or not?"

"Well, if they want to see you, absolutely," Gammick responded.

"I'm not asking you to force anybody to do anything," Mack said.

"Sure, but if they want to see you, that will be arranged."

"Good enough."

Gammick tried to clarify a point to Mack regarding the death penalty, which Mack wanted carried out within one year.

"You mean within one year, you want at least a year?" Gammick asked. "What do you want to do?"

Mack explained that he wanted as part of his condition of stipulating to the death penalty to have access to a computer, printer, and the Internet so that he could access the press and expose the corruption that he believed was being committed.

"I figure that should take about a year to get it all resolved . . . out in the open . . . and you go through all the legal stuff then to get it done at the end of the year," Mack said.

Gammick explained to him that he would have to talk to the sheriff about the computer and the Internet access request during the time that he would be lodged in the Washoe County Jail.

"That's up to their security procedures and everything else," Gammick said.

"Would you give me your word that you'll fight for it for me?" Mack asked. "Not saying that you can get it done, but that you'll support that."

"I can give you my word."

"Listen, I trust you, Richard," Mack said. "You're the one person in the government right now that I trust."

"I will give you my word I will definitely check into it," Gammick said. "I will ask if it can be done. I've got one thing I want from you on this, though. Everything that you are printing or going to be put out or you are sending out, I get a copy of it."

"No problem."

Mack explained again that his purpose in wanting

computer and Internet access while in jail was to "expose what's happening to people in this thing called family court that is destroying people. . . ." He also said that he would talk more about it with Gammick when they had more time.

"Okay, the biggest issue with this one," Gammick reiterated, "is it's going to be a security issue. I'll tell you that right now. So I've got to have access to everything you're doing so it can be checked for security, because we have guys up there (in jail) that will be arranging for people to get hurt, jail breaks, all kinds of stuff. Okay?"

"Yeah, I have no problem with you," Mack said. "I trust that you're not going to get in the way of what I'm trying to accomplish. I trust you on that, so I have no problem with you being able to see everything."

"I'm not going to get in your way with what you are trying to accomplish as long as it doesn't physically hurt anybody else, and as long as it's safe," Gammick said. "That's the only two things I'm going to be looking at, okay? I know you want to get your message out. I've got that in mind."

Mack's next condition was that he did not want to do any prison time. He apparently wanted to remain in the Washoe County Jail until his death sentence could be carried out, should it be granted. He said that he would "not play the game, and appeal, and all of that." Gammick, however, said that he could not make a guarantee on that condition.

"I know you can't," Mack responded. "All I was asking for is, look, if somebody wants to have to go through all of this, I don't want this thing to turn into a big thing all about me and fighting for my, you know, coming up with some crazy defense. I did what

I did, I'll tell you what it is, and if I need to die for it, I will—that's it."

"Okay, I want your word that you will support the truth being exposed, nothing more, nothing less," Gammick said. "I've always done that or you wouldn't be calling me."

"I know that," Mack said. "I just wanted to hear it from your lips."

"Tell me something, will you? Because I'm dying to, trying to figure it out. Where the hell is the car?"

"Um, I will give you . . . the keys to the car when I meet you," Mack replied. "I'd like to meet you on Thursday."

"Okay, if that's what we got to do," Gammick said. "You just got me dying because we've been looking for that car and can't find it."

"I know. . . ."

"Okay, tell me what you want to do on meeting, and then give me time to check into it. If everything is copasetic, we'll do it."

"Okay."

"You need to understand there's a little bit of a security concern here," Gammick said. "I will meet with you personally. That's no issue. We've just got to make sure nobody else gets hurt on this whole thing."

"Nobody'll get hurt," Mack said. "I—I am completely unarmed, you have my word on it. You've known me long enough to know that . . . I wouldn't do anything to ever hurt you or anybody around you, or any police officer."

"Well, I didn't expect the thing to happen last Monday, either, buddy."

"I understand," Mack said. "Hey, listen . . . you have my word as much as you can trust it at this point that . . . I'm unarmed. There'll be nothing but a peaceful surrender. All I ask is the same thing. I don't want to . . . have my teeth bashed in. . . . I don't have a problem if you want me to lay down and have them frisk me and do everything they want. . . . Have a sharpshooter sitting on me . . . I don't care. All I'm saying is I'm going to come in peacefully. Otherwise, I wouldn't be calling you. I could stay away for a long time."

"I can guarantee you a couple of things," Gammick said. "One, I'll be there. And two, you will be treated exactly the way you asked to be treated. So if you're cool, everything is mellow. You will not be manhandled. You will not be hurt. If you go nuts on me, then they're going to—"

"I won't go nuts on you. You have my word."

"You swear?"

"I wouldn't be calling you, Dick, if I was going to. I mean, I would just stay underground."

"All right. I understand that. . . . We'd have fun looking for you, I'll tell you that."

"This phone card is gonna just go out, so you got like twenty-two seconds," Mack said.

"Thursday. When and where?"

"Meet me in Mazatlan, Mexico," Mack said. "I will call you at noon, Mazatlan time, and tell you where . . . I'll meet you, and if something gets screwed up, uh, let's see here, um, I will call Mike on his cell phone. Just have him have it there if somehow we get screwed up."

Apparently, Mack's phone card ran out of minutes, causing the phone to go dead. However, a few minutes later, Gammick's phone rang again, and it was Mack. After making apologies for the phone abruptly hanging up, the fugitive and the district attorney confirmed their plans to meet in Mazatlan at noon on

Thursday, June 22. Gammick wanted to know how they would connect, once Gammick was in Mexico.

"I don't know," Mack replied. "You got a cell phone that will work in Mexico?"

"I doubt it very seriously," Gammick said. "I'm going to have to find one. . . . Let's do this. Why don't you give me until . . . tomorrow to get that arrangement made, and then you tell me when you want me to be here, and call me back here at the office and I can give it to you then."

"Um, I'll just call Mike's cell phone," Mack said. "I'm sure he'll want to come."

Mack was referring to Mike Laub, an attorney who was also a friend.

"Just have him make sure it's set up so it works here," Mack continued. "If something gets screwed up, I will call your office." In that event, he said, they would work through Gammick's assistant.

"Okay," Gammick agreed. "And you know I'll probably have people with me, you understand?"

"Yes," Mack said. "You're going to have armed people, or marshals, or whatever you have to do . . . to take me. I don't have a problem with that."

"Well, I just didn't want you going, 'Oh, my God, look at this. You lied to me.' And take off. I don't want that happening."

"No, no, no, I'm not going to do that. I know you are going to have people that have to protect . . . I'm just letting you know that there's nothing going to go down."

Gammick asked Mack how many airports there are in Mazatlan, and Mack replied that he did not know.

"Okay, I understand," Gammick said. "I've got one of my guys sitting here who's working on this who says there is one there. I've never been there, so we'll be in

at the airport, noon Thursday, and go from there. . . .
Don't get real weird on me . . . like back in the . . .
brush hills, down in the canyons, and crap like that."

"Oh, no, no, no," Mack said. "I'll do it in public so
that . . . this is just what it is. . . . You've known me
long enough, other than the incidents that happened the other day, that . . . I can't even think of a
reason why I would do anything other than what I'm
offering to do."

"Now you're sounding like the Darren I know,"
Gammick said. "So . . . I'm pretty good with that."

During the next few minutes, Gammick asked
Mack whether he would want to talk with him on the
flight back to the United States, and whether he
would have any problem with him recording their
conversations. Mack acknowledged that he did want
to talk with him. However, after mildly protesting
about having their conversations recorded, Mack
agreed that they would talk and Gammick would take
notes. Mack said that he would submit to being
recorded later. Mack also stated that he did not have
a problem if Gammick wanted to bring someone from
the press with him. Gammick remained noncommit-
tal on that issue, but asked Mack what his expecta-
tions were on when he would be interviewed by the
media. Mack said as soon as possible, and it was
agreed that it would be done later, when he got back
to Reno. Gammick indicated to Mack that he did not
want him to feel like he had been "screwed" during
any of the process that was about to begin, and assured the fugitive that he would not lie to him.

"Okay, I guess I'm getting a trip to Mexico on
Thursday, huh?" Gammick said.

"You are . . . and then all I ask is that you don't . . .
start a big hubbub down here," Mack said.

"We will react exactly as whatever you do," Gammick assured him. "If you are mellow and cool, it will go down that way."

"I will be . . . mellow and cool," Mack said. "Listen. If I'm a whacko and get all whacked-out, then you do what you have to do."

"You don't sound like you're doing that to me. So . . . just be cool, everything will go cool. . . ."

"Everything will be cool, I promise," Mack said. Mack promised he would not try to hurt anyone, including any police officers who might be present during his surrender.

"Those guys are all heroes in my book," Mack said. "I don't have anything against any one of them, and I don't want any of them hurt or anything else."

13

The next day, Tuesday, June 20, 2006, as he prepared for his trip to Mexico to bring his friend Darren Mack back to Reno to stand trial for murder and other charges that had not even been laid yet, Richard Gammick waited in his downtown office for yet another telephone call from the fugitive pawnbroker. Gammick had been considering his options regarding Mack's surrender, particularly regarding where the surrender would take place—he, along with others, including Mack, had wanted to try and keep him out of *federale* custody, and therefore out of a Mexican jail. He wanted to make Mack's transition from fugitive to prisoner transpire as smoothly as possible, to keep things simple. As a result, he wanted Mack's surrender to occur at a U.S. Consulate, which is the same as being on American soil, and the closest United States Consulate General to Mack's currently believed whereabouts was in Guadalajara, inland from Puerto Vallarta.

There was another concern. Gammick, adhering to the laws of the state of Nevada, and at Mack's own request, would be seeking the death penalty against

Mack. If Mack suddenly found himself in the custody of the Mexican police and changed his mind about surrendering, there could be a problem with returning him to the United States to stand trial. The treaty between Mexico and the United States does not fare well in death penalty cases. If Mack suddenly decided that he did not want to come back, Mexico might decide not to honor an extradition. Under the extradition treaty, Mexico would not necessarily have to send Mack back to the United States to face a potential death penalty if he did not want to go. It therefore seemed more crucial than ever that the surrender take place at a United States Consulate General.

It was about 10:25 A.M. when the call Gammick had been expecting came through. After mutual greetings and confirmation that Mack had received Gammick's message regarding the potential complications of their meeting outside of a United States Consulate General, they got down to business.

"We've been doing some brainstorming here, and I'm sure we're on the same sheet of music," Gammick said. "There's no way in the world that we want . . . to notify the Mexican authorities when we're coming in and what we're up to. There is no way in the world we want the *federales* to get their hands on you if we can help it. I imagine you're in the same boat."

"Right," said Mack. He indicated that he was in agreement with Gammick about inadvertently falling into the hands of the Mexican authorities.

"Okay, what we'd like to do is have you meet us at a U.S. Embassy," Gammick said, adding that he had some that he suggested Mack take a look at.

"Well, let me give you a different . . . city that I'm closer to," Mack said. "It's, uh, Puerto Vallarta."

"Okay, Puerto Vallarta does have a consulate,"

Gammick said. But it didn't have a United States Consulate General, only a United States Consular Agency—the closest consulate general to Puerto Vallarta was Guadalajara, and the U.S. Embassy was located in Mexico City. Gammick sat on that fact for a moment or two. "So you want to plan on that?"

"Yeah, that's fine," Mack said. "But what do I do? Just go, go to the consulate gate?"

Gammick explained to Mack that he had "one of the federal guys" in his office, a person who dealt with these types of situations, and said that they were working out the details. He also then brought up Guadalajara.

"We've been talking to Guadalajara, and they're inland a little farther," Gammick said. "But if you want to do Puerto Vallarta, we're going to need to call them and get all the details, exactly what needs to be done."

Gammick did not go into details at that point about the differences between a consulate and a consular agency, but he clearly preferred that Mack go to Guadalajara. Instead, he asked Mack to call him back in about two hours after he had time to call the consulate in Puerto Vallarta to see what needed to be done to pick up Mack there.

"Yeah, I'll call you back at twelve-thirty P.M.," Mack said.

"Hang on," Gammick said. "I've got another question for you."

"Yeah."

"Is there any chance that you can get back across the border to the United States?" Gammick asked.

"Um, I don't know," Mack replied. "Coming back through is probably a little bit more challenging. . . ."

"Do you have fake identification? Or are you using yours?"

"Well, neither one," Mack said.

"Neither one? That wasn't the answer I was looking for," Gammick said. "You don't have any ID with you?"

"Well . . ."

"I'm not . . . I don't care what it is—"

"I'm not . . . I'm not . . . using any ID," Mack said, obviously choosing his words carefully and feeling his way along to see where his friend, the district attorney, was heading with the subject.

"Okay, well . . . I just want to know, if you had fake ID, if you could get back across the border. . . ."

"No, I can't," Mack stated matter-of-factly. "I don't have fake ID."

"Okay. Think about Guadalajara," Gammick said. "Let us check on Puerto Vallarta, and I'll look for your call at about twelve-thirty P.M."

"If it's going to be Guadalajara, it would . . . We'll have to rearrange the time frame."

"Okay," Gammick agreed. "So if it's going to be Guadalajara, it would have to be later?"

"Yeah," Mack said. "I have to figure out a way to get there."

"Okay. Puerto Vallarta you could make Thursday at noon still?"

"Yep."

"Okay . . . call me back in two hours, would you?"

"I will."

"All right, thank you," Gammick said.

"All right, bye."

It had taken barely a day for the proposed meeting with and surrender of Darren Mack to change from Mazatlan, to Puerto Vallarta, and now possibly Guadalajara. However, later that day when Mack called back, he rejected the idea of going to Guadalajara to surrender, but agreed to surrender at the United States Consular Agency in Puerto Vallarta.

* * *

Meanwhile, a number of judges back in Reno began expressing their concern that additional security was needed for the judges and courtrooms there. Superior family court judge Charles McGee went public and told a reporter for the *Reno Gazette-Journal* that he was afraid to return to work after what had happened to Judge Chuck Weller. He had, after all, heard the glass shatter in Weller's office and had heard the judge when his body fell to the floor.

"I was afraid up there," McGee said. "I was more afraid than Judge Weller, and I don't want to go to work afraid, because if I've got that emotion, I can't be that clearheaded."

McGee, along with senior family court judge Scott Jordan, was critical of the media attention given to the hate messages that had shown up anonymously on a number of websites.

"We are concerned that the extensive media coverage of this week's tragic events in Reno also resulted in wide dissemination of several comments about Judge Weller that were written by people with questionable motives," McGee read from a prepared statement. *"Giving a legitimate venue to those comments gives credibility to anonymous, one-sided and emotion-fueled tirades which deserve none and can easily inspire others who are disgruntled with a divorce settlement to decide that taking matters into their own hands is acceptable, and it is not."*

McGee also spoke briefly to reporters about the bailiffs who typically do a good job by being proactive in looking out for people who might be inclined to cause problems. When a potentially dangerous defendant is brought into a courtroom, additional bailiffs can be assigned when needed. There was one case that particularly had bothered him, one in which an office supply store owner—who had appeared calm while in court—had threatened him later.

"He killed his girlfriend," McGee said, "and announced he was on his way to Reno to kill me and his ex-wife, when he got into a battle with a SWAT team somewhere in Northern California, and, I think, committed suicide by cop."

McGee indicated that he believed incidents such as had occurred with Judge Weller might be prevented before ever making it to the courthouse through mediation, in which people could "vent their terrible pent-up emotions without getting into a courtroom, which seems to exacerbate that." He also indicated that training sessions for judges, particularly new ones, might be helpful to prevent violence against those serving the community.

"I think some of it has to do with learning you can assert the authority of the court in a very formal way," McGee said. "You can talk to the loser and say, 'You may not understand any of this, but I'm going to explain to you what decision I made, why I made it, and what legal principles were involved. I don't care if you hate me, I just want you to go out of here understanding it was a rational process and not one that was the result of outside influence or some kind of bias on my part.'"

During the same week that Mack had killed his wife and had shot Judge Weller, the U.S. Senate approved an amendment spearheaded by Senate Minority Leader Harry Reid that provided additional funding for bulletproof windows, additional security forces, and certain other safety enhancements to courthouses throughout the United States.

14

The untimely murder of Charla Mack and the shooting of Judge Chuck Weller clearly placed the family court system, particularly in Nevada, into the spotlight as professionals and laypersons alike debated about how well the system was working, or how poorly it was working. Those in support of the system praised the work of Weller and other family court judges and raised questions regarding how well they would be able to do their jobs in their often highly charged, emotional, and sometimes dangerous environment, particularly in the aftermath of Weller's injuries. On the other hand, those who thought unfavorably about the system argued that there was little on the books that could be used to hold judges accountable for their actions, and that the entire family court system was in dire need of repair. Furthermore, said critics, the system provided little, if any, recourse for people who believed that they had been victimized by the system during the course of a judge's decision. Those same critics, and Darren Mack was certainly one of them, contended that the Nevada Commission on Judicial Discipline had received nearly 1,700

complaints over an unspecified ten-year period in
which the Commission had handed down only approximately twenty orders of punitive proceedings.
Why so few? many people had asked. One reason
given was that the commission lacked adequate funding, while the more vocal opponents said that it
lacked courage and moral fiber to be truly effective
against judicial misconduct, real or perceived.

Whether he had been treated unfairly or not,
Darren Mack obviously believed that he had been.
However, in fairness to Weller, precedents had been
set in previous rulings by other judges that made
Weller's ruling in the Mack case seem normal and appropriate. Arguing that a divorce ruling, such as the
one Weller had made, should never be used to ration-
alize any kind of violent reaction, Billie Lee Dunford-
Jackson, a codirector at the National Council of
Juvenile and Family Court Judges, said Weller's custody and support order in the Mack case seemed appropriate. When an act of violence is committed by
one of the litigants, it was typically a matter of that
person wanting control of the situation.

"I'm not speaking to this case in particular, or
second-guessing any judge's order," Dunford-Jackson
said. "But I do know that a common trait of people
who are perpetrators of domestic violence is that
they're motivated by power and control. And when
someone, like a judge, steps up and tries to take the
power and control in the relationship, they often
react strongly."

Bonnie Russell, a spokesperson for the Web-based
Family Law Courts site, which is not always friendly
toward the family court system, and has referred to
the system as the "divorce industry," said that Weller
had done "the right thing" in the Mack case.

"Usually in these cases, the one who spends the most wins," Russell said. "But in this case, he (Mack) was not winning, and it pissed him off. So he decided to demonize the judge because he was not getting the result for all of the money he spent. . . . People are getting killed. If you can, it's best to stay out of the courts. Your emotional health will be saved, and your bank account will be saved."

However, according to Paul Mozen, a spokesperson for Nevadans for Equal Parenting, Darren Mack, who had become involved with the group, had felt ineffective and helpless in Weller's courtroom.

"When Mack came to the meetings," Mozen said, "he was convinced that (the judge) had made up his mind prior to coming to court. He said he thought Weller did not like him, and no matter what he did, Weller would rule against him. He felt like he was getting screwed by the court. . . . It's a court of allegations, and the judge has to decide what the truth is. . . . Judges have no accountability for their decisions. If the judge doesn't like someone, who's there to look at it?"

Darren Mack apparently had told Nevadans for Equal Parenting that he planned to use videotapes of the hearings between himself and his wife, presided over by Weller, that would depict the unfairness to which he claimed he was being subjected. He had been very outspoken about his feelings toward Weller, and had also met with his friend DA Richard Gammick a number of times to seek help or advice about how to deal with his case.

According to Judge Dale Koch, president of the National Council of Juvenile and Family Court Judges, family court cases sometimes get very ugly. When they do, it's typically the spouse that becomes the target and *not* the judge.

"The part of the case in Reno that was unique," Koch said, "was that the person allegedly shot the judge. The part that was not unique was that the person allegedly killed the spouse. When one side believes they're not getting their way, they're angry, and some people really are not able to cope with it. They feel they are losing control. It is scary to realize that is going on, and every one of the judges who do family court work realize they are potential targets. It is an unfortunate occupational hazard."

Coverage in the *Reno Gazette-Journal* revealed information about another case that Weller had been involved in, a case that Weller said that he did not remember, that brought Darren Mack and another opponent of the judge together. The case in question had involved a young boy who, the father believed, was being abused by the child's mother in another state. The father had the child seen by a Reno psychologist. The child then said to the psychologist, namely, that he had *finally admitted . . . the serious behaviors and actions that definitively is sexual abuse and emotional abuse,* according to a temporary protective order (TPO), which the father apparently had asked for. It was granted, and it would keep the child out of his mother's custody until an investigation could be completed.

The behavior that prompted the father to take the boy to therapy included the child washing his hands many times each day, as many as thirty times, and that the skin on his hands had begun to look like that of an eighty-year-old man, "wrinkled and cracking."

The boy's sibling told therapists that the child purportedly slept with the mother and allegedly fondled her breasts. When the sister had asked their mother about her brother's behavior, the mother allegedly said that if she told anyone about it, the mother would be put in jail and "would end up killing herself." However, within days of the approval of the TPO, the mother filed an emergency motion to regain custody of the boy. If approved it would require that he be sent home.

Judge Chuck Weller presided over a hearing regarding the motion to send the boy back to his mother.

"You have the power," the man told Weller during the proceeding. "You have to make sure that a child is not in danger."

Without hearing any testimony from a psychologist or a sibling of the boy's, who were prepared to give testimony, Weller ruled that "emergency jurisdiction does not exist" and that the situation had already been determined by a court in the other state. He also said that because a judge in the other state had ruled that the claims being made had no value, Nevada, therefore, had no jurisdiction in the matter. Furthermore, Weller said, the Uniform Child-Custody Jurisdiction and Enforcement Act (UCCJEA), adopted by the Nevada Legislature in 2003, essentially prohibited a court in one state from making rulings that had already been decided in the state where the case was initially heard. It was designed to "deter interstate parental kidnapping" and to discourage parents from "forum shopping" if they were unhappy about a ruling. Although the man's attorney attempted to utilize a statute that would have permitted an investigation to determine whether the child might be in danger, Weller told the father that he could go to jail if he did not take the child to a sheriff's office so that he could be returned to his mother.

The father claimed that it had been at that moment that Weller had become his enemy.

"I freaked," the father said. "And then I started looking at this guy Weller. He is dangerous."

The man related to his friend and neighbor, Darren Mack, what had happened, and the two men began a mission with the objective that they would begin taking actions to bring the judge's reputation into disrepute. Both men had decided that they wanted Weller to be removed from the bench.

"This was something that Darren carried around with him for the past year," the man said. "He knew my son. He knew the circumstances, and he said if this could happen to me, anything can happen to anyone. . . . Darren felt there were people . . . who understood what he was going through."

Weller was clearly not a popular judge—certainly not with many of those whose divorce cases he had presided over. He had a large number of critics, and had received low scores in a survey of family court judges that had been conducted by the Washoe County Bar Association. He was reportedly the only family court judge to receive less than satisfactory choices on the survey sent out to lawyers. The questions being asked of the attorneys on how well they thought judges were doing in their jobs had a rating scale of between 1 and 5; 3 was labeled "satisfactory." The lowest ratings for Weller pertained to a question regarding whether he was "patient and courteous" to those he dealt with in his courtroom, i.e., attorneys, litigants, and witnesses. Half of the lawyers surveyed indicated that he should be retained, while the other 50 percent indicated otherwise. Weller was the only family court judge in Washoe County to receive a less than satisfactory rating in the bar association's surveys, since 1998. Weller reportedly responded to his rating by saying that he was not out to placate lawyers, but he instead focused on doing the right thing for the families that came before him. He said that the low ratings were a result of the election and did not accurately reflect his performance as a judge. He said that he had come through a difficult election process. He ran against a county commissioner that some in the political machinery might liked to have won, instead of Weller.

"I think people chose sides in the election," he said. "It doesn't surprise me that I had critics coming out of the election. That's a factor. . . . This talks about how we select judges. If you come through an ugly race, you have some enemies when you reach the bench."

But he was not without his supporters, either, one of whom was fellow family court judge David Hardy, who had also worked with Weller in a private law firm before either was elected a judge.

"I don't know how to explain what appears to be a lot of discontent," Hardy said. "I know he has a zeal for this job and an energy that's manifest in his long work hours and his attention to the details of each case. . . . He brought a great energy to his work and he wants to be a good judge."

Meanwhile, as Northern Nevadans pondered the shooting of Judge Weller and his ratings, Darren Mack made preparations to reach his rendezvous destination of the United States Consular Agency in Puerto Vallarta, located in the city's old downtown area, to surrender to Washoe County district attorney Richard Gammick, whom he had known for about twenty years, and others who were accompanying him. Even though Gammick was going to Mexico to bring Mack back, he had already begun preparations to recuse himself and his office from prosecuting Mack. Instead, he would turn the case over to the Clark County District Attorney's Office in Southern Nevada, where it would be prosecuted in Las Vegas.

Although he had told Gammick during one of his telephone calls that he was close to Puerto Vallarta, his precise whereabouts at the time the surrender meeting was set up were not truly known by authorities. If he had not yet crossed the Sea of Cortez on a ferry bound for Mazatlan, he still had an all-night journey to make to reach the resort city, where, in all likelihood, he would have to board a bus that would take him to Puerto Vallarta in an approximate eight-hour ride. The trip would take him from an arid desert landscape to that of a very humid area with rain forest characteristics.

Despite having come to terms regarding his surrender to Gammick, Mexican authorities—including the *federales*—launched an immense search effort to try to find the fugitive before the surrender could occur. The roads going into and out of the large tourist city of Puerto Vallarta had police and military checkpoints set up with photos of Mack, which were also distributed to local and state police agencies. On the day prior to the surrender, police officers searched one resort after another, starting at the city's north side and moving southward toward the small bayside village of Mismaloya, where legendary Hollywood director John Huston filmed *Night of the Iguana*. Huston and star Richard Burton got falling-down drunk on *raicilla*, the local moonshine, during filming. Officers showed Mack's photo to various resort employees, including desk clerks and room attendants, to no avail—no one had seen him. If they had seen him, they had not recognized him.

According to Reno PD detective Ron Chalmers, one of the resorts looked at was the Grand Velas All Suites & Spa Resort, a luxurious hotel located north of Puerto Vallarta, in Nuevo Vallarta. The Grand Velas was situated in a growing and newly developed community. Rooms cost from $600 to more than $4,000 per night. It was a resort where Mack and another woman had stayed after he had filed for bankruptcy. The cops had found out about that trip from Mack's female companion, who contacted the police after learning that Mack had been charged with murdering his wife. The woman told Chalmers that she had gone with Mack on that trip to Mexico because she had been looking for a serious romantic relationship. However, when it became apparent to her that Mack was not interested in love but was fascinated with the swinging lifestyle, she broke off the relationship and moved on. During her conversations with Chalmers, she said that she had not heard from Mack. Chalmers pointed out that the woman who had accompanied Mack to the Grand Velas All Suites & Spa Resort was not the same woman who had gone with him to Cabo for the Eutopia swingers convention.

15

The United States Consular Agency in Puerto Vallarta, where Mack's surrender was supposed to have occurred, at approximately 8:30 A.M., on Thursday, June 22, 2006, encompasses a small office in a downtown building in a busy tourist area, not far from the beaches of the Pacific Ocean. The Malecón beach wall, with its familiar arches that overlook the ocean, is located across the street from the agency, which has since been moved north to Nuevo Vallarta. The area is filled with shops, selling handcrafted items to the tourists, and restaurants, with strolling musicians looking for gratuities from dining patrons. An occasional mariachi band can be heard outside on the streets as the balmy but fresh sea air blows in from the ocean, and the tourists routinely dodge the droppings of the well-fed seagulls that fly overhead.

The minutes ticked by, however, as FBI agents and Mexican police officials watched the streets outside the consular agency for Mack's arrival. As they looked up and down the much-traveled streets, some historic cobblestones, and tried to remain inconspicuous, thirty minutes soon passed the agreed-upon meeting time;

still, there was no sign of Darren Mack. After an hour had passed, most of those involved agreed that he was not going to show up. No one, however, had any ideas about what may have happened—if they did, they were keeping their thoughts to themselves. In Reno, where police officials had been eagerly awaiting word of Mack's surrender, feelings of frustration began to creep back. When it was clear that Mack was a no-show, Reno police chief Mike Poehlman called a news conference.

"He did not follow through with the agreement he had made with us to surrender himself this morning," Poehlman said. "That only leads us to believe he has gone off in a completely different direction, changed his mind."

Poehlman reiterated that police believed that he was traveling under the names "Darren Stone" and "John Smith," but declined to elaborate on what led investigators to those false identities. He also said that investigators had reason to believe that he was not in short supply of money.

"Our belief is that he has a large sum of cash with him," Poehlman said.

Poehlman said that detectives still were not sure how Mack had traveled from Reno to Mexico. There were no records that he had used his passport, or that he had used a passport or other identification under the purported assumed names.

The last communication that Mack had with anyone in Reno had been the previous day, Wednesday, June 21, 2006, at 6:00 P.M., during which he had agreed to the 8:30 A.M. meeting to surrender. However, no one had heard from him since that last telephone call.

Gammick, who was at the Thursday news conference—and not in Mexico as had previously been discussed

and agreed upon with Mack—explained the chain of
e-mails and telephone calls that he had exchanged
with Mack earlier in the week, but he remained elusive about their exchanges.

"I'm not going to discuss what we discussed," Gammick said. "We take one step at a time. At the time I
had discussions with Darren Mack, we never talked
about any negotiations whatsoever on any charges.
There was some discussion on the penalty, but absolutely no decisions have been made, and they will
be made at the appropriate time."

Gammick said that Mack appeared to be keeping
up with what was going on with his case by following
media accounts. He said that although Mack had
seemed "pretty straight up" and "concerned" during
his conversations with him, Mack had not asked about
his children, but he had asked Gammick to give a
message to the Mack family.

"He did ask me to call the family and relate to
them, to send his love to his mother and brother, and
that he was in good health," Gammick said.

Gammick said that aside from the sighting of Mack
at the resort in Cabo, he really had not been certain
of his whereabouts. He said, however, that he had
some ideas about where he was, based on things that
were said during their telephone conversations.

"He would not tell me where he was at," Gammick
said. "I picked up that information through conversations on where he was supposed to be. We were negotiating a meeting place, and through that, we found
out various locations."

Now that Mack had obviously reneged on his
promise to surrender, he had lost considerable credibility, Gammick asserted.

"If he does call back," Gammick said, "I'm going

to have a heart-to-heart with him to see where we're going to go. Obviously, he's dealing all the cards."

During the news conference, the questions and answers turned toward the death penalty, and whether Mexico would extradite a person facing capital punishment. Gammick told reporters that he was not sure about Mexico's policy involving a treaty between the United States and Mexico. He said that Mexico would not extradite a Mexican national to face a potential death penalty, but he admitted that "when it comes to an American citizen, I don't know what their policy is.

"It seems to be flexible," Gammick added. "But I'll worry about that when and if I get there. He's got to be in custody before we can talk about extradition."

Gammick, however, had said previously that Mack could face the death penalty for the murder of his wife. There was no mention at the news conference that Mack had expressed to Gammick during one of their telephone conversations that he wanted to receive the death penalty.

As far as the treaty between the United States and Mexico was concerned, the treaty would protect an American citizen or a citizen of any other country that faced possible execution if returned to the United States, according to Sandra Babcock, a professor at Northwestern University School of Law, who also serves as counsel for the government of Mexico on capital punishment cases.

"There's an extradition treaty between Mexico and the United States that allows Mexico to refuse to extradite anyone who faces the death penalty," Babcock said. "If a person is being extradited, Mexico asks for assurances that they will not face the death penalty."

United States Department of Justice (DOJ) spokeswoman Donna Sellers also said that the treaty between the two countries allows for protection in death penalty cases.

"The treaty does not bar extradition if the crime is death penalty eligible," Sellers said. "Instead, it allows denial of extradition if the requesting country fails to provide an assurance that the death penalty won't be imposed. If this assurance is provided, then extradition should not be denied."

In the face of disappointment of everyone involved in trying to bring Mack in, Judge Weller issued a brief statement on behalf of himself and his family: *It is our greatest hope that no further bloodshed occur in this matter. The Mack family, and in particular Darren Mack's mother and children, along with the family members of Charla Mack, have suffered enough loss and grief in this tragic episode.*

As a result of Mack being a no-show, officials in Mexico fanned out and began checking public transportation outlets, such as bus stations, the airport, taxi stands, anywhere there might have been a reasonable expectation for him to seek a way out of Puerto Vallarta. Unfortunately, by early evening, there had been no sign of Mack—no one questioned by police had seen him, despite the photographs of him that had been circulated throughout the area. Police officials, in Mexico and the United States, were even more frustrated that they had failed in their efforts to flush him out. Of course, with all the traffic and tourists coming in and out of Puerto Vallarta, it was always possible that he was still there, essentially hiding out in plain sight.

On June 22, 2006, the same day that arrangements had been made for Mack's surrender, Nancy Grace, of CNN, was reporting on the air about the negotiations between Mack and law enforcement, and pointed out on national television some of the details surrounding Mack's surrender plans—including the fact that the moment he stepped into an office of the U.S. Consulate he would officially be on U.S. soil. In such a scenario, the extradition proceedings with Mexico would suddenly no longer be an issue, leaving prosecutors with the ability to seek the death penalty. It was pointed out by a defense attorney guest on the show that it would be in Mack's best interest to somehow get himself into a Mexican jail, somewhere that would enable him to negotiate his situation and avoid the possibility of a death sentence.

While Darren Mack was still making news on national television, including such shows as *48 Hours* and *Dateline,* among other programs, the Reno PD said that it was still trying to determine precisely where Mack might be in Mexico, if he was even still there at all. They were also still looking for the SUV he was believed to be driving when he fled the United States. Although they admitted that they really did not believe he had the vehicle with him in Mexico—if he was truly still there—the RPD stated that they wanted very much to find it for the evidentiary value involved.

Police Chief Mike Poehlman, who also appeared on Nancy Grace's program, announced in response to Grace's questioning that the vehicle that Mack allegedly drove into a parking garage at the Sacramento International Airport was only there for ten minutes before leaving, according to the payment information obtained from Mack's corporate American Express credit card. Poehlman theorized several possible scenarios about why the vehicle was there for such a short time, including that Mack may have dropped someone off or had picked something up there. There had been no indication that another vehicle had been stolen from the parking facility, at least not yet.

According to Poehlman, the police investigation was looking at the likelihood that Mack was carrying a significant amount of cash with him. During divorce proceedings, Charla Mack had speculated that Darren had transferred money outside the United States, and others expressed their belief to the police that he had a considerable amount of "disposable income" available to him. Precisely where he was, no one could say. But according to Poehlman, detectives believed that he was somewhere along Mexico's west coast, as of June 21, 2006, in part because of credible sightings in Cabo San Lucas. In addition to having been seen inside the health club at one resort, he was also spotted twice poolside—but alone. A possible timeline that investigators had put together placed him at Cabo San Lucas on June 15, and then in La Paz, along the Baja peninsula, two days later. They believe that he then crossed the Sea of Cortez from La Paz, which placed him at Mazatlan, and then later to Puerto Vallarta, where the surrender was to have occurred. Poehlman said that there were a number of active leads that the detectives were still following up on, mostly bits of information that were coming in from Mexican officials.

"The investigators are working closely with FBI officials inside Mexico to locate and apprehend Mack, who may have moved since his last contact," Poehlman said on television. "It's been over twelve hours since we had our last contact, and he can obviously travel a great distance in that time. In addition to the warrant for his arrest for the murder of Charla Mack, and the federal warrant charging unlawful flight to avoid prosecution, we, the police, have probable cause now to arrest Mack for the attempted murder of Reno Family Court judge Charles Weller in the sniper shooting of the judge in his third-floor office on June the twelfth."

In response to questions posed by Grace, Poehlman told the national audience that Reno investigators really had no firm ideas as to how or precisely when Mack entered Mexico. When she pressed the police chief on whether he had a theory about Mack's presumed visit to one of the Sacramento airport's parking facilities, he admitted that he nor his investigators were really certain that Mack had actually entered the parking garage in question. He said that "the assumption is that he was there when that credit card was used," but the chief admitted that they had no hard evidence that it was Mack. When asked who else had the authority to use Mack's credit card, Poehlman said that he "could have given it to anyone. . . . That could be a way to try to lead us in a false direction."

During the remainder of the Darren Mack segment of the news show, it was pointed out how Mack may have been attempting to create a ruse by contacting District Attorney Richard Gammick and attempting to set up a deal to turn himself in, a ruse that could further throw the cops off his track if he decided to make another flight from facing justice. He may have seen on the news in Mexico that the cops were looking for him there, and then decided that he would try another attempt at escape. After all, it only stood to reason that a fugitive wanted on a murder charge would seek advice from a defense attorney, not the district attorney. Neither the cops nor Richard Gammick was buying that line of reasoning to explain away Mack's failure to surrender, as previously planned. Nearly everyone close to the case believed that they would hear from him again.

16

Later that same evening, the mystery surrounding Darren Mack's whereabouts, and why he had not shown up at the United States Consular Agency in Puerto Vallarta, was revealed. According to one of his lawyers, Scott Freeman, Mack had not shown up to surrender, as originally planned, because he and Freeman were still discussing his options—particularly the concerns that Freeman had stressed regarding the death penalty and extradition. Even though Mack had previously told Gammick that he wanted to receive the death penalty for his criminal actions, discussions with his attorney had apparently altered his outlook on the subject. Although Mack had not changed his mind about surrendering, his attorney wanted to make sure that they had covered all of their bases legally, and that Mack fully understood that Mexico would not have to extradite him if he faced the death penalty. Following consultations with Freeman, Mack was ready to surrender that same evening. However, the plans now had Mack surrendering on Mexican soil, and that would require that he be placed inside a Mexican jail.

Many of the officials involved, including FBI agents, had checked into the Casa Magna Marriott in Puerto Vallarta, located near the beach. It was an ideal location for their purposes, particularly since it was only about five minutes from the airport. Since the consular agency had closed for the day, hours earlier, the agents scrambled to determine an appropriate location where Mack could turn himself in. Finally someone suggested that perhaps the best place for Mack to surrender would be in the lobby of the Marriott itself, because it was convenient for nearly everyone concerned. It was agreed by everyone, including Mack, that the surrender would occur there later that evening, around midnight.

Mack showed up at the Marriott early, however, at around 11:30 P.M. Police officials were already in place, and they were watching as Mack entered the hotel lobby. Looking haggard, he appeared to be weary and somewhat unkempt, with beard growth, apparently having been unable to shave for a couple of days. He was carrying a green suitcase, and was dressed in jeans, a pullover shirt, and wearing a red Los Angeles Angels baseball cap. He walked confidently through the lobby, past the front desk, and headed toward an area where there were a number of public telephones. Watching him carefully from approximately twenty feet away, agents held their positions as he reached for one of the telephones to call Freeman. After finishing his conversation with the attorney, he walked back to the front desk, where agents promptly surrounded him and informed him that they were "the guys you're looking for." Desiring to keep public attention to a minimum, the police officials promptly escorted him outside and to a waiting police van. Before placing him inside the van, the cops frisked him to make certain that he was not carrying any weapons or anything that could be used as a weapon. Then they placed him in handcuffs. Although they had not found any weapons on him, they did find a bus ticket from Ensenada to La Paz in one of his pockets, along with approximately twenty credit cards, and $36,200 in cash. He was also carrying his driver's license and passport, but did not appear to be in possession of any fake identification. He was subsequently driven to the local jailhouse, located northeast of Puerto Vallarta, in Las Juntas, an economically strapped part of town. He was booked into the jail at approximately 1:00 A.M., on Friday, June 23, 2006.

Constructed of concrete and painted white, with iron bars on the windows and gates, and a law enforcement sheriff-style star painted near the double-door entrance, the place certainly looked like a jail. Armed with submachine guns, officers guarded the entrance. Mack had been escorted to the jail by Mexican immigration officials, *federales*, local cops, and FBI agents; it was now very clear that Mack was in Mexican government custody. He had not made plans for this earlier in the week during his discussions with Gammick.

The jail was dirty inside, and Mack was placed inside a cell with only a toilet—there was no bunk or bed, and nothing to sit on except a filthy tiled floor, which he ended up having to sit upon for the rest of the night. Jail officials did not provide him with a blanket. Mack was hungry and in need of something to eat and drink. Police officials went out and bought him a taco, water, and soft drinks, which he had to drink with a straw out of plastic bags, because jail regulations prohibited cans and bottles from being brought into the cell area. After providing him with the meager sustenance, the police officials left him alone. If everything went off as planned, he would only have to spend a few hours in the Mexican jail before leaving for the United States. He had already been booked on an American Airlines flight from Puerto Vallarta to Dallas, Texas, scheduled to depart at 9:48 A.M.

According to Reno police chief Mike Poehlman, police officials believed that Mack had decided that he wanted to give himself up, but he might have done it out of fear.

"We believe, based on what we know, that he was aware that things were tightening around him with the checkpoints that the Mexican authorities were running," Poehlman said. "They were aggressively checking public transportation. And that led him to contact his attorneys."

"It was always his desire to surrender," countered one of Mack's attorneys, Scott Freeman. Las Vegas attorney David Chesnoff was also representing Mack now. "It was always his lawyers' advice that he surrender. However, we wanted to explore the options with Mexico, and that created the delay."

Freeman said that he had discussed Mexico's extradition policy thoroughly with Mack. Mack had made the decision to surrender voluntarily and "was not apprehended," and all of the parties involved had agreed to cooperate to accomplish the surrender. He said that Mack's "concerns for his family and his children" weighed heavily in his decision to give himself up and return to Nevada. He also said that Mack's mother and brother were relieved that he had turned himself in to authorities.

"The most important thing is that their son and brother is alive," Freeman said. "They're grateful this ended peacefully. . . . It was his desire to come back and defend the charges."

Police officials consisting of a U.S. agent and a Mexican immigration representative, who were assigned to return Mack to the United States, arrived at the jail to pick him up at 7:00 A.M. After arriving at the airport, Mack's transporters fed him a breakfast burrito, coffee, and orange juice purchased at a fast-food outlet inside the terminal. Soon after finishing his breakfast, a handcuffed Mack boarded the plane and was placed in a seat at the rear of the aircraft.

Approximately two and a half hours later, Mack landed at Dallas/Fort Worth International Airport, where airport police officers met him as he stepped off the plane and arrested him on the Washoe County warrant that charged him with murdering his estranged wife, Charla, eleven days earlier. He was held at a secure location as Reno investigators flew to Texas on a jet owned by the state of Nevada, loaned to them with approval from Governor Kenny Guinn, to retrieve him and bring him back to Nevada.

Upon their arrival, Mack waived extradition from Texas to Nevada and he was promptly flown back to Reno with detectives and police officers on either side of him. Shortly before midnight, he was transported inside an armored SWAT vehicle, with an escort by police in two cruisers, and taken to the Washoe County Jail. Before being allowed to exit the police van, a half-dozen police officers, armed with assault rifles, stood outside, prepared to shoot in the unlikely event that he decided to make a break for it. There were a number of detectives, including Jenkins and Chalmers, as well as another dozen or so sheriff's deputies who escorted Mack inside the jail, where he was booked. Once inside and secure, he met with his attorneys, until approximately 3:00 A.M., on Saturday, June 24, 2006.

A short time later, a warrant was obtained by police that allowed them to search his suitcase. Inside, they found the key to the 2006 Ford Explorer that he had been driving, but its whereabouts were still unknown to the investigators. Also in the suitcase was the key to his Hummer, which he had left behind inside the garage at his Reno townhome, and nearly two dozen phone cards, which he had purchased to make long-distance calls from Mexico. They also found a pair of binoculars and the accompanying carrying case, and a pair of tan Rockport shoes, each of which bore red stains, according to a police search warrant document. A black T-shirt and a black belt, both stained with a dark substance, were also inside the suitcase—these items, along with the shoes, would be tested at the state crime laboratory to identify the stains. The cops had also retrieved Mack's Treo PDA and were examining its contents. They were not yet revealing whether there was anything pertinent, such as incriminating e-mail messages, on it or not.

Shortly after learning that Mack had been taken into custody, a number of people close to the case, including Judge Weller and Charla Mack's family members, expressed their relief that Mack had been apprehended. They thanked those in the law enforcement community for their kindness and generosity at a time when none of them felt really safe with Darren Mack on the loose. Weller, who was still recuperating from his wounds at an undisclosed location, issued a statement that he was *overjoyed that [he] and [his] family will be able to resume [their] lives*. He also said in a statement that he and his family were *grateful that Mr. Mack*

*has been apprehended and that this tragedy has been resolved
in a peaceful manner without further bloodshed.*

Chris Broughton, Charla Mack's brother, and
Soorya Townley, her mother, had learned of Mack's
surrender late Thursday evening.

"We are greatly relieved . . . but not surprised . . .
that Darren Mack has been apprehended without additional senseless bloodshed, and we look forward to
justice being served, for my sister's murder and for
the shooting of Judge Weller," said Broughton at a
press conference held after Mack's return to Reno,
with his mother looking on by his side. "Our family
has been forever destroyed by the barbaric and
heinous acts of June twelfth. But in spite of these
acts, we have also experienced great goodness here
in Reno."

Broughton said that even though Darren Mack had
fled to Mexico, Broughton and his family never believed he would "get very far" because of all the efforts
being made by law enforcement to bring him in.

"Nothing will bring my sister back," he added. "We
are still in mourning and we are still in great sadness.
However, we don't have to look over our shoulders for
the rest of our lives."

Townley, who had been residing in California, was
making plans to relocate to Reno so that she could be
closer to her granddaughter and be involved in her
life. The child, at that time, was living with Darren
Mack's mother.

Up until they had learned of Mack's plans to surrender, Mack's family, particularly his mother, Joan,
and his brother, Landon, did not even know that he
was still alive. Although they had received a lot of support from the community where they had lived for

nearly fifty years, as well as from family and friends, they had been taken down a dark road by their fears.

"I've been in shock," Joan Mack said with tear-filled eyes. "We just have to put one foot in front of the other and pray. Lots of prayers. We hope everybody can pull through this for the best interest of the children."

Her son Landon agreed that it was about what was best for the children.

"We love their family," he said in a reference to Charla's parents and brother. "We want to stay a family."

Joan Mack described Darren as having been a "good son," and added: "Both of my sons, they've been model citizens. They've always been there for people." She said that they had always been community oriented and had helped out with fund-raisers and youth activities. She said that she was grateful to the community.

"The support of the community has been amazing," she said. "Everybody has called, asking if there's anything they can do. It's so gratifying to hear people in the community remembering the good times. We want to thank the community for all of its support. . . . You see things on TV and hear things on the radio, but you never think you're going to be involved in anything like this."

Mack's motive for killing his wife and shooting Judge Weller, according to a friend that had talked to police, was simply that he had reached "the end of his rope," and had become "extremely frustrated and angry with both his estranged wife and Judge Weller," as was stated in one of the search warrant affidavits. The witness apparently had told detectives that Mack had "discussed hiring him to follow Judge Weller in the hope of proving that he was corrupt."

According to District Attorney Richard Gammick, there were many issues that his office faced in the prosecution of Darren Mack, including whether to seek the death penalty or not. Gammick indicated that he would be involved in that process. However, there would likely be other challenges presented by Mack's defense team, which would need to be dealt with, including a potential conflict of interest because of the friendship between Mack and Gammick, as well as the telephone calls and e-mails between the two while Mack was on the lam. Gammick said that all of the issues would be addressed.

"We work really hard to try to avoid as many of these legal issues as we can," Gammick said. "But the attorneys on the other side are aggressive, and I'm sure we're going to see challenges on just about every single thing that can be challenged. . . . I owe my allegiance to the people of this county, and this case will be handled just like any other murder case would be handled."

PART III

BACK IN RENO: THE LEGAL WRANGLING BEGINS

17

Although Darren Mack was now back in Reno and behind bars, the investigation into the brutal murder of his wife and the attempted murder of Judge Weller continued at full speed. As investigators David Jenkins, Ron Chalmers, and others continued their work in attempting to show that Mack's actions on June 12, 2006, and afterward, were the result of a very methodical and well-thought-out series of events, interest in the case among Reno's residents did not seem to wane. After all, as a millionaire businessman, he had been thought of as a pillar of the community—one who had managed to get himself on the FBI's Ten Most Wanted Fugitives list. FBI Director Robert S. Mueller had given Mack top billing on its website, having described him as a man who should be considered armed and dangerous and one who had access to all types of weapons. Interest in the Mack case was not going to go away anytime soon.

A number of Reno residents were happy that Mack had been taken into custody peacefully, including business owners and managers of businesses that had been locked down two weeks earlier while downtown was seemingly under siege. One employee at a downtown restaurant, who was at work the day of the shooting incident, reflected on that day's events as he recalled the fear and excitement as the cops locked down the area.

"I was here the day the whole thing went down," the employee said. "We were locked up inside for three hours, and the cops were outside with their guns. . . . I guess it is a good thing that he was caught. There is that relief. Now people can eat in peace."

Another resident said that it was "reassuring" to know that Mack was in custody, which, she believed, brought "some closure for the community."

Other residents said that they had not been concerned during the ten days that Mack was on the lam.

"I never felt unsafe while he was on the loose," said one of the other residents. "People who target other people for harm usually are on a mission and do just that, and not much else. It's not like a serial killer."

"I didn't know he got caught," said yet another resident, who apparently had not heard any of the news about Mack's arrest. "But I feel safer. Yeah, totally."

"We're happy he was caught peacefully," said a Washoe County Courthouse security officer, who had been in the middle of the perceived downtown siege.

As people who experienced the traumatizing downtown ordeal involving the shooting of Judge Weller felt relieved at the news of Mack's arrest, allowing their lives to begin to return to normal, many of Charla Mack's friends and acquaintances took time out to reflect on what a special person she had been. Some recalled how on the Friday before her murder, she had been at her daughter's elementary school, helping out in various ways, including serving lunch to the children. Then, to everyone's shock and disbelief, she was viciously stabbed to death in the garage of Mack's townhome, while their daughter was upstairs watching television with a friend of Mack's who had agreed to look after her, not knowing about the carnage that was to take place that fateful morning.

"Everyone loved her," said a friend, the former director of the Montessori school where Charla volunteered. "She would walk in the room and the energy inside would shift. She was bright and vibrant, energetic and giving."

Charla, as well as Darren, had served on the school's board, and Charla had been involved in fund-raising activities for the school.

"She's one of the reasons why I came there," said the former director. "She was beautiful, inside and out. . . . I am absolutely blown out of the water by any accusation for this behavior [of Darren's], because I will tell you, I love him, too. I loved both of them and knew them as a unit, not separately."

Another staff member and friend at the school had met Charla when she was pregnant, shortly after she had married Darren. She described them as the typical newlywed couple, and she was shocked when she first heard that Charla had been killed.

"Oh, my God" had been her first thought. "The worst part is that I can't get their pictures out of my head. It's unreal," she said.

The friend said that the last time she had seen

Charla had been about a month before Charla was killed. She said that Charla had told her that she was going through a "pretty ugly divorce," but, otherwise, had looked good and had said that she was trying to "put her life together."

"Charla was always vivacious and had a lot of energy," she said. "She was always smiling and was just a good person."

The friend said that she had seen Darren Mack about a week before the killing. He had been at a juice bar in Reno, and he was holding his daughter on his lap.

Both of the friends described Charla as a good mother, and said that she had a positive and close relationship with her two stepchildren from Mack's previous marriage, which seemed disparate from the court records in which Charla had charged that Darren had tried to keep the stepchildren away from her.

"I can't tell you how special her children are, and that did not happen by accident," said the former school director. "She was the best mother. She put a lot of energy into being a mom. It's not an easy thing to be a stepparent. I saw a lot that others did not see, and saw how hard she worked to make her family situation work."

Although Charla liked to spend time at home, putting together scrapbooks and photograph albums, her friends from the school insisted that she was much more than a stay-at-home mom with an often lavish lifestyle.

"She wasn't a nobody who just depended on this man," said the school staff member. "She was not a lazy woman who just sat in a million-dollar home

Reno, Nevada, as it looks from an area near Virginia City. *(Author photo)*

The entrance to the upscale Fleur de Lis townhomes where Darren Mack lured his ex-wife, Charla, so he could kill her. *(Author photo)*

View of Darren and Charla Mack's Tudor-style home. *(Author photo)*

The Mack family business, Palace Jewelry and Loan, only a few blocks from where Darren Mack shot Family Court Judge Chuck Weller. *(Author photo)*

The parking garage from where Mack shot Judge Weller. *(Author photo)*

Back view of the Mills Lane Justice Center. *(Author photo)*

Investigators remove the remains of a window, shattered by a bullet that struck Judge Weller at the Washoe County Courthouse complex. *(Photo courtesy of AP Images/Rich Pedroncelli)*

Reno Deputy Police Chief Jim Johns *(second from right)* makes a statement during a press conference about the search for alleged sniper and murderer Darren Mack. With Johns are *(from left)*: Washoe County Assistant Sheriff Craig Callahan, Reno Police Chief Mike Poehlman, and Washoe County District Attorney Richard Gammick *(Photo courtesy of Marilyn Newton/Reno Gazette-Journal)*

Reno Deputy Police Chief Jim Johns points to the parking gallery where Darren Mack allegedly fired a shot that struck Judge Weller at the Family Court. *(Photo courtesy of Marilyn Newton/Reno Gazette-Journal)*

SWAT team members make their way along Sierra Street toward First Street, looking for the sniper who shot Judge Weller that morning. *(Photo courtesy of Marilyn Newton/Reno Gazette-Journal)*

Police move along First Street as they search for the sniper.
(Photo courtesy of Marilyn Newton/Reno Gazette-Journal)

Two Reno policeman, armed with semiautomatic weapons, guard a perimeter around the area where the suspected sniper was thought to be.
(Photo courtesy of Marilyn Newton/ Reno Gazette-Journal)

Two Reno police officers keep a close eye on the Palladio Condominium project under construction at First and Sierra Streets as SWAT team members search the building. *(Photo courtesy of Marilyn Newton/ Reno Gazette-Journal)*

Arch Rock at Cabo San Lucas, one of the exotic locations in Mexico where Darren Mack lived a life of luxury while on the run from the law. *(Author photo)*

Washoe County District Attorney Richard Gammick listens to a question from the media after he announced that Clark County (Las Vegas) would try the Darren Mack case. *(Photo courtesy of Andy Barron/ Reno Gazette-Journal)*

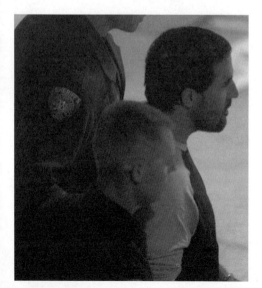

Darren Mack is led into the Washoe County Jail upon his return from Mexico. *(Photo courtesy of Liz Margerum/Reno Gazette-Journal)*

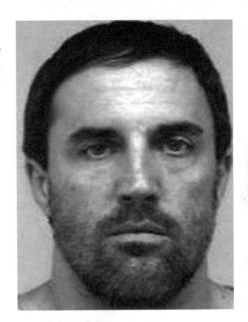

Mug shot of Darren Mack. *(Photo courtesy of AP Photos/Dallas County Sheriff's Department)*

Darren Mack being escorted by police to court. *(Photo courtesy of Andy Barron/Reno Gazette-Journal)*

Darren Mack is escorted out of court by Washoe County Deputy John Edwards after his motion to withdraw his guilty pleas was denied. *(Photo courtesy of Marilyn Newton/Reno Gazette-Journal)*

Soorya Townley *(left)*, mother of stabbing victim Charla Mack, and Chandra Mayer, Charla Mack's best friend, listen tearfully to testimony by family court judge Chuck Weller. *(Photo courtesy of Marilyn Newton/ Reno Gazette-Journal)*

Joan Mack, Darren's mother, reacts to statements made during closing arguments. *(Photo courtesy of Marilyn Newton/Reno Gazette-Journal)*

Presiding Judge Douglas Herndon listens as Darren Mack tells his story from the witness stand. *(Photo courtesy of Marilyn Newton/ Reno Gazette-Journal)*

Darren Mack testifies at his plea withdrawal hearing.
(Photo courtesy of Marilyn Newton/Reno Gazette-Journal)

Mack tells his side of the story in court.
(Photo courtesy of Marilyn Newton/Reno Gazette-Journal)

Darren Mack's attorney, William Routsis *(left)*, was accused of misconduct by Special Prosecutor Christopher Lalli. *(Photo courtesy of Marilyn Newton/Reno Gazette-Journal)*

The Mack family waits in anticipation for the judge to make his decision in the plea withdrawal hearing of Darren Mack. From left to right: Mack's son, Jory; his brother, Landon, and his mother, Joan. The woman in the front is not identified. *(Photo courtesy of Marilyn Newton/ Reno Gazette-Journal)*

Charla Mack's mother, Soorya Townley, spoke before the sentencing: "When I awake, I feel a thick, deep-seated depression that's hard to shake off." *(Photo courtesy of Marilyn Newton/Reno Gazette-Journal)*

Special Prosecutor Christopher Lalli reflects during the Darren Mack trial. *(Photo courtesy of Marilyn Newton/Reno Gazette-Journal)*

Prosecutor Lalli offers summation while defense attorney William Roustis takes notes and Darren Mack watches. *(Photo courtesy of Marilyn Newton/Reno Gazette-Journal)*

Family Court Judge Chuck Weller wipes tears from his eyes as he testifies about being shot by Darren Mack and how his life had changed as a result. *(Photo courtesy of Marilyn Newton/Reno Gazette-Journal)*

Judge Weller listens to a question during a news conference at the National Judicial College in Reno, Nevada. *(Photo courtesy of David B. Parker/Reno Gazette-Journal)*

Judge Weller points to Darren Mack during his testimony to identify Mack as the man who had shot him. *(Photo courtesy of Marilyn Newton/ Reno Gazette-Journal)*

and did nothing. Charla was always involved helping someone. . . . I want people to understand what a loss to the community this is. This is just horrendous."

After having met with Mack during the early-morning hours of Saturday, June 24, 2006, his lawyer Scott Freeman met with him again later that morning to begin preparing his defense. Mack was kept in a separate cell, segregated from the other inmates. He was kept under close surveillance. Aside from his attorneys, he was not yet allowed to have visitors, according to a spokeswoman for the Washoe County Sheriff's Office. He was also scheduled for a physical examination, after which he would undergo a psychological evaluation in an effort to determine his current state of mind. Although the law required that he be arraigned on the charges he was facing within seventy-two hours, a court date had not yet been set. However, everyone connected with the case, including his lawyers and the district attorney, expected that the arraignment would occur within the time frame mandated by law, and that he would likely be in court on Monday, June 26, 2006.

As it turned out, Mack's first court appearance did, in fact, occur on Monday, June 26, via video from the jail. Having showered and shaved, Mack, dressed in the typical red jail jumpsuit, appeared with Scott Freeman by his side. However, Freeman refused to recognize the murder and attempted murder charges against his client at that time, and stated that the case would need to be moved out of Washoe County and the Second Judicial District due to a number of reasons, including a conflict of interest. As a result, no plea was entered, and the court appearance ended rapidly. Although no one knew it yet, Mack would not enter a plea to the charges until September, more than two months away. In the meantime, the legal wrangling was only beginning.

18

Although Darren Mack had been arrested and charged with murder and attempted murder, people were still talking about the major crisis that had occurred in downtown Reno on June 12, 2006. Residents still brought up in conversation how Reno police and Washoe County sheriff's deputies had converged on the downtown area, effectively closing it off to anyone who was not already there and locking down the two courthouse buildings, where more than two hundred employees were forced to remain until after 4:00 P.M. and were cautioned during the lockdown to stay away from the windows. Unless an employee brought his or her own lunch and had easy access to it, no one could eat lunch that day, according to Kathy Rogers, Judge Steven Kosach's secretary.

"It just takes your breath away," Chief Judge Jerry Polaha recalled. "You don't think about this sort of thing happening. You say good-bye to the kids and the wife in the morning and come in to work, and boom. You want to do a public service, but you don't realize there are people out there who want to shoot at you."

Nevada Supreme Court chief justice Bob Rose recalled that he held similar feelings.

"It is a slap against lawful authority and an attack not just against a judge, but against everyone," Rose said. "The shooting of a judge, who was dedicated to helping citizens resolve their disputes, is one of the most despicable and cowardly acts imaginable . . . a tragedy and an outrage."

A number of people doing business at the two courthouses had been sent away after the shooting but prior to the lockdown.

"We were . . . told . . . to get away from the windows," said one person who had business related to a restraining order. "Then they told us to get out and get down the street. We were trying to get something done in the court, and now it has to wait."

A man who had entered the courthouse to pay a traffic fine had just gone through security when he was told to leave the building.

"I was just putting my belt back on when we were told to evacuate the building," the man said. "They told us to leave, but they didn't say why."

A family law attorney who had witnessed much of the melee explained that family court tends to be more unpredictable than other courts by its very nature.

"Dealing with divorce, child custody, child support, guardianship, these are things that all of which are highly emotionally charged," the attorney said. "We can all imagine, based on the subject matter of the family court, what might have prompted this."

The scenario had been similar at other places of business, including nearby restaurants. Many dining establishments were locked down for hours. Many of the businesses lost considerable revenue amounting to thousands of dollars due to the lockdown. Although managers and business owners complained about the lost revenue, they admitted that it was all for the best—public safety had to take priority.

A hoist operator working at a nearby condominium project was told to shut down his operation and to take refuge.

"I heard the shots, and then all of a sudden, I saw the cops running in," the hoist operator said.

It was not uncommon for losers in family court cases to become emotional, according to family law attorney Ronald Logar, who had practiced the specialty in Reno since 1961. Cases involving decisions that affect the disposition of families are simply more volatile than criminal court cases.

"I can tell you that often . . . the litigant that is unhappy with the outcome of their case is more likely to blame the other spouse and the judge rather than accept any responsibility on their behalf," Logar said. "The ones that believe they lost can't accept responsibility themselves, and they're looking at everybody else to blame."

According to a number of lawyers, shouting matches between the litigants are commonplace, but only rarely do such altercations escalate into violence. One Reno attorney, Clifton Young, recalled that a woman had to be restrained physically and removed after trying to attack him inside a judge's chambers.

"There's an old saying," Young said. "In criminal court, you see the best side of the worst people, and in family court, you see the worst side of the best people. . . . [In family court], that raw emotion is different than the emotion involved if you are injured in a car accident, or you're an employer and your employee embezzled money, or if you're suing your business partner for breach of contract. There's always emotion involved to some extent, but in family law, it's raw, unbridled."

According to Logar, it is important that attorneys on both sides of a case remain aware of clients who might become a problem, and to pay particular attention regarding their behavior inside and outside of the courtroom so that they can warn each other of potential dangers when a client might react abusively, or even violently, to a judge's decision. In a case several years earlier, he had received a warning from another attorney regarding a threat that had been made toward him.

"I got a call from the other attorney who said, 'I want you to know when my client walked out of the office today, he was mad and said he was going to get you,'" Logar recalled. "He was concerned enough and he knew his professional responsibility to warn me."

Logar said that the threat had been the closest he had ever come to having an act of violence committed against him by a losing client. He said that it is important for lawyers and judges to choose their words carefully. Careless words have the potential to set people on a path of violence due to the fact that their frame of mind is already one of anger and despair over their situation. He said that it is important not to call them "a thief or . . . a liar.

"All you have to do in your papers or in court is to say that the money is gone and it is missing and it was in control of one of the parties," Logar added.

Chuck Weller, who had become a judge because he apparently believed that judges "can help a lot of people," had handled hundreds of divorce cases, both as a lawyer and as a judge, but he had never been physically attacked before—much less shot from a distance by an angry man with a high-powered rifle.

"There are a number of cases that are hopeless, but that's a small percentage," Weller said.

Darren Mack's actions on June 12 were ample proof that his and Charla's case fell into that small, hopeless percentage. Not only had it turned out to be a tragedy, but it had literally turned the justice court system in Northern Nevada upside down by placing a level of fear among those involved in its day-to-day activities that had never been seen before in that area of the country.

Weller's shooting was an all-too-vivid reminder that physical danger comes with the job of being a judge. A year earlier, in 2005, superior court judge Rowland Barnes was shot and killed in an Atlanta, Georgia, courtroom by a man who was on trial for rape. The shooter had apparently taken a gun from a guard who was escorting a prisoner into Barnes's courtroom. After shooting the judge, the gunman fled and shot and killed a deputy on the street outside the courthouse. A month prior to the Atlanta shooting, relatives of a federal judge in Chicago were killed inside the judge's home. Although neither of the aforementioned examples involved judges in family courts but instead involved criminal cases, the acts of violence in hindsight—especially after Weller had been shot— served to accentuate further the dangers with which judges have to live. Nonetheless, courthouse security personnel, known primarily as bailiffs, do a very good job in keeping order and helping keep everyone safe.

"The bailiffs over in family court do a pretty good job of keeping things cooled down," a longtime area lawyer said after Weller's shooting. "They are very proactive in helping people when it's time to leave, and getting them to the elevator when it's time to get along. There are people who lose it in court, and that is why the bailiffs are there."

In the aftermath of Weller's shooting, other judges jumped on the safety issue bandwagon and voiced their concerns. One jurist, Washoe County District Court judge Connie Steinheimer, had cause for alarm three years earlier when a police officer warned her that a man had threatened to kill her. Despite the threat and the warning by the police officer, nothing was done to offer her a sense of security and protection, according to what she told a reporter for the *Reno Gazette-Journal.*

"That was it," she said. "Nobody checked my home or my children. Nobody put a tail on my car. I don't get threats all the time, but the volatility of our cases is always on everyone's mind."

Steinheimer and another judge had locking mechanisms placed on the doors to their chambers so that their secretaries could decide whether or not to buzz anyone into their offices. But that left a security hole as well—who was looking after the secretaries? If a person was intent on obtaining entrance to a judge's chambers, all he or she would have to do is overpower, maim, or kill the secretary to get inside.

"We are very, very vulnerable here," Steinheimer said. "We have no buffer between us and the public in this building."

Although all the people working at the two courthouses were making every effort to return to their normal routines, it was not easy for some. A number of employees had asked to have professional counseling, while others, including bailiffs and sheriff's deputies, more carefully scrutinized everyone doing business in the two facilities. Everyone was still clearly on edge, though they tried hard not to show it.

"We deal with hostility every day, so that's not new to us," said Darin Conforti, a court administrator. "We just had a bomb threat two months ago, but the shooting takes it to a whole new level. . . . A lot of action will take place to ensure the safety of the public that uses this facility and the employees who work here."

Conforti said that although security procedures were being evaluated in the aftermath of Weller's shooting, anyone making threats would have to answer to law enforcement authorities.

People who worked in the downtown core area were not only still talking about Darren Mack and how he had shot Judge Weller, but many were still on edge over the incident, wary of the very real possibility that such a violent act could happen again.

"It's still a big event," a construction worker commented while in the vicinity of Wingfield Park, near the courthouse. "But I don't think anybody is ducking when they hear loud noises."

Another issue that concerned a number of people who worked in the Washoe County Courthouse and the adjacent Mills B. Lane Justice Center was the subject of the number of guns being allowed inside the two facilities, particularly inside the courtrooms. One of the issues concerned the fact that District Attorney Richard Gammick wanted his deputy district attorneys, as well as the investigators who worked for them, to remain armed.

"I have great concern for people with guns that bulge out of their sports jackets visible to anybody," Steinheimer said. "Way too many people have guns. We all became aware of it after the Atlanta shooting."

It was Steinheimer's desire to get the issue before the Nevada Legislature to see if a reasonable solution to guns in the courtroom could be found. One of the central problems was for sheriff's deputies and bailiffs to be able to recognize easily who in the courtroom was authorized to carry a gun—a not-so-easy task considering the fact that probation officers, detectives from more than one agency, and narcotics officers all tended to carry guns with them when they came inside a courtroom. It was difficult to know who was who "in a split second," according to Steinheimer. One solution, offered by Washoe County undersheriff Mike Haley, was to have additional gun lockers installed near the courtrooms. But that still left a lot of guns inside the buildings as prosecutors and law enforcement officers in plain clothing entered and left the facilities—and what of the problem if someone else decided to conduct their own sniper operation from a considerable distance, like Darren Mack had done? Should expensive bulletproof windows be on the agenda to help protect Washoe County's judiciary?

The questions were far-reaching and made more complicated by factors such as expense that the legislature would have to consider—building engineers were even called in to assess whether the buildings in question could handle the weight of the super-heavy bulletproof glass that was being considered. But Washoe County District Court judge Janet Berry and a host of others, including Senator Harry Reid—who wanted to increase federal money for courthouse security across the nation—believed that it would be only a matter of time before another judge became the target of someone unhappy over a judge's decision.

"I don't know how many judges and staff members have to be murdered before we, as a society, acknowledge this is dangerous work," Berry said.

There were other risk factors that concerned Berry and others, including the fact that judges and their staff members often came into close contact with defendants and their families and known associates by simply walking down a courthouse hallway or riding an elevator to get to and from their offices—not to mention a parking garage, where security was often only minimal at best.

"This is a horrific tragedy, and it'll happen again, unless we all decide to prioritize the safety of judges and their staff," Berry added.

At the time of Weller's shooting, Senator Reid indicated that legislation was needed to provide the additional funding that would pay for additional security agents and bulletproof windows. At the very least, heavily tinted windows should be considered, Reid and others indicated.

"Judges, like Chuck Weller, their clerks, jurors, and others who are serving their country and upholding the law, must be free to do so without threats to their lives," Reid said during a speech on the U.S. Senate floor within days after Weller had been shot. "Congress should take immediate steps to try to prevent a recurrence of the Reno tragedy in Nevada courthouses, and in courthouses elsewhere in the United States."

"We have seen too many instances in the United States, the latest being in Reno, where judges literally put their lives on the line when they go to work every day," said Jim Denton, a political consultant based in Las Vegas. "We need to provide these jurists the security that they need in order to do their jobs safely and efficiently."

The fact that bulletproof glass was not installed in the newly opened Mills B. Lane Justice Center was "obviously a cost-risk analysis," according to Reno Municipal Court judge Ken Howard. "Then something like this happens," he added, "and the cost is really secondary."

"As far as the windows and this type of situation, that is currently being looked at," chimed in Assistant Sheriff Craig Callahan. "We are going to be moving forward with the cooperation of the chief judge."

A bill that would provide some of the additional funding being sought for security improvements that Reid was pushing was cosponsored by Senator Arlen Specter, a Republican (at that time) from Pennsylvania, and Senator Patrick Leahy, a Democrat from Vermont. The bill, in addition to providing funding for additional security, would also require a periodic review of judicial security. It also would create additional penalties for people convicted of threatening or harassing judges.

"The ability of the judiciary to determine the rule of law without fear or favor is an indispensable prerequisite to our democratic society," Specter said about the bill when he introduced it. "Our judges' personal security, along with judicial independence, must be safeguarded at all costs, and I believe this bill is an important step toward providing those safeguards."

The bill, attached to the Defense Authorization Bill in June 2006, became known as "the Court Security Improvement Act," and was quickly passed.

"We must do all we can to better protect the dedicated men and women throughout the judiciary and the courthouses," Reid said. "These hardworking public servants do a tremendous job under challenging circumstances."

Too little too late seemed to be the key phrase after Weller had been shot, however. In November 2005, a security audit was conducted in part by the Washoe County Sheriff's Office, and a consultant out of California was paid $8,000, which yielded a list of thirty-one security recommendations for Reno's court facilities that had largely gone without any of them having been implemented. One of those recommendations had been to hire a firm to cover the windows of the courthouses with a dark tint that would prevent anyone from seeing in from the outside. Such a move very likely would have prevented the shooting. Another issue involved a row of Dumpsters situated along the south side of the Washoe County Courthouse, on Court Street, that the consultant indicated could "provide great receptacles for bombs." After Weller had been shot, however, everyone—including many judges, the sheriff's office, district attorney's office, and a public-works agency—agreed that the issues uncovered in the security audit would no longer be ignored and would be addressed moving forward.

"What happened . . . brought a lot of things to the forefront," said chief district judge Jerry Polaha. "Things we discovered quite some time ago are still undone."

According to Undersheriff Haley, an order had already gone out to have the Dumpsters in question moved to another location that had been deemed safer by the newly formed security committee.

"We had to get all the players on board," Haley said. "They acquiesced to having the sheriff's office see to their needs. Up until [recently], that power was not afforded to the sheriff's office."

However, Haley did not agree that relocating Dumpsters and placing dark tint on windows would necessarily protect the judiciary from a person bent on getting even.

"There isn't enough money in anyone's coffers to ensure safety in a free society with reasonable access to our public officials," Haley added.

In other words, if a person was determined to kill a judge, he or she would be able to find a way to do so.

Others argued that a possible solution to the problem might simply be to repair flaws in the facilities, such as those that required judges and defendants to share the same hallways and elevators, which in and of themselves create security issues. The answers to the problems, however, lay in the hands of the voting taxpayers, who often vote down bond issues for improvements of public buildings, and in the hands of slow-moving bureaucrats.

It seemed like the lawmaker politicians and judges were wallowing in self-aggrandizement in their concern for their own safety and had forgotten that police officers, as well as cab drivers and convenience store clerks, to name only a few occupations of people who come into contact with violent, dangerous people, live amid a much higher incidence of victimization than do our country's judges. It was a plain and simple fact that called into question whether additional money—which was getting much harder to find—for such judicial safety programs as was being looked at was really justified. With already nearly depleted federal and state budgets at issue during difficult economic times, one had to consider whether judges should receive special protection treatment, particularly at the federal level, when the actual number of judges killed—either on or off the job—is miniscule by comparison to police officers and others. Nonetheless, it was an issue that the politicians seemed hell-bent on pursuing in the aftermath of the attack on Judge Weller.

19

As the investigation into the tragic events of June 12, 2006, continued, Detectives David Jenkins and Ron Chalmers learned more about what may have helped to push Darren Mack over the edge that fateful day. As they delved deeper into what lay behind Mack's anger toward Judge Chuck Weller, they confirmed some of what they already knew—namely, that Mack was not the only Washoe County resident who did not like Weller or the decisions he made as a judge. They found a number of complaints on such sites as *www.legalreader.com* and *www.courthouseforum.com*, posted by parents whose comments did not paint a flattering portrait of the judge—in fact, just the opposite. Some of the posters' messages portrayed Weller as being a monster, abusive, incompetent, tyrannical, and committing favoritism.

[Weller] is increasingly earning himself the reputation of being one of, if not the most, abusive and unfair judges anywhere to be found in America, one poster wrote on the Courthouse Forum site.

I think I got royally screwed by the guy, wrote one angry parent who had gone before Weller in 2005 for a child custody and child support hearing. I don't wish anything like this on anyone, but what happened doesn't surprise me at all.

That angry parent, who was a member of Nevadans for Equal Parenting, as was Mack, said that a number of the group's members had discussed the possibility of filing an official complaint against Weller, but they had not followed through with their discussions. Even if they had filed the complaint, said the parent, the group would be prohibited from talking about it without first obtaining permission from the Nevada Commission on Judicial Discipline. Discussing an official complaint without first obtaining permission, which is rarely granted, could cause a citation for contempt of court to be issued to the person or persons discussing it. According to Dave Sarnowski, executive director for the Nevada Commission on Judicial Discipline, there were no complaints pending against Weller at the time of the shooting. Sarnowski, however, would not discuss whether complaints had been filed against Weller in the past.

"I cannot verify or confirm whether or not a complaint is on file, or has been filed in the past," Sarnowski said.

However, a spokesperson for the Nevadans for Equal Parenting group said that their group had received "a lot of complaints" about Weller, "more about him than the other judges." But does the fact that Weller received more complaints than other judges mean that he was not doing what he was supposed to be doing? Not necessarily, according to Bill Dressel, National Judicial College president.

"Of all the assignments in the judiciary, [family court] is one of the most difficult," Dressel said. "It's not really unusual if you would get complaints on a family court judge. Does that mean he is not doing the correct job? I couldn't say. . . . In our country, we have a way for people to voice their opinion. What may have been the genesis for [Weller's shooting] is just completely abhorrent behavior. There is no justification for violence."

Others, such as a Carson City lawyer, Caren Jenkins, believed that Weller had not been a judge long enough to have developed a trend, such as favoritism toward a particular gender in the cases he heard. In apparent agreement with several others involved in family court, Jenkins also voiced her opinion that family court tends to be more volatile than other courts.

"Dealing with divorce, child custody, child support, guardianship, these are things . . . which are emotionally charged," she said. "We can all imagine based on the subject matter of the family court what might have prompted this. . . . I don't think he (Weller) has had enough decisions to have devoted a trend toward favoring gender or other outcomes yet."

There was little doubt in the minds of the investigators at this point in their probe that Darren Mack had been significantly involved in Internet blog attacks against Weller. Information had turned up from Nevadans for Equal Parenting that had informed Weller prior to the shooting that "one angry man was starting a campaign against him, using friends, associates, the media, and anonymous blogs to ruin Judge Weller's reputation," said political consultant Jim Denton, who also served as Weller's spokesperson following the attempt on Weller's life. Denton also had run Weller's political campaign when Weller ran for judge in 2004. The aforementioned father's advocacy group also issued a statement on its website offering its members' thoughts and prayers to Weller's and Charla Mack's families.

Nevadans for Equal Parenting condemns the violent and senseless crimes which have occurred this week in Reno, the group stated. We hope if any good can come of this tragedy it will be that we take a close look at the current situation in our courts and hopefully make positive changes.

By this point in the investigation, additional information had come to light about the *Big Nickel* advertisement for the sale of a Harley-Davidson motorcycle, which had been taken out by someone who listed Weller's wife's name, and which had provided directions to their home. Whoever had taken out the ad had paid for it with cash. Although Weller had called the police and had reported the incident to court security, essentially all that could be ascertained was that the ad had been placed anonymously.

"Weller owned no Harley and had never placed such an ad," Denton said. "Bikers started showing up at his house at seven on Saturday morning in answer to an ad promising an auction of an expensive Harley motorcycle."

A short time later, Denton said, Weller had been awakened in the middle of the night by their dogs, which were barking loudly and in a manner that had caused some concern that someone may have been outside prowling.

"Therefore, when Weller was shot," Denton said, "he said his first concern was for his family's safety from someone who had his home address."

There was little doubt in anyone's mind who was close to the investigation that Darren Mack had been left angry by many of Weller's decisions in his divorce case, but as investigators learned more about that aspect of the case, it began to seem as if it had been more about the money that he had been ordered to fork over to Charla than anything else. Because he had been so upset, the detectives learned, Mack had called several of his friends and had aggressively asked them to help him try to alter the situation—including attempts to garner support toward discrediting Weller, including, but not limited to, hostile blog postings about the judge.

Mack's longtime friend Dan Osborne had been one of the people who Mack had asked to assist him. Although Osborne had agreed to contact the news media on Mack's behalf, including the *Reno Gazette-Journal,* the response to his efforts had been minimal at best.

According to Rob Dotson, president of the Washoe County Bar Association, people should not give much credence to anonymous blog postings such as those that investigators believe Mack may have been involved in because they seek to defame the person they are attacking and the posters are typically not held accountable for their actions because of their anonymity.

"The problem I see in anonymous posting on blogs is that the person making the postings is not held accountable for the truth of the statement as their identity is not known," Dotson said. "Therefore, in viewing such statements and deciding what weight, if any, should be given to them, I think the anonymity of the authors must be considered. . . . In order for our justice system to operate effectively, it is critical that our judges retain independence. In making their decisions, they must not be influenced by the identities of the parties, nor for that matter, [by] fears for their own or anybody else's safety based upon the ruling they make."

Meanwhile, as Jenkins and Chalmers looked more closely at Mack's Internet postings, particularly those related to swinging and personals, they found that he had set up profiles on Yahoo.com, Match.com, and Cupid.com, in addition to the MySpace site that he had created and dubbed himself "toomuchfun," an egotistical reference. In each of the Internet profiles, Mack had indicated that he was looking for attractive women who were no more than five feet ten inches in height, and insisted that those who responded to him be particularly sexual and daring. In one profile, he described himself as a forty-five-year-old divorced father of three who looked twenty years younger than his actual age, said he was a flirt and the life of a party, that he was in great shape physically, and listed his interests as dancing, travel, and family. He also boasted that he was a business owner who made in excess of $150,000 per year, and claimed that the most important things in his life were his relationships with his children and family. On one of the sites, he described an important aspect of his life as living life so there is [sic] no regrets at the end.

They found one personals posting on Yahoo.com in which Mack stated that he was looking for someone to connect with, enjoy great times together and to explore life outside the typical relationship structure that everyone seems to be so unhappy in. On Match.com, his profile read: I have done a lot of work to become very present and grounded in life. I am successful and happy with my life and am very fun loving. I am looking for a woman who is very attractive, is very happy and complete with herself who would be a partner and companion exploring life together. Must not be controlling, jealous, mean or insecure.

The last sentence of Mack's Match.com profile could have been an apt description of himself: controlling, jealous, mean, and insecure.

20

It is the experience of most, if not all, homicide detectives who investigate spouse murders that have occurred as a result of domestic disputes that violence was a major component of the marriage, often arising from simple disputes that escalate into anger, and then an act or acts of violence. Often when a man kills his wife, such a killing occurs after a heated argument in which one or both parties have been excessively abusive toward one another, and the murder occurs during the heat of passion, or at the height of the dispute when one party loses all control and decides, often in a split second, to kill the other. That did not appear to be the case with regard to Charla Mack's death.

The investigation did not appear to uncover acts of aggression or meanness on Charla's part, but instead showed a high degree of premeditation on Darren's part. There were many factors that pointed toward him having planned Charla's murder, and there was evidence to back up such a scenario. His "to do" list was but one piece of evidence, and it also seemed clear that he had used their daughter as a ruse of sorts to gain access to Charla so that he could kill her. In Jenkins's and Chalmers's opinion, it seemed pretty clear-cut that Mack had carefully planned his actions for the morning of June 12, 2006. Despite his claims of self-defense, it did not seem that he had acted out in the heat of the moment. They also weren't buying his claims that Charla had been verbally and physically abusive and had threatened to kill him if he left her, as he had claimed in the temporary protective order that he had filed and quickly rescinded two weeks after Charla had filed for divorce.

When Mack began challenging Charla's claims in the divorce proceedings, the detectives recalled, he had insisted, according to his court filings, that she was subject to *behavior patterns of wide mood swings, with . . . rage to bouts of incessant crying,* which he claimed had escalated and *her mental stability has rapidly declined.* Just what percentages of Mack's claims were true, if any, remained to be seen, and Jenkins and Chalmers realized that they might not be ascertained at all.

The cops knew Charla had denied Mack's allegations and had claimed that she should have custody of their daughter, which Mack had been hotly disputing. In papers, she had claimed that she was a *fit and proper person to have primary custody* of the child, and the investigators had not found anything besides Mack's allegations to indicate otherwise. Similarly, the alleged acts of violence that he claimed *seemed* to be isolated incidents that bordered on the nonexistent.

In fact, the detectives uncovered evidence that Charla had predicted her own death at his hands as she had fought for custody of their daughter, and had stated as much to friends and acquaintances. She had told others of Mack's potential for violence, and she had described him as a vengeful person who would stop at nothing to get revenge against anyone who got in his way or who had somehow wronged him. She warned one friend that he was out to get her and that "someday he will probably kill me."

"When that happens," Charla had told the friend, "I want the world to know what a son of a bitch he is."

In the end, of course, neither had won custody of their eight-year-old daughter. Charla was dead, and Mack was in jail awaiting trial for murder, attempted murder, and other charges arising from his rampage. As it turned out, a family court judge awarded temporary custody of the child to Darren Mack's mother, Joan, with visitation available to Charla's family.

"This family is destroyed," said Egan Walker, an attorney who represented Charla's mother, Soorya Townley. "Anytime a person chooses violence, it is a selfish act and this entire family, including the Mack family, is just reeling from it. . . . Our focus is trying to calm the hurricane that's blowing around this child."

"We negotiated for liberal visitation for everyone concerned, with the main focus being the best interest of the child," said Scott Freeman, the Mack family's attorney.

"It's just such a nightmare," Townley said later. "I never imagined something like this would be happening."

Soorya Townley was fond of showing photographs of her daughter and her granddaughter, and one of her favorites had been of Charla and Darren's daughter dressed as a fairy in a garden, surrounded by flowers and butterflies, kneeling beside a pool in a staged fantasy setting.

"This was the fantasy world they had," Townley said. "This is the direct opposite of what Darren has now created for his daughter."

As part of the continuing investigation, Jenkins and Chalmers also continued to explore the possibility of whether Mack had anyone helping him—either in carrying out the crimes committed on June 12, or in helping him evade the long arm of the law, or perhaps even assisting him to hide or dispose of the rented Ford Explorer, which still had not been found. As with any of the numerous investigations that the seasoned detectives had conducted, their aim was to leave no stone unturned, including determining whether or not he had an accomplice.

"Through many leads that we are following up on, if it turns out that there is another person involved, who could possibly be an accomplice . . . we would go after that portion of this investigation, too," said Reno police lieutenant Jon Catalano.

One of the many leads that the detectives had followed up on was that of United Airlines pilot Chad Ruff, who said that he had first encountered Darren Mack inside the gym at the Melia Cabo Real hotel and resort in Cabo San Lucas, the day after Mack had killed his wife and shot Judge Weller. The sighting indicated that Mack had moved quickly to arrive at the resort by that time—he had either flown to Mexico or had driven around the clock to have gotten there by June 13. Nonetheless, Ruff said that while he was dressing inside his room after exercising in the gym, he had seen a news report on the television that told about Charla Mack's stabbing death and the sniper attack on Weller. The report also listed Mack's status as a fugitive. He told the detectives that it had "struck" him that he had seen the person who had been the focus of the news report.

Ruff told the investigators that he had seen the man again at the pool, sunbathing with a female companion. Ruff said that he purposely walked by the man several times that day so that he could study his face. Convinced that the man was Darren Mack, he began trying to contact authorities to report the sighting. Unable to get anywhere with Mexican police officials, Ruff waited until he returned to the United States the following day and immediately contacted the Reno Police Department to make his initial report. It had been about that time—the precise details were unclear—that Mack had moved on to another location.

In the meantime, it seemed as if Mack and his attorneys—in planning his defense—would be launching an all-out attack on Charla in an effort to change the way that she had been portrayed thus far. Mack and his attorneys seemed intent on portraying him as a victim, instead of being the villain. They made it known that Mack's defense likely would be one of self-defense. They were clearly out to change her "kind and giving" persona, which was seen in public, and instead portray her as violent and abusive at home. She was being likened as a terrorist of sorts, torturing her husband with custody and monetary demands, all of which Mack felt as abuse. She had even purportedly threatened him with acts of violence, such as cutting off his penis and putting it inside the freezer. She once allegedly told him that she would kill him, that she watched Court TV every day and had learned how to do it. Mack had reportedly gone to a psychic for a reading and had been told to beware of Charla. The psychic told him that Charla would stab him with a knife, and had seen "blood everywhere." But that was all due to come out at trial, which was still a long way off. Mack was clearly in the process of pulling together a unique, if not bizarre, defense, with the aid of his lawyers. It also appeared that he might try to say that when he shot Weller, he was legally insane.

Not only were Darren Mack and his lawyers already thinking ahead to trial, but before June 2006 was over, as Jenkins's and Chalmers's work continued, Washoe County District Court chief judge Jerry Polaha had made a decision about the presence of firearms inside the courtrooms. No one—except police officers—could bring a firearm into a Washoe County courtroom without prior approval from a judge, according to Polaha's order. Polaha's decision was readily endorsed by the police union, the sheriff's department, prosecutors, and other judges. It was also ordered and agreed that plainclothes cops would wear colored badges so that the armed bailiffs could quickly and easily recognize them as police officers.

Darren Mack, the wealthy, handsome bodybuilder, whose sex life was considered over-the-top, had, by his actions, clearly—and not to mention quickly—changed the way business would be conducted inside Reno's courtrooms in the future.

21

By early July 2006, Darren Mack was still busy putting together what many people, including reporters for the *Reno Gazette-Journal*, were calling a "diverse legal team." In addition to Scott Freeman, forty-nine, Las Vegas attorney David Chesnoff, fifty-one, as previously mentioned, had signed on to defend the accused killer. Chesnoff, who was once a law partner of famed Las Vegas mayor Oscar Goodman, who was known for defending a number of mob figures of the past, had become somewhat of a celebrity lawyer himself after having represented such people as Britney Spears, Martha Stewart, René Angélil (Celine Dion's husband), Leonardo DiCaprio, Jamie Foxx, Nate Dogg (a Death Row Records recording artist) in a multiple armed-robbery trial, and Stone Temple Pilots lead singer Scott Weiland. He also was successful in his defense of alleged mob figure Salvatore Scafidi in a federal death-penalty case. Other well-known clients included Shaquille O'Neal, Andre Agassi, David Copperfield, Lindsay Lohan, Suge Knight, and Mike Tyson. He has also represented purported Hells Angels members, poker players David "Chip" Reese, Johnny

Chan, Shawn Sheikhan, Phil Ivey, and Doyle Brunson, as well as U.S. District Court judge Harry Claiborne in Claiborne's U.S. Senate impeachment trial many years ago. Listed on the Super Lawyers website, it seemed that Darren Mack, and his defense, was in good, capable hands.

Freeman, on the other hand, was cohost of a weekly television talk show, *Lawyers, Guns & Money,* with former law partner, David Houston, on the Reno-Tahoe ABC-network affiliate station, KOLO-TV. Freeman's first murder case was in 1992 when he defended Jong Woo Lee, who had been charged with killing his brother-in-law, Park Chong Nam, that same year. Interestingly, Richard Gammick, then a deputy district attorney (DDA), prosecuted the case, and Judge Mills "Let's get it on!" Lane, who was also a former boxer and a boxing referee, heard the case. Freeman placed Lee on the stand, and the jury found him not guilty of the killing. Freeman has also represented Shirley Colletti, the former manager of the Mustang Ranch, which was a Northern Nevada brothel.

He also helped get Nevada's "Son of Sam" law overturned during his defense of Jimmy Lerner, a convicted felon who wrote a book about killing a friend, Mark Slavin, by beating and strangling him. The law permitted victims of felonies to collect money from criminals who had produced books, movies, or other media associated with their crime, but the Nevada Supreme Court found that the law violated freedom of speech and was therefore unconstitutional.

Although both attorneys representing Mack were as different in their personal lives as night was from day, with Chesnoff being an avid poker player who previously had won first place in a tournament at the Bellagio Hotel and Casino in Las Vegas, and Freeman a sportsman who likes to ride bicycles, play golf, and ski, it appeared that Mack was in very good hands despite the mountain of evidence against him. Both of the attorneys had been brought into the case by Darren Mack's family.

"The Mack family knew of my practice and my experience and reached out for me to see if I could help their brother and son," Chesnoff said. "When Darren first called me, he was aware of my lengthy experience in high-profile cases."

Mack was also aware of Chesnoff's experience and positive track record, with regard to death penalty cases.

"Nobody I have represented has received the death penalty," Chesnoff added.

Freeman was asked to be a part of Mack's legal team by several members of the Mack family, in part because of his associations with the family through some of their friends. Chesnoff also asked him to come on board, and he readily agreed.

"I'm personal friends with some of Mack's personal friends, and I knew him as an acquaintance," Freeman said.

"It's very clear that Mr. Mack has been an upstanding citizen and a good family person," Chesnoff told a reporter for the *Reno Gazette-Journal*. "He has made it very clear he's the person people knew before this happened. . . . There's obviously very serious issues that need to be examined. There will be things that have to be presented that, in many respects, will lead us to defending him. That's why he voluntarily returned."

Mack let it be known right away through his attorneys that he wanted his case tried outside of Washoe County, because of the potential conflict of interest.

Freeman went before Justice of the Peace Edward Dannan in late June to argue that point.

"The district attorney's office is a witness in this case and has an actual conflict," Freeman told Dannan. He argued that the presiding judge in Mack's case could not be from the same judicial district as Weller, because, he said in an interview later, "all judges in Washoe County were affected in one way or another by the events of June twelfth, which could affect their impartial view of the case.

"We're just looking for a fair trial," Freeman added.

District Attorney Richard Gammick, however, announced that it was his opinion that a conflict of interest did not exist, and that he and his office would oppose the move out of Washoe County.

"Just because I've known Darren Mack as an acquaintance doesn't mean he isn't going to be held responsible for what he has allegedly done," Gammick said. "If this was in family court before Judge Weller, I could see it, or if this was handled by someone in my office who had a conflict, I could see it. But you can't just do a blanket 'I don't like him.'"

In the Washoe County District Attorney's Office, where Chief Deputy District Attorney Tom Barb led the felony trial team, there was a system in place that decided who got to prosecute a particular case. The system was quite simple, in fact. The deputy district attorneys took turns carrying what they referred to as the "homicide cell phone." In Mack's case, DDA Elliott Sattler, thirty-nine, had been carrying the phone on June 12, and was thus chosen as prosecutor. He had handled about fifteen murder cases in his career.

"We have about eight people on the murder rotation, and any one of the eight could do this case [while] standing on their head," Barb said. "If you're on the eight, it shows you're a person who is capable, and who has done six to ten murder cases on their own. . . . It was his (Sattler's) day at the barrel."

"The homicide phone is a cell phone that all local agencies call when a homicide or suspicious death happens," Sattler said. "You carry the phone until you get a case. You're on call for as long as it takes."

Sattler was carrying the phone when Charla Mack's body was found, and after he received the call, the phone was passed on to another of the eight people on the team, who would keep it until he or she caught the next assignment, regardless of how long it might take.

Although Sattler acknowledged that Mack's case was a difficult one, he said that he was looking forward to prosecuting Mack. He considered it a really strong case from a prosecutor's point of view, and he said that he had a lot of support from everyone in his office.

"It's been a very good, multiagency effort," Sattler said. "A lot of agencies put a lot of outstanding work into it."

Being the boss, Gammick oversaw everyone in the district attorney's office, but he did not necessarily work directly on a particular case. However, because he was the district attorney, Mack's attorneys made it clear that they would continue to pursue the issue of conflict of interest, as well as other issues related to the case being prosecuted in Washoe County.

"It goes beyond the personal relationship," Chesnoff said. "There are issues based on what we believe are some conversations [the district attorney] may have had directly with our client prior to our representation of him and after the alleged events, which may make him a potential witness. . . . We're going to be researching and preparing written pleas to the court, which will be filed in the next day or so, in which our position is more clearly put on paper."

Freeman said that he and Chesnoff were not ruling out the possibility that the issue might have to go before the Nevada Supreme Court for a decision.

"Because this is a case of first impression, and these facts have never been decided, the supreme court may be involved," Freeman said.

When Sattler became aware of the early challenge by Mack's defense team, he said that he was not particularly surprised that they had jumped onto it so soon. He also said that he and his colleagues in the district attorney's office were expecting an aggressive defense by Mack's lawyers, and that he would be prepared when it came time to go to trial.

"I guess this (the conflict-of-interest challenge) would be the first shot across the bow," Sattler said, adding that he had no conflicts in the case. "I have no personal relationship with Judge Weller or with Mack."

By the time the month of June was at an end, Darren Mack faced charges of murdering his estranged wife, as well as charges of attempted murder and battery with a deadly weapon in the sniper shooting of Judge Weller.

Although no one quite realized it yet, the fact that Chesnoff and Freeman were preparing to file motions to remove Gammick and the Washoe County District Attorney's Office from the Mack case was just the beginning of a myriad of legal wrangling that would occur before Darren Mack ever went to trial.

22

As the prosecution persisted in its efforts to build its case against Darren Mack, and the defense team continued exploring strategies that might get their client off the hook, the state of Nevada decided that it wanted its money back for expenses related to loaning its ten-passenger, twin-engine Cessna Citation jet airplane to the Reno Police Department for its use in bringing Mack back to Washoe County. The plane costs approximately $800 per hour to operate, and total flying time used in the operation was slightly more than seven hours, according to figures released by the Nevada Department of Transportation (DOT). The total bill was approximately $6,000, which the Nevada DOT said it would bill to the Reno PD. The state typically reimburses police agencies for the costs incurred in extraditions, but this time the costs were considerably more than if a commercial flight had been used. The jet was used because Detectives Jenkins and Chalmers, among others in the police department hierarchy, had said that it was crucial that Nevada authorities be able to get to Mack as quickly as possible under the circumstances. Using the state's aircraft accomplished that in less time than if the detectives had flown commercially to bring Mack back, according to Reno police lieutenant Jon Catalano.

"Earlier, when he was supposed to turn himself in, we had an FBI jet available, but he missed that window," Catalano said. "As soon as he got to the United States, I thought it was important to get detectives there right away, because he hadn't invoked his right to silence or to an attorney. It was our best opportunity to interview him. . . . It was worth doing, when you have a case like this. Sometimes you can get your best interviews on the way back, which can be difficult on a commercial flight."

Although Catalano indicated that the investigators had engaged in "a lot of conversation" with Mack on the way back to Reno, he would not discuss what they had talked about. There was no mention whether the Reno PD would seek to avoid paying the state's bill.

On Tuesday, June 27, 2006, Judge Chuck Weller held a thirty-minute press conference at the National Judicial College, his first public appearance since his release from the hospital. It was evident as he walked into the room that he was still feeling the effects of the shooting. When he sat down, it was apparent that he was making a deliberate effort to sit up straight. He was accompanied by Annie Allison. He had little to say about Darren Mack.

"I have some scars that aren't healed over," Weller said. "I have new skin growing, and if I stand up for a long time, it starts to pull. It hurts a little bit. I'm mostly okay. I'm just healing."

When asked by reporters about Mack's claims that

Weller was corrupt and issued positive decisions to those who had made contributions to his campaign, he chose his words carefully in declining to discuss the charges that Mack had been making.

"I'm not going to respond to his criticism at all," Weller said. "Because I don't know what's in his head, and it's inappropriate for me to respond. I can say that my job is to go into the courtroom and decide cases without bias, and that's what I have striven to do the entire time I've been on the bench. . . . I have given my life to the justice system, and Mr. Mack is entitled to all of the protections that our system affords—due process of law, the presumption of innocence. . . . The court system will appropriately deal with Mr. Mack."

He was also careful with what he had to say about the shooting itself, due to rules surrounding judicial ethics, and he also did not want to say anything that could jeopardize the pending case against Mack. He did indicate that he remembered the shooting as he stood in his office speaking with Allison. He said that he remembered hearing the shot and the glass shattering as the bullet or bullets blew apart the window.

"I dropped to the ground," he said. "Annie got out of the room. I started on the way to the door, and I believe the door opened. I believe the bailiff entered the room and helped me get out. . . . I'd be speculating on the number of bullets, but I think it was more than one. . . . I was hit here," he explained as he placed his hand in the vicinity of his heart. He said that was the bullet that nearly killed him.

Annie Allison described her wounds as well.

"I have shrapnel wounds throughout my body," she said, adding that she was particularly moved by how the judge had handled everything.

"To the judge's credit," she said, "the first thing he

said was, 'Call my wife and family.' That was extremely touching. You think about your injuries—Are you going to live? Are you going to be okay? Is someone still out there?—and he was thinking about someone else."

Weller added that his concern for everyone's safety continued for days after the incident, before Mack had surrendered. He said that he had not known at that time if the violence was over or not, and because of that, and the fact that there had been numerous suspected sightings of Mack while he was on the lam, he had around-the-clock protection from Washoe County sheriff's deputies.

Weller explained during the press conference how much he loved being a judge, and he said that he was hopeful that he would be able to return to work right away. He said that he was supportive of seeing continued positive changes occur within the family court system, which, he said he knew from experience, was an intricate setting that often caused dramatic changes in people's lives. He called the family court system a "place of raw emotion."

"It's important to our democracy that the courts be able to operate in the absence of fear," Weller said, also referencing the Atlanta court shooting. "If this is the future of America, we need to provide more security to our judicial system so that it can operate."

When Weller left the room, he walked slowly, and it appeared that he was still in pain from his injuries.

Mack's lawyers went ahead with their motion to try to get Washoe County judges, as well as the Washoe County District Attorney's Office, off the case, which they formally filed on Wednesday, June 28, 2006, in which concerns were voiced about several lunches that

Mack had had with Gammick and others, and how
Weller had handled the Mack divorce. One of the primary arguments in the motion was how Washoe County
judges had been affected by the shooting of Judge
Weller, and that none of them should hear the case
against Mack. Although Gammick had not seen the motion yet, he argued that having lunch with someone did
not necessarily create a conflict of interest.

"I fail to see why that's an issue," Gammick said. "I
have lunch with people all the time."

The motion described the relationship between
Mack and Gammick as more than mere acquaintances. It said that they had been friends for more
than twenty years, and that within the parameters
of that friendship, Mack had "sought out professional counsel and advice" from Gammick about the
issues of his divorce and the custody battle for his
daughter.

According to information contained in the
motion, Mack and Gammick had met at least three
times over the previous year at the Prospectors' Club,
inside Harrah's Hotel & Casino in downtown Reno,
to discuss Mack's case over lunch. The meetings apparently occurred in June 2005, and in February and
March 2006. Only Mack and Gammick were present
during the June 2005 meeting, but the chief operating officer (COO) of the Mack family business,
Palace Jewelry & Loan Company, was present with
Mack and Gammick during the February 2006 lunch.
Present at the meeting the following month were
Mack, Gammick, and Assistant District Attorney
(ADA) John Helzer.

*As more specifically detailed in the affidavits . . . Mr.
Mack revealed details of his concerns with Judge Weller,*

[and] they were acknowledged and responded to by Mr. Gammick, read a portion of the motion.

The motion also mentioned that Mack showed Gammick and Helzer a document at the March meeting and had asked for their opinion *concerning its contents, as well as matters regarding Judge Weller,* maintained Mack's attorney Scott Freeman.

During their discussions during the March meeting, Judge Weller entered the restaurant and approached the group. According to the motion: *As Judge Weller approached, certain documents that Mr. Mack wanted to provide for Mr. Gammick's and Mr. Helzer's review were quickly assembled and placed from view.*

According to Freeman, he sent Gammick's office a letter after the incidents of June 12 in which he had asked that the district attorney and other law enforcement personnel not contact Mack without the presence of his attorneys. Freeman said that Helzer acknowledged the letter; yet on several occasions prior to Mack's surrender, *Gammick disregarded that letter . . . and engaged in conversations with Mr. Mack on a one-on-one basis.* Freeman said that because of these instances of contact between the parties, Gammick and Helzer had become witnesses in the case and therefore should be disqualified from the Mack case, along with their staff.

Freeman further argued that Mack could receive a fair trial *only* if a judge from another jurisdiction presided over the case. In his argument, he cited Judge Charles McGee, present inside the courthouse at the time of the shooting, who had told reporters and others that he *was scared to come back to work after hearing window glass shatter and the thump of Judge Chuck Weller's body hit the floor. . . . "I was afraid up there . . . and I don't want to go back to work afraid, because if I've got that emotion, I can't be clear headed."*

A judge in this state cannot preside over any proceeding in which a reasonable person with knowledge of all of the relevant facts might reasonably question the judge's impartiality, the motion read.

"Boy, he's desperate, isn't he?" Gammick said about Freeman after the motion had been filed. "I've made no secret of the fact that I am an acquaintance of Darren Mack. He asked me if I knew some names of some lawyers who could help him out. . . . Mr. Freeman needs to refresh his memory," Gammick said about his contact with Darren Mack while Mack was on the lam. "It was Mr. Mack that called me. He called me every time."

"We just want Mr. Mack to have a fair trial," Freeman said. "The judges [in Washoe County] are good judges, but they're also human beings," he added, inferring that they may be affected, and their decisions impacted, by the shooting of Judge Weller. Freeman said that the Nevada Supreme Court should assign a judge from another district so that there "won't be a cloud over the proceedings and we can get on with the business of the case."

Because Weller had had *a significant professional relationship with his fellow judges,* Freeman had written in a motion, there was the potential that a judge, especially one from Washoe County, hearing the case would want Mack *to be convicted and given a very lengthy sentence, rather than be set free, so as to make another attempt to harm another judge of the Second Judicial District.* Freeman further wrote that every judge and justice of the peace in the area *is impliedly biased, and that there is, at the very least, an appearance of bias.*

23

On Thursday, June 29, 2006, despite the efforts of Darren Mack's attorneys to get his case tried before a judge in a different judicial district, with prosecutors from another county as well, Justice of the Peace Edward Dannan denied requests for any further delays and set Mack's preliminary hearing for July 11, 2006. Accompanied by his attorney Scott Freeman, Mack appeared before Dannan via live video hookup in a room at the Washoe County Jail. Freeman had argued earlier that Gammick should have voluntarily disqualified himself and his office from the case, but after Dannan's ruling, he said that he was still confident that the issues he was concerned about would be resolved soon. Calling the criminal complaint against Mack a "fugitive document," Freeman had wanted the proceedings to remain idle until his motion to have Washoe County prosecutors and judges removed from the case could be properly reviewed by a district court judge.

"I believe that date (July 11) will be moved to give all the parties time to review the legal and factual issues related to the defense's position," Freeman said after the brief video appearance.

By the start of the hearing before Dannan, Deputy District Attorney Elliott Sattler and Freeman had agreed that the preliminary hearing should be delayed until July 28, 2006, during which time Freeman's motion could have been reviewed by a district court judge. However, when Sattler made it known that he wanted Mack to waive his right to complain that his preliminary court appearance did not fall within the required seventy-two hours after being charged, Mack's other attorney, David Chesnoff, advised Mack, along with Freeman, that he should not speak prior to a ruling on the motion. Mack's legal counsel was concerned that to do otherwise might be construed as an acknowledgment of the charges against him, thus giving legitimacy to the charges that, so far, had not been acknowledged. That, in effect, had caused Sattler to change his mind about continuing the preliminary hearing until July 28, as he did not want to risk an appeal later on regarding those issues. As a result, he asked Dannan to move forward, and Dannan complied.

As it turned out, however, it did not take long for the district attorney's office to do an about-face and remove itself from the case. On Wednesday, July 5, 2006, Gammick recused his office from Mack's case because of his twenty-year relationship with the murder suspect.

"My relationship with Mack has caused shadows on the case," Gammick said at a news conference. "Now that we've eliminated issues raised so far, we can get to the facts of the case. We don't want to risk the case on it (the DA's relationship with Mack)."

In changing his mind about wanting to remain on

the case, Gammick said that his relationship with Mack had been a "professional" one in which he had known him relating to work with regard to pawnshop issues that typically came before the authorities. He also said that he was acquainted with Darren's mother, Joan, and Darren's brother, Landon.

"He talked to me and a lot of people about the problems with his divorce," Gammick said, adding that he had no regrets about communicating with Mack to help bring about his surrender. "Three or four lunches, that's the extent of it (their relationship). There was no hunting together, or trips. We've had a friendly relationship for a number of years."

Freeman and Chesnoff were, of course, pleased with the new turn of events.

"We're very pleased that Mr. Gammick took the time to review the issues and made an obvious self-examination in terms of his relationship with Mr. Mack and made the correct and professional decision," Freeman said.

"They are dealing with the battle peacefully," Chesnoff added.

"I like to take care of my own backyard," Gammick also said. "But this is the best decision in the long run."

It was not yet known if Mack's trial would be held in Las Vegas or Reno, but at the time that Gammick had recused his office, it would still be held in Reno as far as he was concerned.

"If or when a judge orders a change of venue, the case will stay right here in Washoe County," Gammick added.

As a result of Gammick's decision to recuse his office from the case, it was decided that the Clark County District Attorney's Office in Las Vegas would prosecute it, instead. Clark County prosecutors would now make all of the decisions regarding the prosecution of the case, including whether or not to seek the death penalty. Gammick's office said that the budget from his office would be used to pay for the special prosecutor, but that he would also ask the Washoe County Commission for additional funding.

Mack's preliminary hearing had also been rescheduled from July 28 to August 8, but Mack's lawyers appeared uncertain if it would still occur on that date, after the legal maneuvering that had just occurred. Nonetheless, Clark County prosecutors were moving ahead, at least for the time being, with the August 8 date as they began meeting with the Reno detectives and beginning preparations for the hearing. Clark County district attorney David Roger, who prosecuted the suspects in the Ted Binion case a few years earlier, announced that he had assigned some of his best people to the Mack case. Ted Binion was one of the owners of Binion's Horseshoe Hotel & Casino and was found dead under mysterious circumstances inside his home.

"We're treating this as if it was a case that happened in our own community," Roger said.

Roger said that his office would wait until after the preliminary hearing to decide whether to pursue the death penalty against Mack. In the meantime, he assigned Assistant District Attorney Christopher Lalli, chief of the criminal division, and Chief Deputy District Attorney Robert Daskas to prosecute the case.

Freeman said that he looked forward to working with the prosecutors from Clark County, and he said that he was pleased with their level of experience.

"That will make the job easier," he added.

On Tuesday, August 1, 2006, as had been expected,

Mack's preliminary hearing was pushed back from August 8 to August 30. This was done in agreement with the new prosecutors, which would, naturally, give them additional time to review the case.

During all of this, Darren Mack remained held without bail at the Washoe County Jail.

As the legal entanglements of the case continued, Weller's administrative assistant, Annie Allison, twenty-seven, filed a civil lawsuit against Darren Mack on Thursday, August 10, 2006, through her attorney, Cal Dunlap, because, according to the lawsuit, she had *suffered extreme shock, horror, and terror and fear for her life* when Weller had been shot, and she had been injured by shrapnel. The lawsuit claimed that the shooting had *immediately temporarily deafened her,* and that she now suffered from nightmares and other distress. Allison was seeking unspecified general, special, and punitive damages in excess of $50,000. Allison's lawsuit also claimed that Mack, because of his anger toward Weller, had ambushed the judge and had fired multiple shots into *his judicial chambers in order to scare, terrorize and intimidate, or to hit Judge Weller,* and in the process, Allison had been *negligently and accidentally* struck by the shrapnel. She said in her filing that the incident had left her unable to *move about freely in the courthouse and elsewhere for weeks without fear of further assault and battery and [she] was therefore falsely imprisoned.*

It turned out Allison was not the only person who was planning to file a civil lawsuit against Mack. Soorya Townley, Charla Mack's mother, was in the process of filing a lawsuit of wrongful death against Mack through her attorney, Kent Robison. It also appeared that Judge

Weller was in the process of planning a similar action against the man who had shot him.

Also on Thursday, August 10, additional money matters were brought up in open court, this time by Darren Mack himself in his first in-person courtroom appearance. Mack, through his civil attorney, Mark Wray, was seeking the money in his retirement account so that he could use it to pay for his defense. The argument that Wray presented on Mack's behalf was that the money in the retirement account was not part of Charla Mack's estate, and it should be released to Mack. Wray cited a federal law, the Employee Retirement Income Security Act (ERISA), which exempts any claims to Mack's pension fund, valued at approximately $750,000. That money, Wray argued, should be turned over to the defense fund that was being overseen by Freeman.

"If a former spouse does not have rights to the plan, a deceased spouse doesn't, and the estate does not," Wray argued.

Apparently, probate commissioner Lynne Simons had ordered that Mack's retirement account be frozen for an additional thirty days so that lawyers seeking its monetary contents could file arguments regarding whether or not the matter came under federal jurisdiction. However, convoluting matters even more, Washoe County District Court chief judge Jerry Polaha had undertaken a review of Simons's ruling because her husband worked for a law firm that was seeking Mack's assets in one of the civil lawsuits against him. Because Simons's husband had attended a hearing in which his law partner, Kent Robison, who was representing Charla's mother in her civil lawsuit, had given testimony about Mack's assets, Polaha was concerned about the possibility of an appearance of an impropriety.

Attorney Egan Walker, who represented Soorya Townley in the matter before the probate commissioner, argued that federal law did not protect Darren Mack's pension if Mack, in fact, had killed his wife. Walker stated that the funds should be kept from Darren Mack and, instead, go to Charla Mack's estate and her heirs.

"While no factual determination has yet been made with regard to Mr. Mack's responsibility for the killing of his wife, he should not profit from her estate, pending any such determination," Walker argued in requesting that Mack's pension fund be frozen. Walker said that if Mack is given access to those funds, "he clearly profits from his crime."

Walker had summoned Robison to the proceeding, and Robison had given testimony that he had been working with Townley for approximately three weeks on a planned wrongful-death civil lawsuit against Mack for the death of his wife. Under questioning by Walker, Robison had testified that Mack could be deemed accountable for killing Charla and, thus, would meet the criteria under the "preponderance of evidence" legal standard, which is not as stringent as the legal standard of "beyond a reasonable doubt" utilized in criminal cases. Robison also stated that Mack's combined assets, including his pension fund, were worth millions of dollars.

"As the chief judge," Polaha said, "I'll give her (Simons) the benefit of the doubt. She has integrity, and I'm sure there was no impropriety there. But we are concerned not just with actual, but with the appearance of, impropriety, and we will have to look at that."

Dressed in the typical red jail jumpsuit and shackled

at his wrists and ankles, Mack paid close attention to the proceeding and could be seen whispering to his attorney several times. His mother, Joan, and one of his defense attorneys, Scott Freeman, sat in the row behind him.

For the moment, his money continued to be held in limbo.

24

A little more than two months after being shot, Judge Chuck Weller returned to work on Wednesday, August 16, 2006, amid fanfare and warm welcomes from his colleagues and staff members. Sitting in a chair that had been placed in the middle of his courtroom, where he had invited all of the family court lawyers for an hour-long conversation during their lunch break, Weller was in good spirits as he was greeted by a round of applause from roughly fifty attorneys who had dropped by to welcome him back.

"I'm back at work, and I'm happy to be back at work," said Weller, beaming with an amiable smile at the small crowd that had gathered in his courtroom. Someone asked him if the shooting would affect his work as a judge. "This experience has changed every aspect of my life. It's been a transformative experience. But what I try to do in every case I have is to make the right decision. It's my hope that fair-minded people would look at the facts I've seen and make the same decision."

"We're happy you're back," said Marilyn York, a

family court lawyer, who told Weller and the crowd
that criticism toward him had been unwarranted and
inappropriate. "We're terribly sorry about what happened to you. I know the offensive comments [in-
cluded] 'He deserved it,' and I want you to know they
are coming from about four of the same stupid
people, and it's not okay at all. We're outraged, and
we do not feel that way at all."

Others in attendance agreed with York, saying that
the negativity toward Weller was not well-founded.
Some said that changes within the family court
system were necessary to reduce some of the negative
sentiment and outright hostility. Among the issues
that they discussed that afternoon was whether or not
the system currently in place for issuing a temporary
protective order, essentially a restraining order, favored one gender over another. Currently, according
to one person present, all a person seeking a TPO
had to do was say that he or she had been threatened
by his or her spouse, and the application would be
approved.

"Word on the street is you can get your kids and
child support if you go in and say, 'He threatened
me,'" said one of those in attendance.

"We have people lying on TPO applications all the
time," Weller responded. "I don't know why we don't
have more perjury prosecutions."

Weller, however, said that he was in favor of having
TPOs, and said that one way to determine whether
the TPO system favored one gender over another was
to begin gathering statistics with regard to how they
were issued.

Chief Judge Jerry Polaha told the group that it also
hurt the system when a lawyer denigrated a judge in
front of his or her clients, or shared his or her enmity

about the judge with the client. When that occurred, the client tended to lose respect for not only the judge, but the entire system, with some, like Darren Mack, taking things too far and resorting to violence.

"Lawyers need judges, and judges need lawyers," said lawyer Pam Willmore. "And the community needs us all. Nobody said this would be an easy job, but it was beneficial to have this today."

The motions just kept on coming. On Friday afternoon, August 18, 2006, Scott Freeman filed additional motions including one to continue the August 30 preliminary hearing. He and David Chesnoff did not want the hearing to occur until after their request to bring in a judge from another district had been decided. The defense believed that if a new judge from outside the district was assigned to the case, then the potential existed for any rulings made in the preliminary hearing to be negated.

"Under the circumstances, and based on recent examples, we believe that our motion should apply to all the judges in the Washoe County court system that have anything to do with Darren Mack," Freeman said.

He was, of course, including in his reference the pending review by Chief Judge Polaha of probate commissioner Lynne Simons's ruling a week earlier on Mack's retirement fund. Freeman's new motion argued that Simons had previously worked in the same Reno law firm as Shawn Meador, Charla Mack's divorce attorney, which she should have disclosed, Freeman said, and which Freeman viewed as yet another potential conflict of interest. He said that due to all of the issues, she should have removed herself from the Mack case.

He also cited again the fact that attorney Kent Robison, representing Soorya Townley in her pending wrongful-death lawsuit against Mack, and that Simons's husband, Mark Simons, who was present in the courtroom at the earlier hearing, created another potential conflict of interest.

"Mr. Simons stands potentially to gain monetarily as a member of that firm . . . as a result of Commissioner Simons's rulings favoring [Townley's lawsuit]," Freeman said. "And if Mr. Simons gains, his wife, Commissioner Simons, also gains. Commissioner Simons should have immediately recused herself . . . as soon as Mr. Robison took the stand. . . . It has become apparent to us that both criminal and civil aspects of Mr. Mack's case can be affected by decisions made by the judges in this county," Freeman added.

The defense attorneys also indicated that they could use additional time to go through the large volume of evidence they had received. The defense move to broaden the scope of their efforts to exclude all judges from Washoe County was viewed with disdain by the new prosecutors from Clark County, because they viewed it as a deliberate attempt at distraction by the defense fashioned to delay the case from going to trial even further.

"We want to see this case move through the criminal justice system," Clark County ADA Christopher Lalli said. "And we don't think disqualification is required. . . . It's in their best interest to confuse what is a straightforward murder and attempted murder case. I see a lot of this as distraction, and it's in their best interest to distract and get away

from the real issues. I don't think that has anything
to do with my case."

The following Monday, Lalli filed his own motion
that opposed the defense motions to remove all
Washoe County judges, civil and criminal, from the
case, but he was in agreement with Freeman and
Chesnoff that the Nevada Supreme Court should appoint a judge from outside the district to rule on the
arguments and to hear Mack's criminal case.

"We were very pleased that the Las Vegas district attorney agreed with our position that at least we should
have the matter heard by an independent judge from
another district," Freeman said. "It makes sense that
if you file a motion in one district, that it's not heard
by a judge in that same district."

Lalli's motion, however, went a step further by including additional details of how Charla Mack had
died and how Mack had gone after Weller later that
same morning.

*He stabbed her body repeatedly, striking her with a knife
or sharp object on her leg, forearm, wrist and throat,* Lalli's
motion said. *The resulting injuries included the severance
of Charla's left carotid artery, her esophagus and her trachea. He also inflicted injuries that resulted in blunt force
trauma to large portions of her body.*

Lalli's motion then described how Mack had gone
to the parking garage, near the courthouse where
Weller worked, where he could shoot the judge from
a distance: *He removed an assault rifle from the vehicle and
aimed it in the direction of the courthouse. When Judge
Weller emerged in the window of his chambers, the defendant
fired at least one round, striking the judge in the chest, bringing him to the ground.*

Lalli also argued that there was no foundation on
which all judges in both the district and justice court

systems should be disqualified from the case. Lalli was careful to point out that Mack had targeted one judge only—Weller—and not all of the judges in the two neighboring court buildings. He wrote that it was *quite apparent that the defendant's motivation stemmed from his divorce proceedings,* and argued that Weller's professional relationship with the other judges in the district, which included *regular and casual contact,* was not sufficient grounds, even as a victim, to remove all judges from hearing the issues surrounding Darren Mack's legal problems.

Recusal is required, however, where the level of personal relationship increases to the point that the judge cannot be impartial or a reasonable person would question the judge's impartiality, Lalli's motion stated, where he quoted from another case that set the standard for removing a judge or judges from a case, in arguing that the defense motion be denied.

On Friday, August 25, 2006, Chief Judge Jerry Polaha sent a request to the Nevada Supreme Court to appoint a judge to rule on the motions by Darren Mack's attorneys to remove all Washoe County District Court judges on the grounds of bias or the appearance of bias. Before the day was done, supreme court chief justice Bob Rose had ordered Senior Judge J. Charles Thompson, based in Las Vegas, to rule on the motions.

Thompson, who served as a Clark County District Court judge from 1975 to 1995, and served as Clark County assistant district attorney from 1996 to 2004, had ties in a professional capacity with Lalli, who had worked under Thompson in the district attorney's office for a period of time. Lalli said that Thompson had not been his direct supervisor, but that he had been Lalli's "boss's boss" and he "absolutely" did not see a problem with Thompson deciding the issue about whether to disqualify the Washoe County District Court judges.

By the following Tuesday, Thompson ruled that Justice of the Peace Edward Dannan, of Reno, could proceed as planned with Mack's preliminary hearing. However, he said that it was likely that the Washoe County District Court judges would be removed if Mack was bound over for trial for shooting Judge Weller, but that it was premature to make such a ruling because the case had not yet arrived in district court. Thompson wrote that he believed that a reasonable person, after having learned all of the facts of the case, might *question whether or not the District Court Judges of the Second District would be entirely impartial when one of their own is the victim of such a serious offense.* The implication was that disqualification of the judges would be required under the code of judicial conduct.

That same day, yet another motion was filed by Scott Freeman requesting that Darren Mack undergo a competency evaluation before proceeding with the preliminary hearing, which essentially acted as a request for a continuance. When asked why the defense had waited so long before making the request for the competency evaluation, Freeman said they first wanted to know which justice of the peace would be hearing the case.

"We have been advised by two mental-health experts that this is something that should be done at this point," Freeman also said.

Freeman said that he and David Chesnoff had begun questioning Mack's competency based on conversations each of the attorneys had had with him, but they declined to provide Dannan with anything more specific, invoking attorney and client privilege. However, Dannan refused to grant the continuance and instead ordered that Mack be held pending the outcome of his trial. It was a blow to the defense, but one that the attorneys had anticipated. Nonetheless, they indicated that they would proceed with seeking the competency evaluation.

Among the items gone over during the preliminary hearing included a statement made by Annie Allison that Mack, at one point during the divorce proceedings with his wife, had given her "the look of death." Judge Weller later made a similar statement about a look of hatred or glare by Darren. Testimony was also heard about Mack allegedly giving out Weller's e-mail and home addresses after placing a phony advertisement in the *Big Nickel* publication, and it was recalled that others, besides Mack, may have had issues with her boss. Earlier, Allison had provided investigators with three other names in addition to Mack's.

The court also heard some of the details that Mack's friend, Dan Osborne, had provided to police about the events on the morning of June 12, including how he had later been asked to meet Mack at a Starbucks, near Mack's townhome. Testimony was also provided by one of the investigators who had been involved in the search of Mack's townhome, which included details of the items found, including the purported "to do" list, which presumably was in Mack's own handwriting, and which eventually would lead detectives on a trail from the townhome to the parking garage downtown. A forensic pathologist also provided details of Charla's wounds and described some of them as defensive injuries. By the time that Dannan had been ready to make his decision to deny the defense request for a continuance, ample evidence had been provided to show sufficient reason to bind Mack over for trial.

On Thursday, August 31, Judge Thompson, just like he had indicated he would do if Mack was held for trial, disqualified the judges from Washoe County from hearing any of the issues surrounding Mack's criminal case. Still at issue was whether to disqualify Washoe County judges from hearing the pending civil cases against Mack.

All the judges of the Second Judicial District are acquainted with Judge Weller and have a significant relationship with him as a fellow judge, Thompson wrote in his ruling.

"Although judges in Washoe County are very fair . . . this case is unique and unusual and touched everyone's professional and personal lives," Freeman said after Thompson's ruling. "For Mr. Mack to get a fair trial without any doubt or concern, it just seemed logical for us to request the judges be disqualified."

Still at issue was the possibility, even likelihood, of a change of venue that would be requested by Mack's defense team. However, under Nevada law, a change of venue cannot be granted until a jury has been selected. Nonetheless, Scott Freeman and David Chesnoff were already discussing such a possibility.

* * *

On Tuesday, September 5, following Thompson's decision to disqualify all of the judges in Washoe County from hearing Mack's criminal case, Nevada Supreme Court chief justice Bob Rose selected Clark County District Court judge Douglas Herndon, forty-two, a former prosecutor, to handle the case. Upon learning of Rose's decision, Herndon only said that he had been very involved in another high-profile Las Vegas case and had not had a chance to "digest" Rose's decision. He said he knew that Mack's arraignment had been set for the following week, but he had not yet had time to figure out the details involved in traveling to Reno for the proceedings.

Herndon's career as a judge had begun when Governor Kenny Guinn appointed him to the bench in January 2005 to fill the slot left open when Judge Ron Parraguirre was elected to serve on the Nevada Supreme Court. He ran unopposed in the primary election the following August. Prior to becoming a judge, Herndon had become a prosecutor after graduating from law school in 1991, and later served as a Clark County chief deputy district attorney who had overseen the special victims unit that involved child abuse and child homicide, abuse cases involving women and children, and Internet crimes involving children.

"I know him pretty well, and we've been on the same team together," Lalli said after learning of Herndon's appointment. "But we have never tried a case together."

Lalli said that both he and his coprosecutor had asked to provide input prior to Rose's selection, and both had recommended Herndon. Freeman also stated after the appointment had been made that Mack could get a fair trial in Herndon's courtroom.

* * *

On Monday, September 11, 2006, after convening a review committee to discuss the merits, or lack thereof, in pursuing a death penalty case against Darren Mack, Lalli announced that prosecutors would not seek the death penalty. Lalli said that the decision, although made after conferring with others, such as Charla Mack's relatives, had been "an exercise of prosecutorial discretion." Although she said that it had been a difficult decision, Soorya Townley said that she had agreed with the prosecution's decision, in part, because of Mack's children.

"I don't think it (the death penalty) would be good for his children," Townley said. "For the children's sake, it's for the best."

"We didn't believe that it was that kind of case," Freeman said after the decision had been announced. "But it's very good news. Now we have the opportunity to proceed with the case and focus on the arraignment Wednesday."

On Wednesday, September 13, Darren Mack had pleas of not guilty, on charges that he murdered his wife and tried to murder Judge Weller, entered by Judge Herndon at the request of his attorneys. Scott Freeman had asked Judge Herndon to enter the pleas for Mack because he and David Chesnoff said that they were planning to challenge the charges. Freeman also stated that he planned to challenge the earlier decision in which his request that Mack undergo a psychiatric evaluation before proceeding with trial was denied.

Herndon then set a trial date for October 1, 2007,

more than a year away, but he added that he would conduct status hearings every thirty to forty days for dealing with motions, such as the petition to dismiss the charges that he knew were coming, and to handle other challenges that lawyers from either side might initiate.

25

On Tuesday, September 19, 2006, Washoe County District Court chief judge Jerry Polaha asked the Nevada Supreme Court to appoint yet another judge to decide whether Washoe County District Court judges should also be disqualified from hearing the civil cases involving Darren Mack. Among the pending civil cases were who would get custody of the child he had fathered with his murdered wife, the disposition of Charla Mack's estate, which was being handled in probate court, a civil suit filed against Charla Mack by Palace Jewelry & Loan, which was demanding the return of an expensive ring and a watch, and Annie Allison's civil suit against him for her having been wounded by shrapnel related to Mack's shooting of Weller. Still likely coming was Soorya Townley's lawsuit against him for wrongful death, for killing her daughter, and also a possible suit from Weller. (It should be noted that the law firm that had been handling Charla's divorce had filed three claims against her estate for an amount of approximately $110,000.) Now that the criminal case had been taken care of, with regard to the judge issue, Polaha wanted the high court to take similar action in the civil cases before additional work was completed on them.

"We have received the request but have not made the assignment," said Bill Gang, spokesman for the Nevada Supreme Court. "We're working on the wording of the assignment to determine what the judge will rule on and the number of cases involved. It's a complicated matter."

Meanwhile, on Monday, October 2, 2006, Scott Freeman moved to have the attempted murder charge against Mack for allegedly shooting Judge Weller dismissed. Freeman argued that the prosecution had failed to produce sufficient evidence to support the charge: *It is equally possible that it (the shot) came from a weapon discharged by someone other than Darren Mack.*

We know of at least three other people who are or were royally upset with Judge Weller and his rulings, one of whom allegedly has a "personality disorder," Freeman wrote in his motion.

In his argument against insufficient evidence to support the attempted murder charge, Freeman further stated that even though prosecutors had shown evidence of a vehicle inside the parking garage across from the courthouse, it had not shown who was driving the vehicle. Also, Freeman said the shot could have come from someone standing on the ground.

This evidence clearly is not sufficient to establish guilt of anyone beyond a reasonable doubt, Freeman's motion read. *To conclude, even as a matter of probability, that Darren Mack attempted to murder Judge Weller is to engage in pure speculation.*

Freeman also argued that Mack should have been allowed to have a competency evaluation before the

preliminary hearing that had been held earlier in the
Reno Justice Court. He had been denied the evaluation, Freeman said, despite the fact that the defense
team had presented statements from two mental-
health experts who said that Mack might not completely understand the charges he faced, or how to
help his lawyers in their defense of him. The inference seemed to be that he was having difficulty communicating with his attorneys, and Freeman's
argument seemed to center on the concern that Mack
should not be *tried or adjudged to punishment for a public
offense while he is incompetent.*

"I think these are very real issues for the court to
decide," Freeman said after filing his motion to dismiss. "We're anxious to see the state's response."

A few days before he was shot, Judge Weller had attended a training seminar at the National Council of
Juvenile and Family Court Judges in an effort to learn
ways to help neutralize conflicts between couples who
were divorcing *before* they got out of control. Following the educational seminar, Weller had begun talking about producing an instructional videotape that
could help explain what lay ahead in court—and
afterward—for angry couples, like Darren and Charla
Mack, seeking divorce. It had been his hope that such
a video could help couples like the Macks to discover
a way to settle their differences on their own, outside
the courtroom. Weller's idea about the videotape
would include information to show couples precisely
how the family court system worked, what they could
expect from the system, and, most important in his
view, how to avoid going into the family court system
in the first place. Some of Weller's colleagues, such as

Judge Charles McGee, agreed that Weller's idea was a good one and could help make divorce confrontations safer for everyone involved.

"Part of the way you secure the courthouse is not by bricks and mortar or bulletproof glass," McGee said. "It is allowing these people an area to vent their terrible pent-up emotions without getting into a courtroom, which seems to exacerbate that because it is built around a system of law where you try to point out the worst part of someone. Most of these people are not bad people. But they'll start drinking, or maybe she'll be unfaithful, and they'll start using these terms as if they are totally unfit people or parents so they can prove their point and win. . . . Well, there's no winner in a family court case. There's a group of losers, including the children."

It turned out that McGee had handled Darren Mack's divorce from his first wife, which he described as "a real donnybrook," an inference to a large public quarrel.

"Family court judges draw the ire of some people who are incapable of thinking objectively because of the pressures of divorce and custody matters," McGee continued. "The angry party blames the judge. Women may say the judge is biased against women, and men will claim that the judge is biased against men—sometimes in the same case."

McGee said that the issue of the children involved in divorce cases is the most difficult, and he expressed concern for Mack's eight-year-old daughter he had with Charla.

"By the grace of God, Judge Weller is going to recover," McGee said. "But whether that little girl ever has a parent again is a serious question."

Jim Denton, political consultant and longtime friend

of Judge Weller's, also saw the positive attributes of Weller's idea about putting together a detailed, explanatory videotape about the family court system. He thought that such an instructional videotape was a step in the right direction toward helping couples seeking a divorce to settle their issues on their own, before they become blown out of proportion.

"You have to remember," Denton said, "if my wife and I choose to get a divorce and we can settle custody issues, we can [also] settle property issues, we can settle monetary issues, [and] we are never going to see the inside of Chuck's courtroom."

A number of other people involved in the business of divorce in one way or another, including Dale Koch, president of the National Council of Juvenile and Family Court Judges, agreed with the idea of educating people about the family court system before they became involved with it.

"It is our role if people are going to become involved in the system to try to get disputes resolved outside the courtroom rather than inside the courtroom," Koch said. "It is their property, their children, so it's best to create an environment where they are . . . trying to resolve things."

Mary Mentaberry, executive director of the National Council of Juvenile and Family Court Judges in Reno, agreed that Weller's idea to better educate people would serve to keep hostility and bitterness, not to mention violence, out of the courtroom.

"There are a lot of folks out there who don't understand what the court system is," Mentaberry said. "It's really mystical. It could help allay some of that fear, help them recognize the situation and how serious it is."

James Hays, president of the Coalition of Fathers

and Families, located in New York, was not fond of the family court system. However, he was in agreement with others, including Weller, about the advantages of couples being able to settle their differences outside of the courtroom.

"We tell people first off," Hays said, "go put your marriage back together if you can, because you have no idea what you're getting into."

Hays pointed out that he and his group for fathers' rights point to cases like Mack's, as well as other cases where violence is involved, as evidence that something needs to be done to change child custody laws to allow fathers more rights legally. At present, he said, the system has tended to be more favorable toward women.

"We say that the system is creating these people and we get vilified," Hays said on behalf of his group. "We have been warning people about this and it seems like every time we bring it up as an issue, it's like killing the messenger. Just because we point out what is going on doesn't mean we agree with it or advocate it."

Although Senior Judge J. Charles Thompson had disqualified all of Washoe County District Court judges from Mack's criminal case, back in August, a ruling had not yet been made on whether to allow or disqualify Washoe County District Court judges from Mack's civil cases. That all changed on Thursday, October 12, 2006, when Thompson, again selected by the Nevada Supreme Court to make that determination, ruled that all judges from Washoe County would be barred from hearing Mack's civil cases, saying that "the same rationale" that applied to the criminal case applied to the civil cases. His ruling became yet another unprecedented decision in Nevada's judicial history.

There was one possible exception, however, and that was the lawsuit filed by Annie Allison. Thompson agreed to hear arguments from her lawyer, Cal Dunlap, to keep her case in Washoe County District Court. Dunlap argued that there was a process to deal with removing a particular judge from a case rather than simply ordering a ban on all of the judges. He said that to disqualify all of the judges would send the wrong message to people.

"We don't want to set precedents that if someone is upset with a judge they can take aim in order to get a different judge," Dunlap said. "A person should not be able to murder someone and then disqualify the other judges by shooting at one."

Dunlap said that he did not see the need to remove the Washoe County District Court judges from Allison's case—after all, he said, she was not a judge, and it did not appear that she had any close relationships with any of the judges.

Darren Mack's civil lawyer, Mark Wray, told the judge that he found it "hard to believe that a person would assault a judge to get another judge." Wray said that judicial standards should be used in deciding the issue, and he argued that if there is even an implied bias, the judge should be disqualified from hearing the case. He said that even if a judge believed that he or she could be fair under the circumstances, it still might be affected by the criminal case against Mack.

Thompson said that he would take the lawyers' arguments into consideration, but would rule at a later date on whether to allow Allison's case to remain in Washoe County.

In the meantime, Wray and others agreed with Thompson's original plan to impose a blanket ban on the Washoe County District Court judges by saying that he had done the right thing, before hearing the arguments to keep Allison's lawsuit in the county's system.

"It's better for everyone—for the judges, the attorneys, and the clients," Wray told reporters. "Under the circumstances, it's better to not force the judges into a position of having to deal with something this close and personal."

Egan Walker, an attorney representing Charla Mack and her family, agreed that it was best to disqualify the judges, in part because it would help remove later on the possibility of claims during the appeals process that a judge or judges had been unfair.

"There is no doubt in my mind that all the judges in this district could fairly and impartially rule on all cases involving Darren Mack," Walker said. "But given the fact that Darren Mack chose to shoot a judge in his divorce case, there is little doubt that anyone might question the reaction of people in the court system."

On Tuesday, October 17, 2006, prosecutor Christopher Lalli responded to Freeman's petition asking that charges of attempted murder against Darren Mack be thrown out due to lack of evidence. He also responded to Freeman's motion to place the case on hold so that Mack could have a competency evaluation. Lalli said in his response that Justice of the Peace Edward Dannan was correct in his ruling to deny the competency evaluation, because Mack's attorneys had failed to show evidence indicating a *reasonable doubt as to competency*.

The defendant has presented no evidence of hallucinations, delusions, history of mental disorder, attempts at suicide, time spent in mental health facilities or numerous witnesses of the opinion that he is incompetent, Lalli wrote in his response. Instead, Lalli said that a social worker had testified to seeing Mack during several court proceedings in which he was *effectively communicating with his counsel, appropriately interacting with his daughter, able to understand legal forms and terminology, and aware of his surroundings.* Lalli said that the social worker's testimony had *entirely refuted the defendant's position.*

As for the defense motion to drop the attempted murder charges for allegedly shooting Weller, Lalli said that the purpose of the preliminary hearing was to evaluate or determine whether there was sufficient evidence to show probable cause that the crime had been committed, and that probable cause can *be based on slight, even marginal evidence.*

In Mack's case, the standard for showing probable cause had been met—a friend of Mack's had given testimony that Mack had "expressed a negative opinion" regarding the manner in which Weller had handled his divorce, and that Weller's administrative assistant had testified that Mack had given her "the look of death" following one of the divorce hearings. Lalli also cited the photos of the vehicle that Mack had rented that showed it at the parking garage where the shooting was believed to have occurred, and at the time when the crime was believed to have been committed, as well as the handwritten note, the so-called "to do" list found inside his home, which *corroborated his involvement in . . . the charged crimes.*

On the other hand, Freeman continued to contend that the arguments for dismissal and for the evaluation were strong.

"At the time of the preliminary hearing," Freeman said, "we had very aggressively asked the justice of the peace to allow a competency evaluation, and now this issue is very alive. It will be up to Judge Douglas Herndon to decide if that decision was a question of implied bias. And the lack of evidence (in the attempted murder charge) speaks for itself."

Judge Herndon, in the meantime, had scheduled a hearing for November 16, 2006, to consider the motions presented by both sides.

On Wednesday, October 25, 2006, attorneys for the *Reno Gazette-Journal* filed a motion to have approximately thirty exhibits, consisting primarily of photographs, used at Mack's preliminary hearing, unsealed. When Mack's case had been moved to district court and Judge Herndon had been selected to hear the case, Herndon sealed the exhibits in question without being asked to do so by either side. In filing its motion to unseal the exhibits, the *Reno Gazette-Journal* sought to ensure that Mack's criminal case was not kept under wraps, but instead it would remain open for public scrutiny and be conducted in a manner in which most criminal cases were conducted.

Scott Glogovac, the newspaper's attorney, cited the newspaper's First Amendment right *to access the courtroom proceedings and documentary records in this matter.* He also cited the fact that the photographs in question had already been presented in open court during Mack's preliminary hearing, which he termed a *very public proceeding.*

This First Amendment guarantee is based not only on historical precedent, but also on the theory that the public's right to access all aspects of such proceedings is necessary for the proper functioning of the judicial system, Glogovac wrote in his motion. *What transpires in the courtroom is public property. There is no special perquisite of the judiciary which enables it, as distinguished from other institutions of democratic government, to suppress, edit, or censor events which transpire in proceedings before it.*

In arguing for public access to the documents, Glogovac cited that rulings had been made in other courts ensuring public access to *all aspects of a criminal trial* "enhance the quality and safeguards the integrity of the fact-finding process, with benefits to both the defendant and to society as a whole."

The exhibits in question were photographs taken outside Mack's townhome, the blood droplets on his driveway, the breakfast nook area, the so-called "to do" list, which had been found in his kitchen, photos of Weller's chambers, medical records related to Weller, photos taken by video surveillance cameras of the parking garage, near Weller's chambers, various crime scene photos, and photos of Charla Mack's autopsy.

Prosecutor Christopher Lalli said that his office had no objection to the newspaper's request to unseal the photos. However, Freeman objected to the request and in his filing said that the unsealing of the documents would violate Mack's constitutional rights, including his right to *effective assistance of counsel,* not to mention his right to due process and his right to a fair trial. Freeman said that he specifically objected to the unsealing of Exhibit P, the "to do" list, because that exhibit *may be subject to a motion to suppress at a future time.* Freeman said that he also objected to unsealing Charla Mack's autopsy photos.

Due to their graphic nature, he filed, *additional objections may be posited in district court prior to jury trial, related to the prejudicial impact of those photographs on the jury.*

Judge Herndon indicated that he would rule on these matters at Mack's hearing on November 16.

On Monday, October 30, 2006, Judge Thompson ruled on Allison's case by opting for the blanket ban on all Washoe County District Court judges, despite the fact that a local judge had accepted her case and believed that she could rule on it without bias. However, Thompson's concern all along had not been centered on actual bias from a particular judge or judges, but, rather, based on implied bias.

". . . the law does not require a judge assigned to a civil case to be as free from bias as those judges assigned to criminal cases," Thompson said in making his decision. "The canons of judicial ethics do not distinguish between criminal and civil cases. . . . I believe that a reasonable person, having learned the unusual facts of this case, might question whether or not the district court judges . . . would be entirely impartial when one of their employees is the plaintiff, and Judge Weller is a key witness."

Allison's lawyer afterward said that he accepted Thompson's decision and that they would "just abide by the ruling and proceed with the case."

The next step now involved Nevada Supreme Court justice Bob Rose to appoint one or more judges to handle Mack's civil cases.

"The chief justice will make the appointment as

expeditiously as possible to ensure the cases can proceed in a timely manner and resolutions can be reached," said Bill Gang, spokesman for the supreme court. "But no appointments can be made before next week at the earliest, and it may be several days before a decision is possible."

Those appointments were actually made by Rose on Thursday, November 9, 2006, nearly two weeks after Thompson issued the blanket ban on Washoe County District Court judges. As it turned out, Rose assigned Judge David Huff, of the Third Judicial District, to handle four of the civil cases against Mack, including the divorce case between Mack and his deceased wife, Charla, Charla's estate case, a probate case between Mack and his first wife, and the lawsuit filed by Palace Jewelry & Loan.

Rose assigned the remaining three cases to Judge John Iroz, of the Sixth Judicial District. Those cases included the custody issues surrounding Darren and Charla's daughter, Annie Allison's case, and a sealed juvenile case for which no details were immediately available.

Lawyers on both sides of the fence expressed relief that the civil cases, which had been in legal limbo since August, could now proceed.

26

On Wednesday, November 15, 2006, the day before Darren Mack's hearing was to occur before Judge Herndon (who would decide on the motions filed by his attorneys for their much-desired competency evaluation, and their efforts to try to get the attempted murder charges dismissed), the unexpected occurred. The Reno PD announced that the rented 2006 Ford Explorer that Mack had allegedly used as his getaway car had been found in Mexico and returned to Reno. The announcement had been kept under wraps until the much-sought-after vehicle had been returned, and the timing of the announcement—the day before the hearing—caused many who had been closely following the case to wonder if such timing of the revealing information had been deliberate or coincidental with regard to the upcoming hearing.

According to information released by Lieutenant Jon Catalano, the vehicle had been found inside a long-term parking facility, the Cinema Star parking garage, in the northern Baja peninsula town of Ensenada, which is just a bit south of Tijuana. The vehicle

was in good condition, Catalano said, perhaps because
it had been stored at a secure location used by people
who have vacation homes in that area, and are there
mostly on a part-time basis.

The Explorer had been located about a week earlier by a private investigator whose job involved trac-
ing stolen cars in that area for the National Insurance
Crime Bureau, which handles cases for the rental car
company, among many others, that Mack had rented
it from. It had not yet been searched by Reno investigators because they were awaiting the approval of a
search warrant that detectives had requested. It was
taken to the Washoe County Crime Lab. Detective
Ron Chalmers said that he was certain that it was the
same vehicle that Mack had been driving on June 12.
Chalmers did not know if the car contained any
weapons—such as the knife used to kill Charla Mack,
or the rifle used to shoot Judge Weller.

"It has dark windows and is very dusty, so it is hard
to see inside," Chalmers said. "We put it on a flatbed
tow truck and brought it back."

According to Chalmers, however, the investigator
who located the vehicle had discovered a loaded .40-
caliber handgun beneath the passenger seat, and an
ankle holster containing ammunition for the weapon.
Although Mexican authorities had not yet released
the weapon to Reno police, they had allowed Chalmers
and Jenkins, among other investigators, to inspect it
and photograph it when they traveled to Ensenada
earlier in the week to pick up the car. The private investigator told the detectives that he had not searched
the vehicle, but he had seen the weapon as it was
being unloaded from a tow truck when its driver had
removed it from the parking garage.

Known as a Desert Eagle handgun, the .40-caliber

weapon was typically used by target shooters and sportsmen, according to Jenkins, and was not a weapon that would be "a first-choice for self-defense." However, Jenkins pointed out that an ankle holster is characteristically used to conceal or hide a weapon and is not practical for hunting—it was something that a sportsman or hunter would not likely use, in his opinion.

According to an affidavit for a search warrant filed by Chalmers, an agent of Budget Rent A Car had contacted the Reno Police Department with the information that the Explorer had been found. When the detectives followed up on the new information, they confirmed that the vehicle identification number (VIN), as well as its license plates, matched the vehicle that Mack had rented.

When Chalmers followed up on the new information, the attendant at the Cinema Star told him that an American arrived with the Explorer on June 14. Using the name "Tim Nichols," the "white male" told the attendant that he was going on a cruise and needed to leave the car there for about a month. The attendant told Chalmers that the man presented a Nevada driver's license, and described him as "approximately five feet nine inches tall, with short brown hair and a stocky build." Nichols paid the attendant $40 for the car's storage, and left the facility with a black suitcase, which rolled on wheels.

Mexican authorities told the Reno detectives that they had found two receipts for travel on the toll highway that runs between Tijuana and Ensenada. They were dated June 13, 2006, at 10:15 A.M. and 10:32 A.M., and were found on the floor of the SUV.

The investigators' theory regarding Mack's direction of travel after he had fled Reno was that he had driven the SUV west to Sacramento, then headed

south to Mexico, likely crossing the border at San
Diego. Tijuana lies practically on the border between
the United States and Mexico. They believed that
after leaving Tijuana for Ensenada, where he had left
the Explorer, he likely had taken a bus from Ensenada
to La Paz, and then somehow traveled to the Cabo
San Lucas resort, the Melia Cabo Real, where he was
spotted by the airline pilot and remembered by the
female gym attendant. At some point, he returned to
La Paz, likely by the weekend of June 17, where they
believed he had taken a ferry to Mazatlan and began
negotiating his surrender in Puerto Vallarta with
Richard Gammick. Their theory regarding the Mexican leg of his travel route was based in part on the bus
ticket from Ensenada to La Paz, found by the police
at the time of his arrest, or shortly thereafter.

During that same week, Kent Robison, a lawyer for
Charla Mack's estate, made the lawsuit for wrongful
death, which had been waiting in the wings, official
by filing it on behalf of the estate's administrator,
seeking an indeterminate sum of money for compensatory, special, general, and punitive damages arising
from Charla Mack's untimely death. The lawsuit
charged that Darren Mack stabbed Charla *at least
seven times in the body and neck . . . without provocation or
cause . . . [and] from the initiation of defendant Mack's
attack on Charla Mack to the time of her death, [Charla] experienced and sustained physical and emotional pain, suffering, disfigurement and anguish . . . [and died] as a
result of the malicious and intentional attack perpetrated
upon her* by Darren Mack. The lawsuit also accused
Mack of being physically abusive to Charla during
their marriage.

* * *

At the hearing held before Clark County District Court judge Douglas Herndon, on Thursday, November 16, 2006, at which Darren Mack showed up in court wearing a white dress shirt, black pants, and a tie, instead of the usual jail jumpsuit, Scott Freeman argued that Mack had not been treated fairly since first entering the court system following his arrest and return to Reno to face charges. Essentially coining a new term, he said they were continually getting "Macked" by the court, and cited the denial of an evaluation for mental competency as an example.

"The Mack case has taken on a life of its own," Freeman said. "It is the 'Mack mode.'"

Freeman said that whenever a defendant's lawyer asks for a competency evaluation in virtually all other cases in the county, they are approved—except in Mack's case, which Justice of the Peace Dannan was quick to deny.

"He (Dannan) had a mission in the Mack case to get it off his plate," Freeman charged.

However, Prosecutor Christopher Lalli argued that Mack's attorneys had failed to provide firm reasons supported by mental-health professionals regarding Mack's mental condition. Lalli said that simply stating that a person was not competent was insufficient to have such an evaluation granted. Lalli repeated much of what he had included in his written motion, as shown earlier, and charged that Mack's attorneys were merely trying to delay the hearing as a defense tactic.

"Clearly, what Judge Dannan did was one hundred ten percent correct," Lalli said.

When he argued whether there was enough evidence to charge Mack with shooting Weller, he said that when the combination of the two crimes, that of Charla Mack's murder and Weller's shooting, was considered, they both pointed toward Mack as the suspect.

"You have Charla Mack brutally murdered, and you have Judge Weller attempted to be murdered," Lalli argued. "What is the common thread there? The common thread is Darren Mack."

Although Herndon indicated that he might not be in agreement with Dannan's judgment to reject the request for a competency evaluation, he said that it was his job to decide whether Dannan's decision had been rational based on Mack's behavior. Herndon said that unless there was something to suggest that Mack was experiencing mental-health issues, such as hearing voices or being distressed from having delusions, an assertion of incompetency would not be sufficient, and he therefore supported Dannan's decision.

In the final analysis, Herndon said that if each piece of evidence in the case was looked at separately, there would not be enough to charge Mack with the attempted murder of Judge Weller. However, he said that the evidence cannot be viewed "in a vacuum," and indicated that when it was all "combined together," or laid out in a linear fashion, it was sufficient to meet the judicial standards to hold Mack for trial. Herndon cited the surveillance video in the parking garage depicting a vehicle that looked like the one Mack had rented, as well as the "look of death" testimony from Weller's assistant. He said it was sufficient to allow the charges to stand.

Regarding the *Reno Gazette-Journal*'s motion that the thirty exhibits originally sealed by Herndon be unsealed, Herndon agreed that much of the evidence had already been discussed during the preliminary hearing and that now that "the cat's out of the bag," keeping the items sealed would not be of much help to Mack's case. Stating that he was concerned about Mack receiving a fair trial, Herndon said that he would allow the thirty exhibits in question to be viewed and would allow many of them to be copied. However, he disallowed the copying of Charla Mack's autopsy photos, Weller's medical records, and Mack's "to do" list.

Although Herndon's legal decisions set the stage to allow the case to move forward in Nevada's court system, the legal maneuvering on Mack's behalf was not over yet.

27

As the case against Darren Mack fast-forwarded to the spring of the following year, and Mack languished in jail, it turned out that Judge Chuck Weller's administrative assistant, Annie Allison, had a past relationship with Kenneth Lund, the law clerk for Judge John Iroz—who had been assigned to hear Allison's civil lawsuit against Mack following the disqualification of the other Washoe County judges. That past relationship, according to attorney Mark Wray, who was representing Darren Mack in the civil case, had created an appearance of bias against Mack. Because of the appearance of bias, Wray argued, Judge Iroz should recuse himself from the case because the rules for the judiciary were clear on the point that people in such positions must do what was necessary to avoid a conflict of interest whenever personal bias or prejudice had become a concern.

Wray pointed out that Allison and Lund had dated each other in 1995 and 1996 while attending Galena High School, had attended their junior proms together, worshipped at the same Mormon church, and had associated with each other while attending Brigham

Young University. They had shared a class together at Brigham Young in 1999, and began spending time together. Lund said that he had also visited her apartment, but Allison said that their relationship had been strictly platonic.

In her lawsuit against Darren Mack, Allison said that she had suffered from *extreme shock* and feelings of *horror and terror and fear for her life* as a result of Judge Weller's shooting. She sought general, special, and punitive damages in excess of $50,000 from Mack's estate.

On Tuesday, March 27, 2007, Cal Dunlap, Allison's attorney, argued at a hearing before Judge Iroz that Lund and Allison had never been involved romantically, to which Lund also had testified, and that they had not seen each other for several years, since 2000. Lund testified that he would not allow his friendship with Allison to influence him during his work on the case, and said that he had informed Iroz about his past history with Allison. Lund also testified that he had worked as a law clerk for Iroz since August 2006, and in the course of his work, he researched cases for the judge, prepared draft orders, and discussed cases with him.

Dunlap argued that Iroz should not have to recuse himself. Iroz sided with Dunlap, and said that he would remain on the case. Iroz had been assigned to the case in November 2006, along with the sealed juvenile case involving Mack's eight-year-old daughter, and said that his rulings on pretrial motions would be based on "the facts and the law," and that the case would be decided by a jury—not by him.

"I don't believe there are any grounds to recuse myself in these cases," Iroz said.

The attorneys for both sides also filed motions regarding whether Allison's civil case should be postponed until Mack's criminal case, scheduled for October 2007, had concluded. Iroz did not decide on those motions immediately, however, and said that he would rule on that issue in April.

The next legal maneuver came in April 2007, but it was initially instigated from the other side. Attorney Egan Walker went to court on behalf of Charla's estate before Third Judicial District judge David Huff and argued that Darren Mack had killed his wife in order to get out of paying a nearly $1 million divorce settlement, which he had verbally agreed to before Charla's death. Now he should be ordered to pay up instead of being allowed to use the funds for his own defense. Mark Wray, however, told Huff—who had been assigned to the Macks' divorce case after the other Washoe County judges had been removed—that the settlement agreement, which Mack had contested, was no longer valid because one of the parties to it was deceased, even though Weller had instructed Charla's lawyer to write the order. However, the order had not been written, and therefore nothing signed, due to the criminal circumstances of the case—Charla's murder and the attempt on Weller's life. The settlement agreement, in which Darren had agreed to pay Charla $480,000 in cash within forty-eight hours of signing the agreement, and an additional $500,000 in monthly installments of $10,000 from his pension fund, had also fallen apart when Darren Mack's mother, Joan, had said that she would not sign global releases that would have essentially ended any remaining legal matters between her and Charla.

"If you make a promise under oath and on the

record, you ought to have to keep it," Walker argued. "A person should not be able to fund his criminal defense for the murder of his wife with funds he had promised his wife."

Wray, however, argued that such verbal agreements were typically written up in the form of an order and signed to render such agreements legally binding, but due to the circumstances of Mack's case, that had never been completed.

"This is an unprecedented attempt to rewrite history," Wray argued. "You can't write the order that never existed."

Furthermore, Wray said, Mack was innocent of the criminal charges until proven guilty. Huff indicated that he would rule on the matter in a timely manner.

Also in April 2007, Mack's criminal defense lawyers, Scott Freeman and David Chesnoff, had filed motions asking that Mack's statements to Richard Gammick be thrown out because Gammick had been aware that Mack had retained attorneys, and that Gammick should not have even been talking with him. The attorneys also argued that Gammick had illegally taped his conversations with Mack, and that as a result, those recordings should not be allowed or admitted as evidence at trial. However, at a hearing in May 2007, the prosecution offered its own motions.

The defendant admitted to Gammick that he had killed Charla, Special Prosecutor Christopher Lalli wrote in one of the motions. *He said that he had "thrown out" the knife used in the brutal killing. . . . The defendant further admitted that he had shot Judge Weller. He indicated that he wanted Weller alive to expose the corruption that drives thousands of men to commit suicide each year.*

In response to the recordings Gammick made of his conversations with Darren Mack, Lalli said that it was Gammick's right under federal law to do so. Lalli also said in his motion that the prosecution did not intend to use the recordings at trial, and therefore did not have a problem with Mack's objection to the tapes. However, Lalli argued that Mack had admitted his crimes to Gammick prior to the recordings being made—and prior to any discussions about Mack retaining an attorney—and that the statements Mack had made to Gammick could be used at trial. It seemed clear that Lalli would be calling Gammick as a witness against Mack.

Since no attorney-client relationship existed during the period in which the defendant contacted Gammick and confessed his crimes, Gammick could not possibly have violated any rules of ethics, which apply exclusively to communications with represented parties, Lalli argued.

Darren Mack's lawyers had also previously argued that items collected from Mack's home following Charla's murder had been obtained illegally and should not be allowed at trial. However, Robert Daskas, co-counsel with Lalli in the case, insisted that police officers and, later, detectives had entered Mack's home with sufficient cause.

Based on the presence of blood on the driveway and the information provided by Osborne, [investigators] believed there was a likelihood of a seriously injured person inside the residence, Daskas had written in his motion. Police personnel were also uncertain whether Mack was still inside the townhome when they arrived, Prosecutor Daskas said, and therefore they were justified in their decision to enter the residence without a search warrant.

The prosecutors also indicated that they opposed

moving Mack's trial out of the Reno area, arguing that the court had no authority to do so before the process of interviewing prospective jurors had begun to determine whether or not a fair and impartial jury *could be* seated. They also opposed Mack's attorneys' motion to split the murder of Charla Mack and the attempted murder of Judge Weller into two separate trials, citing that the *relevance of the two events is obvious.*

On Thursday, June 14, 2007, Judge David Huff ruled that the nearly $1 million divorce settlement between the Macks would take effect, stating that under Nevada law, an oral order, such as that issued by Weller, could be placed into effect, if adjudication had occurred while all of the parties were alive. In the Mack case, Huff said, the hearings with Weller had established "that Judge Weller made a decision on the facts of the case concerning property distribution." Weller had questioned the parties, and had "accepted the agreement and stated that it 'shall be the order of the court,'" Huff said. "Due to the realities of practice, time, and constraints on counsel, or the unfortunate circumstances surrounding this case, the order was not entered." As a result, Huff said, the order would now be entered.

"Darren Mack will pay to Mrs. Charla Mack the sum of four hundred eighty thousand dollars," Huff ordered.

He also ordered that an account be set up to pay Charla's estate an additional $500,000, in installments over a period of five years, and that he would also pay her estate $15,500 "to resolve arrears and support issues," and another $6,500 to resolve a brokerage account. Huff also ordered that Charla's car, as well as the

ring and watch whose ownership had been disputed
earlier by Joan Mack, be returned to Palace Jewelry &
Loan Company.

"The order says Judge Weller's order from the
bench is now memorialized in writing," Walker said
on behalf of Charla's estate.

Walker, however, admitted that he did not yet know
how the settlement payments would be funded from
Mack's pension fund, since it was tied up in court, and
said that everyone would have to put their heads together to come up with a plan to fund the settlement.

Darren Mack's attorney, Mark Wray, said that he
would appeal the judge's decision, which would likely
end up taking the matter to the state's supreme court.

"She was only entitled to that when she was alive,"
Wray said. "You have to ask the higher court to see if
this is right. I don't think there is any precedence for
that. When things like this happen, you have to seek
review."

Although a number of legal issues had been resolved during the first six months of 2007, there were
additional issues that would be addressed before
Darren Mack's criminal trial began in the autumn.

28

Although many of the records in Darren Mack's criminal case had been ordered unsealed by Judge Douglas Herndon, the matter of the *Reno Gazette-Journal*'s lawsuit to have the records of Darren Mack's numerous civil cases unsealed had remained mostly judicially undecided during the first six months of 2007. In one of its motions, the newspaper had argued the public's right to be informed about what goes on inside courtrooms, insisting that there *is great public interest in making sure that all proceedings are conducted fairly and without bias*. The problem, as the newspaper rightly saw it, was that Senior Judge Noel Manoukian, a former Nevada Supreme Court justice, had gone too far in sealing the records of the civil case filed by Charla Mack's family for wrongful death, even though his reason for doing so had been to protect Darren Mack's right to a fair trial. It was pointed out that Manoukian had sealed the records in the case, even though lawyers for both sides had not requested him to do so. In fact, counsel for Charla Mack's estate actually had opposed the sealing of the records. The judge had sealed the case, he said, "out of an abundance of caution and concern that media coverage of this civil proceeding could adversely affect . . . [Darren Mack's] fair trial rights" in his upcoming criminal case.

However, on Tuesday, July 24, 2007, Judge Manoukian granted the *Reno Gazette-Journal*'s motion to unseal all of the documents in the wrongful death lawsuit against Mack, and prefaced his decision with a letter to the attorneys on both sides that read, in part: *I believe that most of you will agree that we never stop learning. This is the first First Amendment case I have had, at least in this context.* He alluded to the fact that the arguments made for *very interesting reading,* and concluded by saying that he hoped his decision *does justice* to the newspaper's arguments.

Manoukian had also suggested that Mack had wanted the case unsealed to help him obtain a change of venue in his criminal case.

The court does speculate that by requesting the unsealing of the proceeding, Manoukian wrote in his order, [the] *defendant wishes to further "fuel" or factually support his motion to change venue. Even if true, it would not be appropriate for this court to keep the . . . case file and proceedings sealed.*

Parties on both sides indicated that they were pleased with the judge's decision, particularly Mack's civil lawyer, Mark Wray.

"Darren has always wanted the civil cases in which he is involved to be open to the public," Wray said after the judge's ruling had been made public. "Not just this case, but the other case where he has been sued. Hopefully, someday the public will see what has happened in all of his cases. . . . Open and public court proceedings are integral to the American system of justice."

* * *

However, despite the judicial decisions that had been made, the legal battles involving Darren Mack continued to rage on. A short time after Manoukian's decision to unseal the case files pertaining to the wrongful death lawsuit against Mack, additional details of an agreement signed in April 2007 by Soorya Townley, Charla's mother; Randall Kuckenmeister, trustee for Charla's estate; and Joan Mack, Darren's mother, were made public. Among those details included a plan relating to monetary and custody issues, which had been included in an earlier ruling but without specifics being readily available for public scrutiny. For example, among the specifics now revealed that led to the earlier decisions was that Joan Mack had agreed to drop her lawsuit against Charla regarding the ring and watch issues. Also, jewelry items would be sold by Palace Jewelry & Loan, and the proceeds would be applied toward Darren Mack's bankruptcy case. Furthermore, Joan Mack agreed that she would purchase her son's assets from the bankruptcy and, following liquidation, she would place some of the funds into Charla Mack's estate. The remaining funds would go into a trust for Darren's three children.

The aforementioned agreement included an order written by Judge John Iroz, in which he had decided that Darren Mack's parental rights would *remain intact and not be terminated*. Soorya Townley would also be granted primary custody of Darren and Charla's daughter. The order also called for shared visitation in which Townley and Joan Mack could each have their granddaughter in an alternating weekly schedule arrangement. Darren Mack would also be required to pay Townley $1,500 per month in child support out of his estate funds. The agreement also stipulated that none of Charla Mack's heirs, nor Joan Mack or any of her heirs, could file any additional legal claims beyond what had been included in the settlement.

The order, Wray argued in a motion to dismiss, made the wrongful death lawsuit against Mack a moot issue. But Kent Robison, a lawyer for Charla's estate, saw things a bit differently and was critical of the April settlement agreement, in part because he had not been a participant in it and had only seen the details of it after it had been made public. One of the issues that Robison brought up was the fact that Judge Manoukian had appointed a special guardian for the Macks' daughter regarding legal issues, and that the other parties to the agreement did not have the authority to make legal decisions on the child's behalf. Robison argued against Wray's motion to dismiss the wrongful death lawsuit, citing the aforementioned issues.

"All of the personal injury and wrongful death claims were not invited to the settlement conference," Robison said. "Nobody in that forum had the right to compromise [the child's] claims and legal rights."

To call the case a tangled legal web would have been an understatement. But that's what it was, plain and simple, and it was showing no signs of becoming untangled anytime soon.

On Thursday, July 26, 2007, Mack's attorneys asked that murder charges against their client be dismissed, citing that Mack's rights had been ignored by Richard Gammick when he, the county's district attorney, had held a news conference in which he had mentioned the confession that Mack had made to him. Gammick's news conference was particularly troubling because it had been held after Judge Herndon had ruled that Mack's confession to Gammick could not be used at trial because it would be "overly prejudicial."

In his motion to dismiss the murder charges, Scott Freeman and David Chesnoff stated that Gammick had *flagrantly, blatantly and purposefully engaged in outrageous misconduct in derogation* of the defendant's *constitutional right to due process, a fair trial, and the orderly administration of justice.* The attorneys further stated that Gammick's actions had *violated his legal and professional responsibilities as a district attorney.*

In arguing against the defense motion to dismiss, the prosecutors said that Gammick's actions in making public comments had been a logical effort to explain his actions at a time when Mack had contacted him and stated that he had killed his wife and had shot Judge Weller.

If the court is concerned that Mr. Gammick acted imprudently, then it should admonish both Mr. Gammick and defense counsel, particularly Mr. Freeman, to cease making public comments regarding each other's character, Prosecutor Lalli answered in his response to the motion to dismiss the murder charges against Mack. Lalli also said that Mack's attorneys should also be admonished to not make *personal attacks* in their pleadings.

August 2007 passed quietly, as did most of September, with little of substance occurring in Nevada's courtrooms regarding Darren Mack's cases, civil or criminal. In fact, it was not until Thursday, September 27, 2007, a mere four days before Mack's criminal trial was set to begin, that anything substantial surfaced. Mack's criminal defense attorneys, Scott Freeman and David Chesnoff, challenged an e-mail that

Mack had sent to Richard Gammick that included incriminating comments Mack had made about the killing of his wife, Charla, and the subsequent shooting of Judge Weller. They did not want this admitted into evidence.

In the e-mail, Mack had laid out his conditions for surrendering to law enforcement in Mexico, and had included a demand that he receive the death penalty for his actions—all the while claiming that he had killed Charla in self-defense. Because Judge Herndon had earlier thrown out the tape-recorded conversations between Mack and Gammick, in which Mack had allegedly confessed his crimes, the defense team was hopeful that Herndon would do the same with the e-mail. Their argument was that the same rules that prompted Herndon to rule that the taped conversations were inadmissible also applied to the e-mail. Chesnoff referred to the e-mail as "fruit of the poisonous tree" and said that it should be thrown out. However, prosecutors Christopher Lalli and Robert Daskas argued that the district attorney would have been "remiss" in his duty to the public and in his role as prosecutor if he had chosen to not read the e-mail from Mack.

"This is something that fell on Mr. Gammick's lap," Lalli argued. "This is not something that he reached out for. . . . If he was doing his job, there is absolutely no reason to punish him."

Lalli said that a ruling making the e-mail inadmissible would be akin to suppression of evidence and "punitive" in nature.

It was reiterated that Gammick had been on his way back to his office on June 19, 2006, when his secretary called him on his cell phone and told him that Mack was on one of the other lines. Gammick said he would take the call, and his secretary transferred it to him. Gammick had said that Mack had asked him, "Have you received my e-mail?" Gammick said that he told Mack that he had not received it, and asked him to send it again. When Gammick got back to his office, he saw an e-mail that listed the sender's name as "Kerry Walburg," with a subject line that read Darren Mack's Surrendering Himself. Gammick said that he had opened the e-mail because of his telephone conversation with Mack.

In saying that he would take the arguments into consideration and would render a decision on the matter soon, Herndon also said that there were reasons other than punishing anyone for misconduct in disallowing the e-mail in question into evidence, such as sometimes protecting people, particularly defendants, from themselves. He said that the legal rules were there, in part, not only to punish misconduct but also to establish when it was permissible for prosecutors to have contact or conversation with a suspect.

Prior to the opening of Darren Mack's criminal trial, Herndon issued his decision on the e-mail that Mack had sent to Gammick—it could be introduced as evidence because it had been sent to Gammick unsolicited. Herndon's comments made it clear that he had agreed with the prosecutors on this issue, in that Gammick would have been "remiss" in his duties if he had not opened and read the e-mail from Mack. At this stage, Gammick was aware that the defendant was still at large and, as such, continued to pose a potential danger.

By the Friday prior to the Monday opening of Mack's criminal trial, which would, naturally, begin with an attempt to seat a jury as soon as possible, the prosecution's witness list had grown to more than two hundred people and included such notable names as Washoe County district attorney Richard Gammick, Judge Chuck Weller, Soorya Townley, among many others whose names were by now also familiar with the reading public throughout much of the West Coast. Less-known witnesses, however, included a woman who had shared a resort room with Mack at a swingers' convention held in Mexico, an airline pilot, a fitness room attendant, Mack's previous wife, and so forth. The prosecutors also indicated that they might call an additional fifteen or so people as expert witnesses. It seemed a good bet that prosecutors would also call a number of attorneys who had been involved in various aspects of the numerous legal issues that had occurred between Mack and his wife's estate, and, of course, those involved in their divorce proceedings. A number of Darren Mack's family members, as well as a few of his close friends, were also on the prosecution's witness list.

The defense team's witness list contained considerably fewer names, but they made it clear that they would likely call some of those testifying for the prosecution. The defense also made it known that they planned to call several mental-health experts, since Mack had pleaded not guilty and not guilty by reason of insanity. They were also prepared to place a psychologist on the stand who would present details of a psychological profile of Charla Mack, should they find themselves arguing a case of self-defense. No one on Mack's team, however, had publicly committed to which path they might go down in defending their client.

PART IV

TRIAL

29

On Monday, October 1, 2007, the much-anticipated trial for Darren Mack finally got under way inside the Washoe County Courthouse in downtown Reno, Nevada, barely a block away from the Mills B. Lane Justice Center, where Judge Chuck Weller had nearly been assassinated. Even before 9:00 A.M., many local residents who had been sent a jury summons, and had responded to it correctly, began lining up to be checked in, wondering if they would actually be chosen to sit on the panel that would ultimately decide Mack's fate. Hundreds of people were involved in the selection process. One by one, they entered the old courthouse to take their turn at answering questions from the prosecution and defense teams in an effort to determine whether—or, probably more accurately, how much—they had been influenced by the extensive media coverage throughout Northern Nevada and much of the state. The goal was to seat twelve men and women, and a handful of alternates, if the prospective jurors had not already reached a conclusion regarding Darren Mack's guilt or innocence. It was very clearly a weeding-out process, and even a hint of a relationship with any of the witnesses that both sides planned to call could easily be grounds for disqualifying a potential juror from serving. Most of the officials involved expected jury selection to last three or four days—if a Washoe County jury could even be selected. That would place delivery of opening statements most likely at the beginning of the following week.

If too many prospective jurors turned out to be too opinionated and firm in their beliefs, there was, of course, the possibility that a local jury could not even be seated. In the event that it appeared that seating an impartial jury might be a problem, the defense team would most assuredly ask once again for a change of venue. Judge Herndon had indicated previously that he would be open to this option if the need arose. In Nevada, it is required by law that a court attempt to select and seat a jury before granting a change of venue.

It had not taken long for David Chesnoff and Scott Freeman to enter their motion again for a change of venue, just prior to beginning the interview process of prospective jurors. Chesnoff presented Judge Herndon a copy of that morning's edition of the *Reno Gazette-Journal,* which had a large photograph of Darren Mack when he had earlier been led into a courtroom by sheriff's deputies. The subject of an article accompanying the photograph was about the beginning of the jury selection process. Chesnoff also presented Herndon with a number of news articles, as well as news items that had appeared on blogs and information about Mack's case that he had obtained from websites.

Chesnoff and Freeman's motion urged the judge to grant the change of venue right away, primarily because the media attention surrounding the case had been so extreme.

"There's a compelling need to give the defendant a fair trial," Chesnoff said. "I ask you to consider, as a matter of due process, transferring this to another part of the state to avoid even the possibility of having to do this again."

DDA Robert Daskas, however, did not want a change of venue granted, at least not yet. He asked the judge to wait and see how the selection process progressed before making such a decision.

"Our point is, let's at least try," Daskas said. "If we can't get Mr. Mack a fair jury, we'll pack up and move."

Herndon said that he understood the concern over all of the publicity, and agreed that it was indeed significant, but he was reluctant to approve the venue change request prior to giving the selection process a chance to work, like the law required.

"There's a lot of people who don't watch that much news," Herndon said in announcing his decision. "I have to agree with the state."

Selection got off to a shaky start. The first prospective juror that was questioned was asked if he could accept whether any mental-health issues by the defendant may have contributed to the crimes committed on June 12, 2006, and whether or not he could be open to a possible insanity defense. The juror unhesitatingly responded negatively.

"The insanity plea? No," he said. "I think he's a totally sane person."

The juror, of course, was excused.

And on it went throughout much of the day, with an objective of selecting thirty-three possible jurors.

After those thirty-three people had been selected, each side—the prosecution and the defense—would eliminate nine people each through the peremptory challenge process, leaving fifteen remaining jurors—twelve to sit on the panel, and three standing by as alternates, if needed. Of course, that was how everyone hoped it would be, if the process ran smoothly.

To sum it up, during the early hours of the first day of the selection process, a group of fifty possible jurors were questioned as a group. Those fifty people had been selected from a group of four hundred potential jurors that had previously been sent questionnaires to determine how many of them had watched the news, how many had learned about the case from the news, and whether they had already formed strong opinions about the case. In addition to trying to nail down how much media coverage each prospective juror had been exposed to, the process also entailed finding out their views regarding the judicial process, what they thought about bias, any experiences they may have had with divorce in their lives, and, of course, what they thought about self-defense in addition to the questions about an insanity plea.

Five of them were promptly dismissed, including the first juror questioned. Another juror was dismissed due to a family health issue, and the other four were dismissed for a variety of reasons that mostly related to whether they could keep an open mind about Mack's mental health or whether they had been influenced by all of the pretrial publicity. One man said that he did not know "how anyone could avoid being swayed" by the media coverage, and said that he could not be "impartial." A young woman was excused because she was a full-time student at UNR, and being on the jury would interfere with her class schedule. Another woman said that it was her desire to come into court with an open mind regarding the case, but eventually said that she had read and heard too much about the case to remain unbiased. The remaining forty-four people were brought back in the afternoon to be questioned more thoroughly by each side, a process intended to glean additional details regarding each potential juror's ability to sit on the panel in judgment of Mack's fate. By the end of the day, however, the process had gone almost ideally, with the approval of three men and three women who would participate in the remaining process.

Among those who were seated on the jury by the end of the first day were two women who both indicated that they had not formed a definite opinion about Darren Mack's innocence or guilt, and another woman who had questioned why a defendant would flee the country "if he's innocent." The woman was allowed to remain on the jury at this stage after she clarified that her opinion of the media's ability to provide accurate information was not a positive one, and that like the other two women, she had not formed a definite opinion regarding his innocence or guilt. One of the men who had been approved was a former doctor who had traded in his practice in order to trade stocks. He agreed that he could keep an open mind to an insanity defense and "do what's right." The two additional male jurors were a teacher and an unidentified man whose opinion about the possible insanity plea was permissible.

By the end of the second day of jury selection, which was moving along very slowly, at least seventy potential jurors had been dismissed because their responses to all of the lawyer questioning indicated that they had preconceived notions about Mack's guilt, as well as other typical reasons. The latter usually related to a personal hardship of some kind that would be made worse due to the time it would take to sit on a jury for what would likely be a month-long murder trial.

Even though she said that she could be fair and impartial, and knew very little about the Mack case, one woman was excused because she revealed that an ex-husband had previously threatened to file kidnapping charges against her in a child custody dispute. Another potential juror was excused because he had made it clear that he thought that Darren Mack was a "spoiled rich kid" who could afford the best attorneys and, as such, could influence justice.

By Wednesday, October 3, twelve jurors had been seated, and an additional thirty-four prospective jurors were brought in to attempt to finish the process. Although an additional juror had been seated, the day ended without any results, because one juror who had been selected previously was dismissed because it turned out that he had made some statements that had been untrue. By the end of the day, Herndon, as well as the lawyers for both sides, appeared a bit stressed and disappointed that Wednesday's efforts had failed to produce any new results.

The next morning, Judge Herndon announced shortly after entering the courtroom that he had decided to grant a change of venue and move the trial to Las Vegas, some 450 miles to the south of Reno. There were likely many more potential jurors with less knowledge about the case, he said. He had given up on the previous optimism he had held that the trial could be held in Washoe County, commenting that the prior day's efforts had been a "net gain" of "zero."

"This case has caused me to lose a lot of sleep over the past few nights," Herndon said in announcing his new decision. "I think it's apparent there's a reasonable likelihood that an impartial panel cannot be found here. . . . Yesterday was just a disaster."

Herndon stated that he had not expected the jury pools to be so aware of the case, and he was disappointed that many of the people they would be selecting the jury from had continued reading newspapers and viewing television news stories about Darren Mack's case. In making his decision, Herndon had cited earlier cases in Nevada that had been much sensationalized, cases in which a change of venue had not been granted. He referred to "sex slave" killer Gerald Gallego, who needs no introduction to true-crime readers, and to the 1980 Thanksgiving Day rampage of Priscilla Ford, who was convicted of killing six people and injuring twenty-three others after driving her Lincoln Continental down a crowded downtown Reno street. She had received the death penalty and had been the only woman on Nevada's death row until her death in 2005 from emphysema. Herndon also mentioned the case of Michael Sonner, who killed Trooper Carlos J. Borland, of the Nevada Highway Patrol, in 1993. While the cases he cited tended to justify his earlier decision to keep the Mack case in Washoe County, Herndon based his decision for the change of venue on a much older murder case that had been overturned primarily because a change of venue had not been granted.

The cases cited by Herndon had received considerably less publicity than the Mack case had gotten. Ford's case, for example, Herndon said of his research, had only turned up sixty-six newspaper references. Ford, Sonner, and Gallego, Herndon said, had not been well-known in the community. Mack, on the other hand, a wealthy business owner, was well-known. Herndon said that research, in part from documents submitted by Mack's defense team, had turned up references to 144 newspaper articles and 242 television news stories on the case, not including the websites and blogs, and there were several that contained information about the case.

"I don't think you can go anywhere without having knowledge about the case," Herndon said, adding that there were approximately one hundred thousand potential jurors residing in Washoe County—too small of a number from which a jury could be successfully chosen for a case that had been publicized as much as Mack's. "But in Clark County," he continued, "you have over one million people from which to choose jurors. I think moving it to Clark County makes sense."

Herndon looked at Darren Mack, who sat quietly next to his attorneys.

"Would you agree that a move to Clark County would be in your best interest?" Herndon asked Mack.

"Very much so, sir," Mack replied. "Absolutely, sir."

Although the attorneys for both sides had been somewhat expecting Herndon to change his mind about moving the case to Las Vegas, Freeman and Chesnoff were elated at the decision.

"We're very, very excited," Freeman said after the decision had been announced. "This is something we worked hard for. It became apparent that as we had anticipated, it would have been difficult for people to set aside their opinions that they probably had."

Prosecutors Christopher Lalli and Robert Daskas were also pleased with the judge's decision to move the trial.

"What we're pleased about," Lalli said, "is that we

maintain the trial date and we continue on. I would have been very concerned if the trial would have been continued six months down the line."

Before adjourning, Herndon set Wednesday, August 15, 2007, as the date that jury selection would begin anew, this time in Las Vegas.

30

Jury selection began slowly, again, on Monday, October 15, 2007, this time in the Las Vegas courtroom of Judge Douglas Herndon, on his own turf. Based on a seven-page questionnaire that two hundred prospective jurors had filled out the week before, thirty had been dismissed. Following a several-hour delay in the individual questioning of prospective jurors due to a mix-up in scheduling, the case eventually got under way later that day, with Herndon calling the process "deliberate and . . . slow-going at times." Nonetheless, the first juror selected this time around was a woman, an office manager for an air-conditioning company. Darren Mack, dressed in a dark suit, watched the entire proceeding. At this early stage, his attorneys had not yet decided if they would place him on the witness stand to testify in his own defense.

And so it went. By the end of the third day, a total of fifteen possible jurors had been selected, including a former newspaper editor and a former nurse, who had gone through a divorce following her experience with a husband who had been addicted to drugs. When all was said and done, they had just under half the number of people they needed to move forward—nearly a repeat of what the jury selection experience of weeding out those with biases or too much knowledge of the case had been in Reno. Unlike in Reno, however, many of those questioned in Las Vegas told the lawyers that they knew little about the case, making the process of finding prospective jurors a little easier. Finally, after five days of the selection process, they had a jury of twelve people, with three alternates.

Following clarification of certain issues and the ironing out of how the case would proceed, opening statements began on Wednesday, October 24, 2007, shortly after 10:00 A.M., in District Court Courtroom 10D. Prosecutors Christopher Lalli and Robert Daskas told the jury that the case was a simple one, and provided a detailed timeline, as well as a motive and method, of how Mack had allegedly committed premeditated murder when he killed his wife, Charla. Daskas also provided details of Mack's so-called "to do" list of things, which he believed, he needed to do to carry out the crimes.

The prosecutors told of how the handsome former bodybuilder had earned millions of dollars by running his family's downtown Reno pawnshop, Palace Jewelry & Loan Company, and described Charla as a brunette beauty who had acted in Hollywood movies. They both drove luxury cars, resided in a large Tudor-style million-dollar home on several acres, with a man-made lake in the backyard. They also engaged in a sex life that could best be politely described as "swinging," which nearly everyone knew about. But their harmonious life together had not lasted, and their open marriage began to suffer, despite the fact that they had been raising a young daughter. The sex and the money that had fueled their marriage during the early years suddenly turned against them as they began having bitter fights and arguments that eventually led to a rancorous and vengeful divorce. As their lives continued to spiral downward in battles over who would gain custody of their daughter, and fights over who would get which assets, their disagreements led to accusations of mental instability. They began also to fight over what some considered their sexual excesses—especially Darren's. After Darren had been left the major loser in the divorce proceedings, with nearly $1 million going to Charla, Mack had become so upset that he literally surprise-attacked his ex-wife and stabbed her to death. Then he attempted to kill their divorce judge—all on the morning of June 12, 2006, before fleeing to Mexico almost immediately afterward.

Prosecutors contended that Darren and Charla's story had been a sad one, but one that had not been all that unusual, a story where their love for each other had somehow turned into hatred, and then violence. Charla had accused Darren of spending money from their joint assets to take women on trips to exotic places, including some locales where swinging conventions were held, and in which he had participated. Darren, on the other hand, had said that Charla had threatened him with violence.

Daskas also went into detail about how Darren Mack intended to kill Judge Chuck Weller, and carefully laid out the scenario of the downtown Reno shooting for the jury's benefit. He also introduced photographs of the two crime scenes, which were shown to the jury, and included videotaped statements made by Mack.

Some of the photographs were gruesome, and showed Charla lying on the floor of Darren Mack's garage, with a wide-open slash wound near the base of her neck.

All the while, Darren Mack listened intently as prosecutors laid out the gruesome scenario, and at one point, his face began to flush as the prosecutors described how Charla died on the floor of his garage while their daughter was upstairs watching television with one of Darren's friends.

In one of the videotapes, made nearly three weeks before Mack's wife was killed and Weller was shot, which prosecutors used to help them bolster their case against Mack for shooting Weller, Darren Mack was seen with an advocacy group comparing Nevada's family court system to the despotism that had contributed to the American Revolution.

"It's time to take a stand," Mack said on the videotape. "It's time to not let this tyranny go under the wraps, keep it quiet. If our forefathers in 1776 stood by [and said], 'Just keep quiet, maybe England will go away,' we would be sipping tea right now. At what point do we . . . stand up to this absolute unconstitutionality and state, 'We're not going to take this anymore'? Where do we draw the line?"

"The defendant's anger brewed," Daskas said of the videotape. "Darren Mack had a problem, and eighteen days later, he found a solution to that problem."

Daskas indicated that the evidence against Mack in both crimes was overwhelming, and the state was prepared to bring in evidence that would connect Mack to both of the crimes, evidence that included DNA, fingerprints, gunshot residue, video surveillance, boxes of bullets that were of the same type used to shoot Weller, the rental car agreement for the Explorer, the empty knife sheath found inside his bedroom that had held a four-inch, double-edged fixed-bladed dagger, his "to do" list, witnesses such as Osborne, and so forth. By the time they were finished presenting their case, Daskas contended, the jury would convict Mack of both crimes. To sum up, the prosecution contended that it would prove that the stabbing of Charla Mack and the shooting of Judge Weller were both part of a deliberate plot by Darren Mack to end the bitter breakup with his estranged wife and to send a strong message to the legal system that he believed was corrupt and had wronged him. Daskas showed photos of the so-called "to do" list to the jury, and said that Charla's murder was summed up by the words *End problem* and *Parking garage—if yes*. Both he and Lalli described Mack as a methodical, cold-blooded killer who thought he could put an end to his divorce problems by plotting to murder Charla and assassinating Judge Weller. It had been a solution, he mistakenly believed, that would allow him to avoid paying the enormous divorce settlement.

"It was a plan formulated and memorialized by the defendant in his own writing," Daskas said, again referring to the "to do" list. The prosecutor also referred to the words that Mack had written on his list, *Put lex in garage,* an apparent reference to move Charla's Lexus from the driveway and into the garage. Both prosecutors argued that Darren Mack had committed cold-blooded, premeditated attacks that fateful day in June 2006, and that he should be found guilty.

* * *

"Ladies and gentlemen, you've heard from the state," Freeman said in his opening statement. "They told you their version of the events, and now it's time for the defense to tell you their story."

During his opening statement, Scott Freeman painted a picture of Darren Mack as an abused husband, and contended that Mack was a victim—not a nasty piece of work as he had been portrayed by the prosecution. He also contended that Charla's death was not murder, but was a result of self-defense. Freeman portrayed Charla as a woman who had a split personality, and said that Darren was fearful of her. He described their relationship as highly contentious, which came into play during their divorce proceedings.

"She can be kind and giving in public," Freeman said. "She could be violent and abusive at home. It was too much for Darren to take."

Freeman also described the defense team's version of events on the day Charla was killed and Judge Weller was shot, and told the attentive jury that Charla had attacked Darren and that he was defending himself against her attack. Freeman described her as a terrorist of sorts, and said that she used the divorce proceedings to demand money and custody of their child. According to Freeman, she had threatened her husband with violence.

"'I will cut your penis off and put it in a freezer,'" Freeman quoted Charla as having said to Darren. "'I will kill you. I watch Court TV every day, and I know how to do it.'"

Eventually, Freeman said, Darren began to believe that Charla would make good on her threats, particularly after a psychic told him to take precautions when around her. Freeman even described what the psychic purportedly told Darren.

"She said," Freeman paraphrased, "'There's blood everywhere. You can't turn your back on Charla. She will stab you with a knife.'"

Shortly after that, Freeman continued, Darren purchased a knife with which he could defend himself.

According to Freeman, on the morning of her death, Charla had demanded that Mack and his family pay her money, according to the terms of the divorce settlement, or else Mack would never see his daughter again.

"She came to threaten Darren into submission," Freeman said.

Charla and Darren began fighting in the garage of his townhome on the day of the murder, presumably because she had learned that Darren intended to appeal Weller's ruling, Freeman said. Apparently enraged, Freeman said, Charla's "split personality" came to the surface, and she began name-calling. When Darren turned his back on her to walk away, she attacked him from behind by striking him on the right side of his face and pushing him. He fell over onto his right knee, and they began struggling. A gun that Darren had been carrying with him for protection fell out of his pocket, and Charla grabbed it. According to Freeman, Charla looked at the gun, pulled the hammer back into firing position, smiled, and pulled the trigger. However, nothing happened—the gun had misfired. When she started to cock the gun again, Darren lunged at her, but she moved quickly, and Darren had only grabbed a handful of hair. She rolled to her left, Freeman said, and they were both on the floor at this point. Darren believed he was going to die, and he had become terrified. That was when he reached for his knife. Charla kicked at him from her position on the garage floor as Darren tried to get the knife out. As the two continued to struggle, Darren plunged the knife into her neck, and into her carotid artery.

"Darren plunges the knife into her neck once," Freeman told the jury. "Charla's violence has stopped."

Knowing that the jurors would be wondering about Mack's "to do" list, and why it existed if Charla's death had not been premeditated, Freeman attempted to explain it by saying that Darren was distraught and temporarily out of his mind following the fight with Charla. He had made the list *after* the killing to help him organize his thoughts.

But would the jury believe that Darren composed the "to do" list after killing Charla? And how would the defense attorneys explain the reference to *Parking garage—if yes,* which had been scribbled onto the list? Only time would tell.

When Freeman had finished his self-defense remarks and had opened the door for his client's plea of not guilty by reason of insanity, attorney David Chesnoff continued the defense opening remarks by telling the jury that the fight with Charla in his garage had caused Darren Mack to "snap," and that Charla's display of hatred toward him that morning had essentially pushed him over the edge. He also told the jury that the partying lifestyle that they had shared during their marriage, in which Darren had used drugs at times, had damaged his reasoning ability.

"Darren's mind was essentially raped—by the drugs—of his reason and judgment," Chesnoff said. "Darren Mack was suffering from a recognized mental disorder."

Chesnoff told the jury that Mack suffered from a

delusional disorder that sometimes prevented him from seeing reality and caused him to believe things that a reasonable person would not necessarily believe. He said that Mack had been out of his mind when he shot Judge Weller "to send a message." To help prove his point, Chesnoff said that Mack shot Weller because he believed that the Second Amendment allowed for people to use weapons against tyranny. He said that the prosecution had already provided evidence of Mack's unbalanced state of mind when they had shown the interview videotape Mack had made with the support group, urging fathers in the group to revolt against the "tyranny" and "injustice" of the family court system.

"If that's not delusional, I don't know what is," Chesnoff said. "He was basically comparing himself to Benjamin Franklin. . . . God is telling him to exercise his Second Amendment rights and end this tyranny. . . . Darren acted upon his delusions in shooting Judge Weller, and the disease he suffers from caused the delusions to control his actions."

After Mack's friend and daughter left the residence through the front door on the morning of Charla's death, Chesnoff said, Darren Mack went "on autopilot" and began thinking about various possible escape plans, including living in the mountains of Northern Nevada. Instead, however, Mack began driving toward the airport, but along the way, he saw the Mills B. Lane Justice Center and decided to send a message to the family court system.

The problem with that theory, which was not pointed out by the defense team, of course, was that the Reno-Tahoe International Airport was located several miles southeast of the Mills B. Lane Justice Center. He would have had to go a considerable distance out of his way to get to the justice center, if he had been heading toward the airport, which was located closer to his home than the downtown justice center.

Another hole in that defense theory was the "to do" list onto which Mack had scribbled, *Parking garage—if yes.* If Mack had not planned in advance to shoot the judge, and had only decided to commit that crime while en route to the airport, why had he scribbled the note at his townhome sometime before leaving? That scenario just did not make any sense, primarily because it did not fit cohesively with the known facts. Even if Mack had planned to leave town via a flight from the Sacramento International Airport, the route to Sacramento would not have taken him past the justice center, where Judge Weller worked, although it would have placed him in the vicinity, if he had taken surface streets north from his home to hook up with Interstate 80.

31

At one point early in the trial, Judge Douglas Herndon had expressed concern over Darren Mack's decision to have his attorneys argue that jurors acquit him in the murder of his wife on the basis that he had killed her in self-defense, and to find him not guilty by reason of insanity for the attempted murder of Judge Weller. His attorneys, Herndon indicated, had advised Mack to pursue an insanity defense on both counts instead of pursuing a "split" defense. Herndon questioned Mack on his decision to disregard his lawyers' advice.

"Against their advice, you wish to pursue the two defenses to two different acts. Is that correct?" Herndon asked.

"Yes, sir," Mack responded.

Following the clarification on the so-called split defense strategy and opening statements presented by both sides, the prosecution began calling witnesses from its list of more than two hundred people. The first to take the stand was forensic pathologist Dr. Katherine Raven, who had performed the definitive autopsy on Charla Mack's body. Photos of how

Charla's body was found were displayed by Daskas, and it was a grisly sight—even for the most seasoned law enforcement professional. Nonetheless, Raven took the jury through her findings.

Raven said that Charla Mack had died as a result of at least seven different stab wounds, including one to the neck, near her collarbone. The wound near her collarbone, Raven said, had cut a large artery. In fact, it had "cut her esophagus in half, and nearly cut her trachea in half," Raven said, and her carotid artery had also been cut. The pathologist also described the wounds that Charla had sustained to her forearm, wrist, elbow, and lower legs—wounds that were consistent with a victim trying to fight off an attacker, Raven said. All in all, she said, there were seven wounds to Charla's body.

In contrast, Daskas said, Darren Mack had not sustained any injuries as a result of the violence on the morning of June 12, and no injuries had been observed on him when he was arrested in Mexico. This was likely because of his large stature and build at five-eleven and two hundred pounds, compared to Charla's petite five-foot-four-inch, 120-pound build—he had easily overpowered her during the attack. When he surrendered in Mexico, there had been no injuries to his hands, his forearms, or his face. The prosecution introduced photos of Mack and the aforementioned anatomical areas of his body to help prove its point.

"He did not have an injury on his body," Daskas said. "Not a cut, not a scratch, not a nick."

Their unorthodox sexual practices were brought up again with regard to which of them had instigated the partner swapping, with the defense contending that Charla had been the instigator and that Darren had gone along with his wife's "fantasies." The prosecution said that it had been Darren who had urged his wife to participate, to which she had "reluctantly agreed."

At another point, the defense attorneys, in trying to prove Mack's mental decline, said that Mack had become convinced that their divorce judge had been sleeping with his wife, and that many of the attorneys were involved in a conspiracy against him. However, the prosecution put a relative of Mack's on the witness stand who testified that he had seen Mack approximately half an hour prior to the attack and he had seemed fine and was behaving normally. Under cross-examination by the defense, however, the same relative testified that he had seen Charla punch Mack during a fight that they had while on an ocean cruise.

During the early days of the trial, Dan Osborne, a longtime friend of Mack's, related his observations the morning that Charla was attacked, and recounted how he had been watching television with their young daughter upstairs while Mack and Charla met downstairs, in the garage. Osborne testified that it had been Mack's daughter who had first heard the faint sounds of Osborne's mixed-breed dog, Rusty, which was part bullmastiff and part Labrador, barking downstairs.

When he went to see why the dog was barking, Osborne said, the dog came up the stairs from the garage, holding his head down and his tail between his legs. Mack was right behind the dog, with a towel wrapped around his hand. Mack had not uttered a word, but shot Osborne "a weird, scared kind of look."

As he tried to understand what had happened downstairs, Mack's daughter pointed out blood on the dog's coat.

"His muzzle had blood on it," Osborne said. "The chest area and then down toward the feet. And, at that point, I thought, 'Something has gone wrong here.'"

"Freaked out" over the incident, in part because of his recollection of how Mack had frequently complained bitterly about his estranged wife, Osborne said that he then picked up the child and headed out the front door.

"Did he say, 'My wife just attacked me'?" Daskas asked the witness.

"No," Osborne responded.

"Did he say, 'My wife tried to shoot me'?"

"No."

Osborne said that Mack did not have any visible marks or injuries on his body when he had seen him come upstairs from the garage, and he had not mentioned having had a fight with his wife. Osborne also said that a cursory inspection of his dog showed that the dog had not been injured. Instead of looking inside the garage to determine what had happened, after Mack's daughter had seen the blood on Osborne's dog, Osborne said they left immediately and headed toward Mack's mother's house.

Osborne said that Mack called him on his cell phone about five minutes after he and the child had left the townhome. Mack asked him to bring his daughter and meet him at a Starbucks located nearby. Osborne said that Mack and his daughter talked privately for a few minutes, after which Mack hugged and kissed her. Osborne said that he then took the child to her grandmother's house and called 911.

As Darren Mack watched attentively from the defense table, Osborne testified that he still considered Mack a "good friend," and said that he had known him for three decades. But he also described Mack's recurrent rages against Judge Chuck Weller, and said that Mack had talked about "getting rid" of Weller. Osborne said that he told Mack, "You really don't want to say something like that—it really scares the hell out of me."

When Osborne was cross-examined by the defense, however, he conceded that he thought Mack had just been "blowing off steam" when he made the remarks about getting rid of Weller. Osborne also said that he had not felt threatened by Mack that morning—Mack had not even acknowledged Osborne's presence or that of his daughter.

"Fair to say 'trancelike' in some ways?" Freeman asked.

"That's probably a good description," Osborne said.

Another witness, a self-described "teammate" of Darren Mack's who attended one of the fathers' rights advocacy groups with the defendant, said that both he and Mack had felt like they had been mistreated by Weller's handling of their divorce cases. The witness said that his first act after hearing that Weller had been shot was to call Mack—each of them had shared the same viewpoint that Weller had been unfair with them and that the family court system was "dysfunctional" and needed to be "torn down." When he called Mack after hearing the news, however, Mack told him that he was too busy to talk with him at that time, and that he would call him back.

"We were both teammates trying to tackle a very important issue," the witness said.

"Do you consider yourself delusional?" Lalli asked him.

"I don't think so," responded the witness.

Police witnesses also testified early in the trial and described how a search of Darren Mack's home had uncovered papers concerning Weller and the divorce process, as well as a map that had been obtained off the Internet that showed where Weller resided. Another, similar map had been found for the residence of Charla's divorce attorney, and the computer date stamp indicated that both maps had been printed four months prior to June 12, 2006.

As the week's testimony wrapped up, jurors also heard statements from a witness who said that Mack had placed a telephone call to the company that managed his gated community and canceled his weekly cleaning service. That call had been made less than an hour after Mack had killed Charla.

Jurors also heard that the gun that Charla had supposedly used to try to shoot Mack had been discarded inside a Dumpster, and that Mack had reportedly urged his attorneys to try to find it, but they had refused.

32

When Mack's trial resumed the following Monday, October 29, 2007, Jimmy Smith, a document examiner employed by the Las Vegas Metropolitan Police Department, was among the many witnesses to take the stand and offer forensic testimony. Smith, a balding, bespectacled middle-aged man, testified that Darren Mack was indeed the person who had written the so-called "to do" list, which police had found on Mack's kitchen table during the investigation of the events of June 12. The list, Smith said, had been written on a yellow legal pad, and had bullet points beside the items on it. Smith said that he had compared the list to eighteen pages of Mack's handwriting and had determined that the style of block capital letters were identical to the other pages that he had examined.

"That document was written by Darren Mack," Smith testified.

As Smith went over the list, prosecutors went, almost point by point, showing the jury the meaning of the references printed on the list. For example, when they talked about the bulleted item *Parking garage—if yes*, prosecutors pointed out that the item referred to Mack's plan to shoot Judge Weller inside his chambers from a sniper's point that he had selected in a nearby parking garage. The list also referred to taking their daughter to her grandmother's house, as well as closing the door to his garage.

In an effort to drive home the point that Mack's actions were premeditated, the prosecution also pointed out that Mack's friend Dan Osborne had previously told the police that Mack had asked him on the night of June 11, 2006, to drive his daughter to her grandmother's house the next morning. Osborne had also told the police that the garage door to Mack's townhome had been in the open position when Mack and Charla had begun talking, but that it had been closed a few moments later—another thing that had occurred that morning that had led Osborne to suspect that Charla may have been harmed in some manner.

Throughout much of the day, police forensics personnel testified to their duties and the items that had been gathered as evidence during the investigation, which had begun as Mack fled to Mexico. Some of the witnesses displayed photos depicting many of the bloodstained items retrieved from the garage, where Charla had been killed, which the investigators had collected and catalogued carefully. Testimony was given indicating that DNA tests had conclusively matched the blood inside the garage to Charla, and it was shown that at least one bloody fingerprint belonged to Mack. Traces of Charla's blood had even been found on Mack's shoes following his surrender in Mexico.

The forensic testimony was damning, to say the least, and the accompanying photographs were also shocking for many of the jurors. One such photo depicted Charla's arm, dark with blood, stretched across the garage floor, near one of the neon-yellow-and-aqua sandals that she had been wearing that morning. Another disturbing photo, taken inside Weller's chambers, showed his wire-framed glasses, of which one lens was covered with blood. The forensic witnesses also talked about, and showed photographs of, Charla's blood-soaked T-shirt, on which one investigator pointed out a knife hole in the shirt's neck area.

The prosecution also pointed out, with the help of scientific testimony from the forensics personnel, bloodstains on a lock that led from the garage to inside Mack's townhome, suggesting that perhaps Mack had locked Charla inside the garage before killing her—while their daughter was upstairs.

Because, in part, the prosecution had worked so hard to show that Mack had killed his wife because he was angry and upset over the divorce settlement, and had hoped to get out of paying it, and because they had contended that he had not paid his obligations to her regularly, the defense took the opportunity to focus on two checks, totaling $800, found in Charla's Lexus. The checks had been written from Darren's account, and one had been marked "alimony" and the other "child support," and were proof, suggested one of the defense attorneys, that Mack had been paying Charla regularly what he owed to her.

The next day, Washoe County Family Court judge Chuck Weller took the witness stand to recall the events on the day he was shot. Among the things that he testified to was that, after being shot, he immediately thought that Mack had been the person who had shot him. He was then asked if the man who he believed had shot him was in the courtroom.

"That man, right there," Weller said as he pointed toward Darren Mack.

During his testimony, Weller said that he had been speaking to his assistant inside his chambers when he suddenly heard a loud noise. Immediately afterward, he felt a burning sensation on the left side of his chest. He indicated that he at first thought that his cellular telephone had exploded inside his shirt pocket, but when he looked up and saw the hole in his office window, he remembered that he was not carrying his phone in his shirt pocket.

"It occurred to me I had just been shot through the window," Weller said. "So I threw myself down on the ground."

Weller said that after he had been shot, he remained on the floor and crawled out of his office, shouting for someone to call his wife so that she could get herself and his family out of their home as a precaution, in case the assailant decided to go after his family.

A reference was also made to Weller's last contact with Mack. It had been at a divorce hearing, about a month before the shooting, when Weller had not allowed Mack to back out of the nearly $1 million divorce settlement that he had made with Charla. At that hearing, Weller recalled, Mack had given him a "mean, hateful, ugly glare," which Weller later described to his administrative assistant as "a look of death."

Under direct examination by the prosecution, Weller testified that the accusations that Darren Mack had made against him were unfounded, including accusations that Mack had been treated unfairly by the judge because his attorney had not contributed as heavily as Charla's lawyer to Weller's election campaign. He testified that he had repeatedly ruled in favor of Mack—he had chosen Mack's plan for custody, instead of his wife's—and he had rejected Charla's efforts to get Mack to pay for counseling for their daughter. Furthermore, he said, one of Mack's attorneys had contributed four times more money to his campaign than Charla's lawyer. He also said that he suspected that Mack had attempted to hide his assets, and he had held him in contempt when he transferred his percentage of the family's pawnshop business to his mother.

During Weller's testimony, he was asked a number of other questions—mostly by the defense on cross-examination—regarding the Mack divorce, Mack's finances, Mack's degree of honesty regarding how much money he had, the fathers' rights groups where some of the members, including Mack, had utilized the Internet in an effort to defame the judge. Weller testified that he had been told that Mack had been behind some of the postings on Internet logs that had contained "just horrible attacks on me"—and so forth. At one point, Chesnoff turned his questioning of Weller toward some of the allegations that Mack had made against the judge.

"You hadn't been sleeping with Charla Mack, had you?" Chesnoff asked.

"No, sir," Weller curtly responded.

"That would be crazy," Chesnoff added. "You

treated Mr. Mack differently than other people who appeared before you—didn't you, Judge?"

"No," Weller flatly responded.

"That would also be crazy," Chesnoff said.

At another point, Chesnoff asked Weller to read the 2006 Washoe County Bar Association survey, in which Weller had been given the lowest retention rating among the twelve judges surveyed. He also asked Weller about any social relationship he may have had with Charla Mack's divorce attorney.

"I've never had my reputation attacked the way you're attacking it," Weller retorted angrily. "It's unfair."

After Weller's remarks, Herndon told the jury to disregard Weller's last statement.

"You know better than that, Judge," Herndon told Weller. "This is not the forum for that."

Chesnoff then asked for a mistrial.

Herndon then temporarily halted the proceedings, and asked the bailiffs to remove the jury from the court-room. In discussing his reasons for asking for a mistrial, Chesnoff said that he thought Weller's remark would taint the jury's opinion of him and Mack.

"I don't think it rises to the level of a mistrial," Herndon said. He also said that he had not taken any pleasure in admonishing a fellow judge. "I've got great sympathy for Judge Weller," Herndon said. "The man was shot, after all."

He then ruled that the trial would continue the next day.

When the trial resumed the next day, Chad Ruff, a pilot for United Airlines, took the stand to testify about seeing Mack at the Melia Cabo Real resort in

Cabo San Lucas. It appeared that prosecutors were attempting to use Ruff's testimony to contradict defense efforts to portray Mack as someone who had suffered a mental breakdown after killing his wife.

Like he had told the police earlier, Ruff said that he first saw Mack inside the gym at the Melia Cabo Real resort, but that later, after returning to his room, he had seen a news report on television about Charla Mack's death and the sniper attack on Judge Weller. He realized that he had just seen the person depicted as a suspect in the news report.

"It struck me," Ruff testified, "that I thought I had seen that person."

Ruff testified that he saw the man again, this time at the resort's pool, and he was in the company of a woman. Ruff said that he walked past him several times so that he could study his face before calling the authorities—he wanted to be sure. He said that Mack and the woman left the pool together at one point and walked toward the guest rooms together.

"Was he acting in any unusual way?" Daskas asked.

"No," Ruff responded.

"No bizarre speech? No bizarre movements?"

"No," Ruff said.

Scott Freeman suggested on cross-examination that Ruff had been mistaken and had incorrectly identified Darren Mack, saying that Mack had actually been in another town in Mexico on the day that Ruff believed he had seen him.

"He couldn't be in two places at once, could he?" Freeman asked the witness.

"No," Ruff replied.

33

Following another weekend recess, when Mack's trial resumed on Monday, November 5, 2007, as his defense attorneys were set to begin calling witnesses, the unexpected occurred. Instead of going forth with the defense, his attorneys said that a plea agreement had been worked out during the weekend recess, and that Mack had decided to accept it. He officially pleaded guilty to first-degree murder for the death of his wife, Charla, and entered an Alford plea to attempted murder, with use of a deadly weapon, for the sniper shooting of Judge Weller. Although he had essentially admitted in court that he had shot Weller, by invoking an Alford plea, Mack had acknowledged that there was sufficient evidence for a conviction without admitting guilt.

"I do understand right now in my state of mind that shooting at the judiciary is not a proper form of political redress," Mack said in Judge Herndon's courtroom.

Part of Mack's deal involved an unusual request that he be granted an unlimited amount of time to speak at his sentencing, where it was believed that he would focus much of his speech on Judge Weller, but prosecutors would not be permitted to question him. However, Weller would also be provided an opportunity to speak about how Darren Mack's crimes had affected him, as would members of Charla Mack's family.

"There are some very important things to say, and I've remained quiet through this whole thing," Mack added.

"Mr. Mack wants to express his views on the entire situation unfettered by attacks on him," Chesnoff said. Had he continued with the trial and had chosen to testify in his own defense, he could have undergone severe cross-examination by the prosecution. "He is going to talk about Chuck Weller, not because there's animosity toward Judge Weller, but about how the family court process should be more sensitive to the emotional and personal problems in family court."

In making the deal, the prosecution agreed to remove from the equation the maximum sentence that Mack could have received from the jury, which would have been life in prison without the possibility of parole. Instead, the plea agreement called for Mack to receive twenty years to life in prison for the murder charge, and sixteen to forty years for the attempted murder with use of a deadly weapon charge. Prosecutors Lalli and Daskas indicated that they would ask Judge Herndon to order that Mack's sentences run consecutively, while Chesnoff and Freeman planned to ask that the sentences run concurrently.

Portions of Mack's agreement included a guilty plea to one count of first-degree murder, with regard to the death of his wife, and a guilty plea to one count of attempted murder with use of a deadly weapon, regarding the attempt on Judge Weller's life. Mack entered the plea agreement with the understanding that a life prison sentence would be recommended, with the possibility of parole after serving twenty years, but that he could also be sentenced to life in prison without possibility of parole. It was further agreed that if Mack did not receive a life sentence with parole eligibility after serving twenty years, he would be allowed to withdraw his plea. The state of Nevada retained the right to argue for the maximum sentence, and that the sentences relating to both counts would run consecutively.

Mack also agreed to make restitution to the victims, and to reimburse the state of Nevada for any expenses related to his extradition. The agreement also indicated that he understood that he would not be eligible for probation, and that it would be up to the sentencing judge whether his sentences would run concurrently or consecutively.

As part of his guilty plea, Mack also had to agree to give up several important rights, which was accomplished in the form of a written waiver that had the potential to severely affect his right to appeal. The waiver included the fact that he understood and was waiving his constitutional privilege against self-incrimination, including the right to refuse to testify at trial; the right to a speedy trial free of excessive pretrial publicity prejudicial to his case; the right to confront and cross-examine any witnesses who would testify against him; the right to subpoena witnesses on his behalf; and the right to testify in his own defense. He also gave up the right *to appeal the conviction, with the assistance of an attorney, either appointed or retained, unless the appeal is based upon reasonable constitutional jurisdictional or other grounds that*

challenge the legality of the proceedings and except as
otherwise provided in subsection 3 of NRS 174.035.

By showing that Mack's guilty plea was voluntary
and made after intelligent consideration of its consequences, the prosecution had, it hoped, dotted all
of its *i*'s and crossed all of its *t*'s. Mack also signed a
separate statement of *voluntariness* to his guilty
pleas, which was included in the plea agreement. It
said, in essence, that he understood the elements
and nature of all the charges against him; that he
understood that the state would have to prove each
element of the charges against him at trial; that he
had discussed with legal counsel any possible defenses and defense strategies that might be in his
favor; and he agreed that everything had been fully
explained to him by legal counsel, and that accepting the plea bargain was in his best interest. He also
agreed that his attorneys had answered, to his satisfaction, all of his questions regarding his guilty plea
agreement and its consequences, and stated that he
was satisfied with the services provided by his legal
counsel.

A short time later, Herndon ruled that the case
would return to Reno for sentencing, which would
occur on January 17 to 18, 2008. He set aside two days
to allow Mack plenty of time to say what he had to say,
while still allowing time for Weller's and Charla's families to speak.

"He's looking at life, plus forty years," Lalli said
later, after court was dismissed. Life, plus forty years,
would be the maximum possible punishment Mack
could receive.

"Our goal going into this case was to see Darren
Mack convicted of premeditated murder and of

attempted murder," Daskas added. "Whether it was by
jury verdict or guilty pleas was insignificant to us."

Daskas noted that Mack's agreement waived his
right to appeal.

Calling Mack a "sociopath" who had "hypnotized
himself into believing he's justified, and that he's
the victim," Soorya Townley told reporters afterward that she had been informed of the plea agreement over the weekend, and she had given her
approval of it.

"I'm glad it's over," Townley said. She indicated
that she was tired of the defense attorneys "dragging
her daughter's name through the mud. . . . On the
other hand, I was hoping he could have gotten life
without the possibility of parole. . . . All I could see in
my mind was how my daughter was slaughtered like
an animal."

David Chesnoff and Scott Freeman, however, said
that Darren Mack had agreed to take the deal because
he did not want to vilify Charla's reputation, and because he also wanted to take responsibility for his
crimes.

"This dark night is over, or at least a portion of this
dark night is over," Judge Chuck Weller said in a one-
sentence statement. He refused to take questions
from reporters.

Judge Herndon had set a sentencing date of January 17, 2008, and ordered that the sentencing be
moved back to Reno. Herndon said that he had decided to reverse the change of venue back to
Washoe County for sentencing because it made
more sense financially, and also because of community interest in the case. He also said that now that

the guilty pleas had been entered, pretrial publicity was no longer an issue.

"It's the original jurisdiction," Herndon said. "It is this community's case. They have a great interest in this case."

In the meantime, Mack began making future plans.

34

Less than a month after making the decision to plead guilty to killing his wife and shooting Judge Weller, Darren Mack fired his defense team for what he believed was inadequate legal representation and began making plans to file a motion to withdraw the prior guilty pleas to the murder and the attempted murder charges. According to Darren Mack's brother, Landon, Darren had hired Reno attorney William Routsis.

"Routsis has been retained to correct a huge manifestation of injustice and to withdraw the pleas," his brother told a reporter for the *Reno Gazette-Journal*.

Darren Mack apparently had had time to rethink the consequences of his guilty pleas, in which he faced life in prison with the possibility of parole after serving twenty years on the murder charge. As a result, Routsis filed a new motion in which he stated that his client had been confused and in a state of physical duress when he entered into the guilty pleas agreement. Instead of following through with the agreement, Routsis argued that Mack should be permitted to withdraw his guilty pleas and go back to trial on the charges of murder and attempted murder. During a brief court hearing, Routsis also asked Herndon to vacate the January 17 sentencing hearing and reschedule it, because he needed more time to prepare for it. Routsis also said that Mack had been receiving poor treatment while incarcerated at the Clark County Detention Center during his trial, which had added to his stress and confusion when he agreed to make the plea. Among the alleged poor treatment that Mack had received was having to wait for long periods between meals, inability to obtain relief for back pain, which he was experiencing, and the fact that he had become dehydrated. All of those things, Routsis said, had made it difficult for Darren Mack to think clearly and rationally.

"This man is looking at a life sentence," Routsis said. He said that he needed the delay in sentencing because he was focusing entirely on Mack's motion to withdraw the guilty pleas, which required him to read through thousands of pages of legal documents.

The prosecution, of course, argued against delaying the sentencing. "There are victims and victims' families who suffered greatly," Special Prosecutor Christopher Lalli said. "They want to put this behind them." He asked Herndon to get on with it "for Judge Weller and his family, and the family of Charla Mack" because "there are people's lives who are kind of floating in the wind."

Noting the fact that Routsis had been on the case since the first part of December, and because sentencing was still a month and a half away, Herndon indicated that "there [was] sufficient time" for Routsis to prepare for the January 17, 2008, sentencing date.

It was also pointed out that Lalli was making plans to call both David Chesnoff and Scott Freeman, as

well as Robert Daskas, who was by this time running
for Congress, as witnesses during the proceedings.
Lalli was in the process of preparing a motion that
would allow Mack to waive his attorney-client privilege, with regard to his previous attorneys, so that
Lalli would be able to question them about the plea
negotiations that Mack had entered into under their
guidance.

Noting Mack's plans to try to withdraw his guilty
pleas, Lalli said that he believed those efforts would
not be successful, but he added that he was not particularly surprised by Mack's intention to try.

"Whenever anybody signs up for a sentence of this
magnitude, it's not uncommon to have buyer's remorse," Lalli said. "Unless he can show that the plans
were not knowingly, voluntarily, and intelligently entered, it won't be accepted."

Routsis said that Mack would likely agree to waive
his attorney-client privilege with regard to his involvement with Chesnoff and Freeman, but only insofar
as it applied to the plea negotiations in question.
Lalli, however, said that he understood that the waiving of such privilege under the law would be without
restriction. It seemed that the legal dialogue held the
potential to open up yet another round of legal possibility, but that aspect had yet to be determined.

There was also the issue of a motion that Routsis intended to file regarding an original plea memo written by Lalli, which was later modified after requests
from Mack's original attorneys. Although Routsis said
that Mack had made a mark on the original document, he did not say how else it may have changed.
Lalli told the judge that he did not have the original
document, or a copy of it, and suggested that Freeman and Chesnoff were in possession of it.

Routsis also indicated that he would call "numerous bailiffs" from Clark County as witnesses, as well as personnel from the Washoe County Jail in Reno, where Mack was initially held upon his return to the United States. Some of the witnesses, he said, were familiar with Mack's "state of mind almost immediately after the plea."

In the meantime, Mack's brother, Landon, defended his brother and lashed out at and condemned the media coverage of his brother's case, and criticized both prosecutors and defense attorneys following the brief court hearing. He publicly called for the appointment of a special prosecutor to "thoroughly investigate the unethical and illegal conduct of the Nevada judicial system."

Landon Mack made reference to his brother's claims that corruption in the legal system in Nevada had prevented Darren Mack and others from fair treatment in cases of child custody.

"The manifest injustice that led to and ultimately resulted with the events of June 12, 2006, will soon be described in graphic detail," Landon Mack said. "The unethical, immoral, and illegal conduct that has continued since my brother voluntarily returned from Mexico will also be revealed in hopes that the truth will make a difference in the lives of others and spare others from such tragedies as my family has and continues to endure."

Charla Mack's mother, Soorya Townley, also delivered a statement after the hearing in which she said that she had seen "no remorse from Darren Mack for his barbaric actions or regret for the profound suffering he has caused. Now it appears, with his latest legal machincations, Mr. Mack is attempting to spoil Christmas for us as well."

Additional details regarding the reasons why Darren Mack wanted to withdraw his guilty pleas began to emerge in approximately thirty pages of new legal documents filed just before Christmas, in which he again alleged that Charla Mack had attacked him the morning of June 12, 2006. He said that she had picked up a loaded gun, pointed it at him, and tried to fire it at him, but the gun misfired. He said that he had placed a gun, a knife, and articles of clothing into a Dumpster and had asked his prior defense team to look for the evidence in a landfill because, he indicated, it could have helped clear him of the charges. However, he said that the search for that evidence was never done.

Apparently, another issue for asking to withdraw his guilty pleas was the fact that Darren Mack's previous attorneys had believed that Mack would not make a good witness to place on the stand, but they had assured his family, early in the case, that he would be acquitted of the charges and that everyone would be enjoying beer and margaritas in Mexico at the trial's conclusion. So far, Mack's defense had cost in excess of $1.2 million, and the beer and margaritas in Mexico did not appear anywhere in sight. Furthermore, Mack's new attorney said that his client's former defense team had so far failed to hand over important documents and files that Routsis could use to help him in his representation of Mack.

Mack's brother, Landon, told media representatives that Mack's old defense team had urged Darren to plead guilty.

35

As the case continued to unfold and look more and more like a soap opera, information came out at the beginning of the new year that indicated that Mack had made claims that Washoe Family Court judge Chuck Weller and Weller's attorney, Cal Dunlap, had sought $5 million in return for supporting Mack's guilty pleas. Weller promptly denied the claim, which had been presented in new court documents, and Lalli said that there was no deal like that made through the prosecutor's office.

According to the documents, which had been filed on Monday, January 7, 2008, Mack alleged that his previous attorney David Chesnoff had received a telephone call from Dunlap and was told that Weller and Dunlap agreed with the proposed plea deal. However, according to Mack's documented allegations, Dunlap purportedly called back later, *quite upset,* and said that he and Weller would only support the plea agreement if Mack paid the money to Weller.

I am not in a civil action with Judge Weller for him to be able to demand money from me, Mack had said in his new court filings to support his request to withdraw his guilty pleas.

"I never said that to anyone, and I never authorized anyone to say it on my behalf," Weller said to a reporter with the *Reno Gazette-Journal* in denying Mack's allegations. "I am an honest and an ethical judge. I went back to the bench after being shot by Darren Mack because I believe the judiciary has an obligation to stand up against attacks against it."

Weller also said that he had not decided at that point whether to file a civil lawsuit against Mack.

Lalli said that it was unethical for a prosecutor to "in any way connect a criminal resolution to a civil suit."

"We had absolutely nothing to do about that," Lalli said. "Nothing."

Mack had also reiterated that he had been coerced into taking the plea deal.

Mack's sentencing hearing, which had only been a few days away, was postponed following the new allegations so that Judge Herndon could hear arguments about possibly throwing out Mack's guilty pleas and allowing him to go back to trial. Herndon tentatively rescheduled the sentencing hearing for February 7 and 8.

At another hearing that began on Tuesday, January 15, 2008, William Routsis targeted David Chesnoff by alleging that the defense attorney had a history of pressuring clients into accepting plea agreements. Routsis brought up a 2006 California case in which an accused drug dealer, represented by Chesnoff, had been allowed to withdraw his guilty plea after claiming that he had been pressured into making it by Chesnoff.

"The affidavits, I think, are compelling," Routsis said. "I think it indicates that lightning did strike twice, at least in this case."

Routsis indicated that he would call bailiffs who would testify about things that Mack said after making the plea agreement, including that he had not murdered his wife. Routsis took the issue even further than that, by alleging that problems with Mack's defense went beyond the plea bargain. He claimed that the defense did not do an adequate job of investigating the case, and brought up the promises that had purportedly been made, including that they would win the case. Among the documents included to help him prove his case was a letter from Darren Mack's son, Jory, which said in part: *Right after . . . paying (the defense attorneys) . . . Scott Freeman told my uncle we would win for sure and they were winning everything.*

According to the claims being made, in part, at least, by Mack's family, Darren Mack did not know what he was doing on the day he agreed to the plea bargain. Family members also claimed that they did not know the full details of what had occurred on June 12, 2006, until the deal had been struck. Alecia Biddison, Mack's former girlfriend, also said that she had not known all of the facts until the day of the plea bargain hearing, in which she and members of Mack's family first "heard it from Darren's own lips what transpired on June twelfth."

Landon Mack also stated that he had never been able to ask his brother about the shooting involving Judge Weller: "David Chesnoff and Scott Freeman [said], absolutely, you cannot discuss this case in any way, shape, or form . . . with your brother, your father, your mother, anybody."

Other family members and friends also said at the

hearing in which the former defense team was being blasted that they had not been informed or consulted about the plea bargain that Darren Mack was involved in making, and they believed that they should have been.

"They (the former defense team) used tactics that I believe you will find at the hearing that have no place in a court of law," Routsis told reporters outside the courthouse.

One of the major bones that Routsis indicated he would pick with the former defense team involved Scott Freeman's opening remarks in which he began making a case for self-defense with regard to Charla Mack's death. Routsis said that, according to the law, a defendant needed to be aware and alert to kill in self-defense. However, Routsis said, the defense, specifically David Chesnoff, had told the jury that Mack was a "victim of the delusions created by his mental illness."

Routsis continued, "You just can't do that in a homicide case. Mr. Chesnoff gutted the ability for this man to get a defense on self-defense."

According to Routsis, that was what led up to Mack's plea deal.

According to published reports, Darren Mack was also alleging that his former attorneys had forged his signature on the plea agreement, which is likely one of the reasons that Routsis was attempting to get the original files from the former defense team.

The fact that Darren Mack's family was not allowed to talk to Mack before the deal was made also might have played a part in the deal going forward as it did. Mack's mother, Joan, told reporters that she did not believe that Charla's death was premeditated by Darren. If he premeditated the killing, she said, he would "never have had his daughter inside the house when he did it."

Mack's family said that Mack was looking forward to testifying in his own defense, if Judge Herndon threw out the plea deal and granted him a new trial.

On Wednesday, January 16, 2008, David Chesnoff took the witness stand during the second day of the latest hearing to respond to questions as William Routsis attempted to convince Judge Herndon to allow Darren Mack to withdraw his guilty pleas. Chesnoff said that he became physically ill when Mack described the bloody crime scene in his garage after he had stabbed his wife, and he testified that he had advised Mack against testifying on his own behalf, out of fear that Darren might come across to the jury "like a sociopath."

Chesnoff also disputed Routsis's argument that Chesnoff and Freeman had coerced or bullied Mack into entering into the plea deal, and said that Mack had expressed interest in making a plea agreement, if it meant spending less time in prison. Chesnoff said that he and Freeman went over the details of the plea agreement the weekend before Mack agreed to go through with it. They thoroughly explained the details—as well as the consequences—of making such a deal. He said that Mack was currently suffering from "buyer's remorse" over his decision.

Chesnoff described Mack as being delusional, and testified that he believed that an insanity defense was his only option—if he took the case to trial.

"The only possible explanation, defensewise," Chesnoff said, "was insanity, because he admitted that he did it."

Chesnoff testified that he believed the plea deal was in Mack's best interest for a number of reasons, including the fact that character witnesses that Mack had initially said would vouch that he was honest turned out not to be cooperative. He also said that rebuttal witnesses that the prosecution had planned to call increased the likelihood that he would be convicted.

At one point during the proceeding, Routsis asked Chesnoff if the defense team had made any attempt to find the gun that Mack claimed would help his self-defense argument because it purportedly had, or should have had, Charla's fingerprints on it. Chesnoff's response was that Mack had not mentioned the gun during their early meetings, but Mack later told Freeman that he had remembered it while meditating.

During the questioning, which made it appear that Chesnoff and Freeman had not done as much as they could have to give Mack a proper defense, including the suggestion that the defense lawyers had given up too easily, Routsis asked why Chesnoff had told Mack that the prosecution's case was impenetrable. Chesnoff's response was that he knew the prosecution had planned to call a blood spatter expert who would describe how Charla Mack had "gurgled" blood as she died.

"The other thing was that Darren, in preparing for his testimony, had told us that after he stabbed her, he put his knee on her head and she was gurgling," Chesnoff said. "When he told that to us when preparing for his testimony, I got physically ill."

Chesnoff also disputed the allegations that Mack had not been allowed to spend time with his family prior to going through with the agreement. He said that he had contacted Judge Herndon and had made arrangements for Mack to spend time alone with his family on the morning he was to make the plea.

Chesnoff also said that he had told Mack that he could change his mind about entering into the agreement at any time prior to accepting the agreement in court.

"He specifically told me he wanted to be the one to tell his family," Chesnoff testified.

During the hearing, Darren Mack took the stand and explained why he was alleging that his former attorneys had coerced him into making the guilty plea. Despite David Chesnoff's testimony a day earlier, Mack also reiterated that he wanted his family to help him in making his decision on whether to accept the agreement or not, and renewed his allegation that Chesnoff had forced him to sign the agreement before speaking with family members. Mack also told Herndon that he had lied to the judge during the plea canvass on November 5, 2007, right before making his guilty pleas. The purpose of the plea canvass questions was to help ascertain that Mack had truly made his guilty pleas willingly and that he fully understood the implications of making the pleas.

"I was broken down," Mack said of his purported lies to the judge. "I needed help."

As part of making his case for a new trial, Mack also told Judge Herndon that the experience surrounding his first trial, which ended in his guilty plea, had made him feel like he had been "psychologically raped.

"I have a whole new compassion for women who are raped now," Mack added. "It was almost like being a puppet. . . . My will was broken down. I wouldn't enter a guilty plea on murder one, because I didn't murder Charla."

Mack described Scott Freeman as his "lifeline" during

the time between his arrest and the events that led up
to his trial. He choked back tears as he described how
Freeman had urged him to accept the plea agreement.

"That's when I felt my will break," Mack said.

Mack also admitted that he had taken drugs previously, specifically Ecstasy, also known as MDMA, which
closely resembles methamphetamine, and testified that
he had taken approximately one hundred pills of the
psychoactive drug during his life. The allusion to his
admitted drug usage seemed aimed at diminishing responsibility for his actions on June 12, 2006. Chesnoff
said that he had decided to use Mack's drug use as part
of his defense strategy to further bolster Mack's insanity defense. Chesnoff also said that Mack was "brain
fried," due to his drug usage.

At one point, Special Prosecutor Christopher Lalli
asked Mack if he would have killed his wife's attorney,
Shawn Meador, if he had seen him that same morning. Chillingly, Mack admitted that he had thought
about killing the lawyer.

On redirect examination by Routsis, Mack, calm
and animated during about three hours of testimony,
reiterated what his prior attorney had said in describ-
ing how Charla, allegedly, had pointed his gun at him,
smiled, and pulled the trigger, and how it had misfired
and how he had stabbed her in self-defense. This time
around, however, he said that the gun had somehow
ended up in her hair, and that some of her hair had
become stuck within the hammer mechanism. That's
why, he explained, he had asked Freeman to search
for the gun. He claimed that his request had not been
agreed to because his prior attorneys believed that the
knife he used to kill Charla would have been found
along with the gun.

"I'm not insane," Mack said.

He charged that his former defense team had worn him down psychologically and had used his emotions to manipulate him into agreeing to plead guilty. He claimed that he was a "puppet and would have done anything" by that point in the proceedings.

Scott Freeman, however, testified that he and David Chesnoff never pressured Darren Mack into accepting any deal, and the attorneys had been prepared to take his case to trial. He also noted several times during the proceedings the sacrosanct attorney-client creed, and asked Herndon to clarify that it had indeed been waived or lifted when Routsis questioned him about why he had not notified the police about the Dumpster, where Mack said he had disposed of the gun he alleged that Charla had tried to kill him with, along with the knife that Mack used to kill her. It was obvious that Freeman was uncomfortable talking about things that Mack had told him in confidence.

"When I learn something from my client, I'm not telling anybody," Freeman said. "I'm not telling anybody about any gun. I'm not telling anybody about a knife."

He said that if the weapons in question had been found by the police, they could have confirmed Mack's guilt.

Freeman agreed that Mack had told him about disposing of his gun during one of their meetings at the jail, but he said that Mack had never urged him to try to recover it.

"The word 'landfill' or trying to find the gun had never come up," Freeman said.

Freeman also responded to questions regarding Mack's allegations that he was coerced by Chesnoff and Freeman into taking the plea deal.

"Chesnoff told him at least five times, if he didn't want to take the deal, he didn't have to," Freeman testified. "We are talking about a situation where we had five days left for trial. If he didn't want to take the deal, we would finish the trial. The witnesses were on their way to Las Vegas from Reno."

Freeman later told an Associated Press reporter that his testimony in the Mack hearing was "unprecedented. Never, in twenty-four years, have I had to testify against a client that I defended as zealously as I did," he said.

At another point, when Special Prosecutor Lalli had expressed doubt about Charla Mack even having a gun the day she was killed, Herndon questioned how she could have been pointing a gun at Darren Mack, considering the stab wounds she had sustained to her arms and legs. Herndon opined that her wounds would have been consistent with someone who was trying to fight off a knife attack.

On Friday, January 18, 2008, following four days of testimony, Judge Herndon went into great detail and took nearly two hours to give his reasoning, point by point, why Darren Mack was not entitled to withdraw his guilty pleas for killing his wife and shooting their divorce judge.

"The defendant admitted that he killed his wife," Herndon said in denying Mack's bid for a new trial. "He admitted he shot a judge" and was not entitled to a "do-over. . . . There was no indication whatsoever that there was any issue with him understanding what we were going through in terms of the plea. . . . He stopped me on multiple occasions to ask for clarifications on matters or raise issues he wanted assurances on."

Herndon added that Mack acted "intelligently" throughout the proceedings, and never raised any of his concerns during the trial. Herndon said that Mack's allegation that he was "a puppet" was "completely inconsistent with him engaging in the question-and-answer process with me and raising issues."

During his decision-making process, Herndon said that he believed that Freeman and Chesnoff had fairly represented Darren Mack, and that Mack had fully understood what he was doing when he entered into the deal. He confirmed Mack's sentencing for February 7 to 8, 2008, and indicated that he would accept Mack's plea and go forward with the agreement that Mack had made with the state.

Following the hearing, Special Prosecutor Christopher Lalli indicated that he would argue that Darren Mack be sentenced to a life term in prison. He said that he was "very pleased" with Herndon's ruling, and added that he was looking forward to the sentencing so that the case could be brought to a close finally. He said that Mack's testimony during the preceding hearing would serve to help the prosecution at sentencing.

Lalli, of course, was alluding to the fact that Mack, when he accused his previous lawyers of mishandling his case, had opened the door on the previously closed attorney-client privilege. Due to Mack's allegations and assertions against Scott Freeman and David Chesnoff, several damaging evidentiary details that had previously been off-limits to the prosecution could now be used at his upcoming sentencing hearing.

"We know things about the facts that we didn't know before," Lalli told a reporter outside the courthouse.

"Things he did, things he said, things he thought about."

Among the circumstances of waiving the attorney-client privilege was that it effectively placed items on the record that had not been there before, and these could be used in future legal proceedings, including appeals and parole hearings. In short, it seemed that Mack had simply dug his already deep hole a bit deeper.

Landon Mack was critical of Herndon's decision during a brief question-and-answer session with the media after the hearing. He suggested that the judge was biased. When a reporter asked him why he felt that the system was against his brother, he replied: "My brother shot a judge."

Before the first month of the new year ended, Washoe County judge John Iroz made a ruling that effectively allowed Judge Weller's administrative assistant's civil lawsuit against Mack to begin moving forward. Allison, who sustained injuries when sprayed with glass and shrapnel at the time Weller was shot, had sued Mack for unspecified damages related to those injuries and the psychological effects suffered from the incident. Iroz said that Allison's attorney could now begin collecting information needed for her lawsuit.

36

Darren Mack's attorney, William Routsis, filed a last-minute petition with the Nevada Supreme Court in an effort to block or put off Mack's sentencing for killing his wife and shooting Judge Weller. There were only hours before the two-day sentencing hearing was set to begin. However, the high court refused to intervene, and the scheduled sentencing hearing began on time on Thursday, February 7, 2008.

As previously agreed, Mack took the witness stand and talked for about three hours in his effort to convince Judge Herndon not to sentence him to prison for life. Although a defendant in a criminal case often makes a few statements prior to sentencing—usually words that take the form of an apology, or that a lesson has been learned from a mistake that will not be repeated—Mack's lengthy statement came across as very unusual, if not self-serving. While the prosecution had asked Herndon to follow the recommendations of the Nevada Department of Parole and Probation that Mack be sentenced to at least thirty-six years in prison, Mack continued to attest that he had not voluntarily entered his guilty pleas.

"The way I put it, and I don't mean it too sarcastically, but if you really buy that I did that voluntarily, I got a great bridge to sell you," Mack told Judge Herndon.

Mack continued by repeating what he had said before about his former attorneys, that they had "pressured" him into taking the plea deal.

"I told him (Freeman) flat out, what it was about for me is that 'you stole my choice by what you broke me down into,'" Mack said. "'It wasn't my choice. You guys pushed me so hard,' and when Freeman turned on that last weekend, it broke my will."

Over the two-day proceeding, Mack's son provided statements on Darren Mack's behalf that, at times, brought a higher level of emotion to the courtroom.

"I believe what happened is exactly what my dad said, because I believe he is one of the most credible [people] . . . and has the most integrity of any man I ever met," Mack's son, Jory, told the judge.

Alternatively, words that Charla Mack had said in Judge Chuck Weller's courtroom, nearly two years earlier, were played again by the prosecution, as a reminder of the angry temperament that her husband had shown her during some of their most unpleasant moments together.

"He gets so angry and so whipped up that I just don't feel comfortable right now," Charla's words stated as a testament to how he had sometimes made her feel. Charla's mother followed with a few words of her own.

"This [is a] man who thought he knew a better plan, who decided to play God . . . ," Soorya Townley said in anger.

One by one, everyone, it seemed, got their chance to take a shot at Darren Mack prior to sentencing.

"May he die in prison," Charla's brother, Christopher Broughton, said. He also described Mack as a "brutal butcher. . . . Let him remain caged until the day he dies."

Jan Sampsel, Charla's father, told Herndon that Mack was no longer able to rely on "his money and family social status," and was finally being held accountable for what he had done.

Judge Weller also spoke prior to sentencing, and said that he and his family still lived in fear because of the attempt on his life. He said that he received a death threat around the 2007 Christmas holiday, in which someone promised "to finish the job Mack started." He said that five other judges had also received death threats after Christmas. He also spoke about his relationship with the Macks during their divorce proceeding.

"I did everything legally possible to be fair to both Darren and Charla Mack," he said. "Darren Mack would not accept that."

A videotape of the May 24, 2006, hearing in which Weller had made some of the rulings in the Macks' divorce case was played for the benefit of the judge. In that tape, Weller was seen in an equable and unflappable demeanor toward both Darren and Charla, and one of his rulings had been for Darren Mack. He even told them that they could file appeals if they were unhappy about his rulings, and had said: "I wish I could come up with something that would make you both happy."

Before he finished, Weller told Judge Herndon

that Mack "has demonstrated that he is too dangerous to live in a free society."

Prior to handing down Darren Mack's sentence, Judge Herndon said that Mack had never shown any remorse for his actions of June 12, 2006.

"He never said, 'I am sorry,'" Herndon stated, looking down from the bench at Mack. "That at least would have shown some remorse. . . . You don't automatically get a certain sentence by expressing sorrow to the court for what you've done, but it would have been nice. . . . But there was nothing. That leads me to the conclusion you aren't sorry."

While speaking to Darren's mother, Joan, and Charla's mother, Soorya Townley, about the Macks' daughter, Judge Herndon broke into tears. He said the biggest tragedy of all stemming from the case was the girl, Erika, who, Herndon said, would now be without a mother and, for the most part, would be without a father, while Mack languished in prison. He asked Joan Mack and Soorya Townley to put Erika first by rising above the tragedy, to put their differences aside, and to try to teach the child "good things about both parents.

"She needs to be raised with hugs and kisses," Herndon said.

According to agreements that had been reached, Erika would be spending twenty-two days a month with Townley, and eight days a month with Joan Mack.

Herndon also made a point to note that Darren Mack had not disputed statements made by Freeman and Chesnoff that Mack had said that he felt he had a right to shoot Weller under protection of the Second Amendment of the Constitution. He said that the judicial system in the United States provided remedies for people to settle their grievances peacefully, without resorting to violence.

"There is nothing in the Second Amendment that says you can shoot public officials," Herndon said. "It is not patriotic to shoot a family court judge because you don't like how he does his job."

To drive home his point about citizens being able to settle their grievances peacefully, Herndon cited the fact that Mack had won a favorable ruling from the state supreme court when he legally had challenged decisions that had been made during his first divorce. He also cited the fact that Las Vegas politicians had been punished by the judicial system for their misconduct.

"Four Clark County commissioners went to prison for corruption," Herndon said. "No one had to shoot them to get them out of office. . . . Modern-day patriots are not people that attack government. They're not the Tim McVeighs of the world, or the Darren Mack who shoots a judge."

Judge Herndon also said that he had taken into consideration the fact that Mack had been a good father, a good brother, a good uncle, and a good cousin, but he had also considered the evidence and how it had stacked up against him. He said that he had carefully examined Mack's life prior to his divorce from Charla, and that he had also carefully reviewed the events that had led up to her death and the shooting of Judge Weller. He concluded that because of the nature of Mack's crimes, his case "was, in the court's mind, what could be considered a brutal murder.

"The truth is," Herndon said, "Mr. Mack is guilty of

these crimes, but he doesn't want to hear anything
about that."

When all was said and done, the moment that everyone had been waiting for had come: the pronounce-
ment of Darren Mack's sentence. Herndon sentenced
Mack to twenty years to life for killing Charla Mack, and
to an additional sixteen to forty years for the attempted
murder of Judge Weller with a deadly weapon. Herndon ordered that Mack's sentences be served consecutively. As a result, Mack would be required to serve at
least twenty years on the first-degree murder charge
before being eligible for parole, and, if paroled, he
would be required to immediately begin serving the
second sentence. And, if he made parole on the sentence for attempted murder, he would have to serve an
additional eight years on the use of a dangerous weapon
charge. Even in a best-case scenario, Mack would be required to serve at least thirty-six years behind bars.
Given credit for the 565 days he had spent in jail awaiting trial, Mack would be at least eighty-one years old
before receiving a parole board hearing. Herndon had
given Mack the longest sentence possible under the law.

Mack was also ordered to pay approximately
$30,000 for Judge Weller's medical bills and for
damage done to his chambers.

Following his client's sentencing, William Routsis
said that the next step would be "direct appeal."

Afterward, outside the courthouse, Christopher
Lalli said that he was pleased that Herndon had made
it tough on Mack with the sentencing. Lalli was still
happy about having made the plea deal with Mack.

"I don't regret any of the decisions we made in this
case," Lalli said. "I think they were appropriate decisions."

* * *

In March 2008, Darren Mack lost the wrongful death lawsuit filed by his wife's estate. He was ordered to pay $590 million—$530 million of which would go to his youngest daughter. Erika's monetary award was broken down as $375 million for punitive damages; $185 million for compensatory damages, which included grief and sorrow, loss of companionship, as well as for the pain, suffering, and disfigurement that Charla suffered prior to her death. An additional $30 million was awarded to Charla's estate as punitive damages. It seemed highly unlikely, however, that Charla Mack's estate—or her daughter—would ever see any of those amounts.

A short time later, Routsis filed another motion on Mack's behalf in which he again asked the judge to throw out his client's plea agreement and grant him a new trial. Routsis's motion, however, was not received well—it apparently contained language that Judge Herndon deemed inappropriate attacks of a personal nature. At a hearing on Tuesday, April 15, 2008, Herndon voiced his feelings about the language used in the motion. Even though Routsis apologized for an "immature approach to the practice of law," and said that his written arguments "were not personal" and that he hoped that "nobody took it personally," Herndon let him know his thoughts, and said that the lawyer's apology "rings hollow."

Herndon stated that Routsis's "personal pronouncements . . . were the worst things I've ever seen," and added that they "were not proper for a legal brief.

"You're not writing a letter to me as a scorned

child," Herndon told the attorney. "If you want to act like a petulant child and complain about things with rhetorical questions and personal attacks against people, then do it on your own time, not on the court's time. . . . Even the most wet-behind-the-ears person out of law school understands that is an improper, unprofessional, and disrespectful way of putting forth written proceedings. . . . It's an immature approach to the practice of law. I would strongly recommend that this type of pleading be ended."

After he had finished handing the attorney his hat with his strong admonishment, Herndon said that Routsis had not made any new arguments to support a change in Mack's plea. He unhesitatingly denied the request to allow Mack to withdraw his pleas.

Herndon's latest decision was also sent to the Nevada Supreme Court, where Mack had already filed an appeal of his case.

On Thursday, March 26, 2009, the Nevada Supreme Court upheld the divorce settlement that ordered Mack to pay nearly $1 million to his deceased wife's estate. The justices, in a nine-page ruling, rejected arguments by Mack's attorneys that the settlement was invalid because it had only been verbally agreed to—but never signed—before Charla Mack's death.

EPILOGUE

The story that you have just read is nearly as much an accounting of Darren Mack's voluminous legal issues, both civil and criminal, as much as it is a true-crime investigation that details the events that compelled him to flee the country for a while, apparently to consider his options—or perhaps to have one last fling in a few exotic locales before spending what would amount to most of the rest of his life in prison. Whatever his motivations had been in leaving the country after viciously killing his second wife, Charla Mack, at which time he was already embroiled in brutal divorce proceedings with her, Darren Mack's legal troubles only seemed to increase exponentially after he killed Charla and attempted to kill their divorce judge, Chuck Weller. These assaults happened at a time when fairness was being sought on several levels through the Nevada court system for those, like Mack, who were embroiled in tough legal issues involving the family court system. At times it seemed like his legal battles would never end.

What started out as a story detailing Mack's crimes,

his apparent flight to avoid prosecution, and the path that brought him back to Nevada to see justice served, eventually became a story that also involved those legal battles. At times I attempted to write the story excluding many of the legal issues he faced, but I found that doing so had left too many unanswered questions. Struggling with how best to write the story, and having substantially rewritten the manuscript several times as I attempted to show the reader what actually happened, I finally decided to write the second half of the book yet another time, when it became apparent to me that the only way to tell the story accurately, and with a good sense of cohesion, was simply to put everything in chronological order.

What you now have in your hands, and are now reading, is that final version. I hope that it does justice to this twisted and convoluted tale of real life that had so seriously gone awry, leaving one person dead, another seriously injured, a little girl without her real parents, and countless others heartbroken and many lives literally shattered.

In August 2009, CBS News ran an updated segment of *48 Hours Mystery* in which it was reported that Mack continues to appeal his conviction on grounds that he pleaded guilty under duress. He is also reportedly appealing the $590 million civil judgment awarded to his deceased wife's estate.

At the time of this writing, Judge Weller was the target of a recall effort, and the subject of a class action lawsuit. He has reportedly filed a personal injury lawsuit against Mack, seeking compensatory and punitive damages, and the class action lawsuit against him was placed on hold, pending the outcome of his lawsuit against Mack. He purportedly still has a number of enemies in the state, and has reportedly received additional threats, as have other members of the judiciary.

Mack, however, claims that he has no money left to pay out the civil judgment, or any future judgments, which may arise out of legal actions.

Soorya Townley is reportedly working on a book about her daughter's murder and the associated legal actions surrounding the tragedy. Darren and Charla's daughter, Erika, spends much of her time with her as part of the custody arrangement between Townley and Joan Mack.

A number of people in Nevada, and elsewhere, believe that Darren Mack got off easy with his sentence, while others believe his punishment was fitting. Although Mack was initially serving his sentence at a state prison just outside Carson City, not far from the elaborate estate he once shared with Charla Mack and his children, he was soon transferred to Ely State Prison, purportedly for security reasons. The prison at Ely, which opened in 1989, is designated the maximum-security prison for the state of Nevada. Nearly 320 miles from Carson City, in the eastern part of the state, not far from the Utah border, Mack's new home for the next thirty-six years or so is a five-hour drive from his prior home. Ely's somewhat remote location places it literally out in the middle of nowhere. The once-extravagant multimillionaire now spends most of his time in an eight-by-ten cell equipped with a sink and a toilet. He exercises in the yard with other convicts, and eats his simple meals with the general male population at designated meal times in the prison's dining hall. He is still hoping to rejoin society as a free man. It's a far cry from the swinging lifestyle and the cushy, deluxe global resorts he once frequented.

Acknowledgments

I would gratefully like to acknowledge Michaela Hamilton, executive editor at Kensington Publishing Corporation, for suggesting the fascinating Darren Mack case as a book project, and to Kensington editors Mike Shohl and Richard Ember for helping me keep it all together during the writing process, and for their sharp skill in knowing what to excise and what to leave in. I am especially thankful to Michaela and everyone at Kensington for their patience and understanding as I worked through personal family issues, including two deaths in my family, during the writing of this very difficult project. I am also eternally grateful to everyone else at Kensington for everything they do to help in the publication of Kensington's top-notch true-crime line.

A very special thank-you to Stephanie Finnegan, who ranks at the top among all of the copyeditors I've worked with throughout the many years that I've been writing true crime books. Stephanie's top-notch skills and intuitive nature of knowing what fits and what doesn't has helped to greatly improve my last several books, especially the one you have just read. All authors, regardless of the genre in which they write, should be so lucky!

I am also grateful to Jack Campbell, attorney for the city of Reno, Nevada, for his efforts in reviewing my requests for information and photos related to the Darren Mack case, though many of those efforts turned out to be in vain. Nonetheless, I appreciate all the time and energy he spent in trying to assist me with my many requests.

Thanks also to Beth Ptak, at the *Reno-Gazette Journal* (*RGJ*), who put me in touch with Tim Dunn, at *RGJ*, who, in turn, helped me connect with photographer Marilyn Newton, who took many of the great shots that can be found in the book's photo insert. I am particularly grateful to Marilyn and the other *RGJ* photographers, who captured some really great photos surrounding this case.

I would also like to acknowledge the fine detective work of David Jenkins and Ron Chalmers, both veteran investigators with the Reno Police Department, who were used as composites of sorts through whose eyes the work of many others was shown and helped bring Darren Mack to justice.

As usual, I would also like to thank my agent, Peter Miller, of PMA Literary & Film Management, Inc., and his assistant, Adrienne Rosado, for all that they do to get these projects off the ground. You guys are the greatest!

Last, but not least, a very special thank-you to Teresita, Kirsten, and Sarah for putting up with my eccentricities and less-than-traditional work habits throughout the years. Without your love and understanding, none of my projects would ever have seen the light of day.

MORE SHOCKING TRUE CRIME
FROM PINNACLE